Invitation

This helpful, up-to-the-minute coll.... than fifty opera stories immeasurably broadens your knowledge and increases your appreciation and enjoyment of one of the most popular and stimulating forms of music.

Dr. Harold V. Milligan, an outstanding authority on the opera, has written these stories with simplicity and clarity and provided complete casts of characters, names of famous arias, duets and ensembles for each of the operas covered. This revised and expanded edition of a bestselling opera book contains the most frequently performed operas from the repertory of the world's leading opera companies. Included are the masterpieces of Beethoven and Wagner, the melodic works of Verdi, Puccini, Bizet, and many other popular masters. Here, too, are noted modern operas by such gifted composers as George Gershwin, Benjamin Britten, and Gian-Carlo Menotti.

More complete than program notes, easier-to-follow and less expensive than librettos, *Stories of Famous Operas* offers a valuable means of refreshing your memory before a performance or introducing you to an opera for the first time.

HAROLD VINCENT MILLIGAN, prominent critic, author, musician and composer, served as Associate Director of the Metropolitan Opera Broadcasts, lectured on the history of opera at Columbia University, and wrote *Opera on the Air*, *Opera Quiz Book*, and *Music and You*.

THIS IS A REVISED AND EXPANDED REPRINT OF THE EDITION ORIGINALLY PUBLISHED BY DOUBLEDAY & CO. (GARDEN CITY BOOKS).

Other MENTOR Books of Interest

Stories of
FAMOUS OPERAS

by

Harold Vincent Milligan, Mus. D.

Introduction by
Deems Taylor

A SIGNET KEY BOOK
Published by THE NEW AMERICAN LIBRARY

Published as a SIGNET KEY BOOK
By Arrangement with Doubleday & Company, Inc.

First Printing, October, 1955

Library of Congress Catalog Card No. 55-11511

SIGNET KEY BOOKS *are published by*
The New American Library of World Literature, Inc.
501 Madison Avenue, New York 22, New York

PRINTED IN THE UNITED STATES OF AMERICA

Introduction

As the crowd was making its way up the aisle during intermission time at a matinee performance of *Il Trovatore* at the Metropolitan, I overheard the lady in back of me remark to her escort:

"You know, I'm so glad I don't understand Italian. I love just to sit back and listen to the orchestra and the singers. Who cares about the plot? If I understood the words they would get in the way of the music—take half the glamor out of it."

In other words, the lady doesn't go to the opera. She goes to a three-hour concert in costume. She is not alone. I have heard that point of view towards opera expressed by otherwise intelligent and cultured people—people who would rather *not* know what is going on on the stage. (I have often wondered how they would react if they were offered *Oklahoma!* sung in Italian.)

It is hardly their fault. They have been conditioned, you might say, to that peculiar point of view, owing to the fact that this is the only nation in the world that does not present opera in the language of the audience. As a result, they have never quite realized that opera is a form of the theatre. It is not a concert, and it is not an oratorio. It is a play in the form of music—the *Drama per Musica* of its seventeenth century inventors.

As for the lady who loves to sit back and listen, I think that if she were able to follow the action of an opera, she would have all the excitement of seeing a play as well as the pleasure of listening to the music. In recent years both the Metropolitan and City Center companies have presented certain operas in English translations; but generally speaking we are still compelled to hear most operas sung in a foreign language.

That is where this little book comes in. Since we cannot follow the plot as it is sung, we can at least have it described. Here are detailed synopses of the stories of more than fifty operas, told simply, without excess verbiage or too drastic condensation, by one who was an acknowledged expert in this field.

The book has other minor virtues. For instance, the idea of listing certain operas with alternate titles is a good one. Whether you know Mascagni's masterpiece as *Cavalleria Rusticana* or *Rustic Chivalry,* you can find it indexed under either title. The type is clear and well printed, and is not hard on the eyes.

The price, of course, is absurd. There are other books dealing with the stories of the operas, furnishing no more information than this one does; but without exception they are bulky and expensive—costing ten to fifteen times the price of this little volume. As for bulk, next time you go to the opera, slip the book into your handbag or overcoat pocket (it will fit; I tried it). Then you can take a refresher course during the intermission.

—DEEMS TAYLOR

Contents

Foreword

For real enjoyment and appreciation of opera, whether the performance is seen on the stage, or heard on radio or television, one should be familiar with the story of the opera, the situations, characters, and emotions which inspired the composer to write the music. Program notes are ordinarily too brief and librettos too lengthy for ready understanding of opera plots that are often involved and lacking in easy-to-follow continuity. Hence the need for simple, compact, yet comprehensive and vivid act-by-act stories of favorite operas which are most often produced and most likely to be seen or to be heard on radio.

In this book the author's aim has been to tell clearly and interestingly—with some hint as to the motives and emotions of the various characters—the stories of fifty famous operas selected from the repertory of the Metropolitan Opera House in New York City, the New York City Center, and other American opera associations.

The names of the most famous and familiar arias, duets, and ensembles are mentioned as they occur in the opera, and these titles are usually given in the original language of the libretto and also in their popular if not always exact translations in English. Many of these arias and ensembles are available in recordings, as are also some complete operas.

The sequence and arrangement of acts and scenes in the opera stories in this volume for the most part follow the practice of the Metropolitan in the production of these operas. Also the Metropolitan's preference as to titling of operas—either in English or in the original language—is generally used here.

H.V.M.

EDITOR'S NOTE: In this new edition, we have included stories by Harold V. Milligan of four operas which were not in the original edition but which have recently returned to operatic repertories with increasing popularity. Four operas of lesser importance have been deleted.

At the same time we have added seven opera stories which Miss Quaintance Eaton has written especially for this edition. Two of these are famous older favorites—*Fledermaus* by Johann Strauss, and *La Cenerentola* by Rossini; and five are outstanding operas composed in comparatively recent years—*Porgy and Bess* by Gershwin, *The Love for Three Oranges* by Prokofieff, *Peter Grimes* by Britten, *The Medium* and *Amahl and the Night Visitors* by Menotti.

The operas are grouped according to composers in this new edition of *Stories of Famous Operas*. The order is alphabetical according to the composer's name; and where there are two or more operas by the same composer, these are arranged in chronological order according to date of first production. The reader can readily locate individual operas from either the listing in the Table of Contents, or the Index of Titles on p. 319.

The editor wishes to express his thanks to the following publishers for their cooperation in the publication of this book: Boosey & Hawkes, Inc. for *Peter Grimes* by Benjamin Britten, *The Love for Three Oranges* by Serge Prokofieff, *Salome, Elektra,* and *Der Rosenkavalier* by Richard Strauss; to G. Schirmer, Inc. for *The Medium* and *Amahl and the Night Visitors* by Gian-Carlo Menotti; and to Gershwin Publishing Corporation for *Porgy and Bess*.

Fidelio

by LUDWIG VAN BEETHOVEN (1770-1827)

Two Acts. Libretto by Sonnleithner.
First produced in Vienna, 1805.

Florestan, a Spanish nobleman	*Tenor*
Leonora, his wife (disguised as Fidelio)	*Soprano*
Don Pizarro, governor of the fortress-prison near Seville	*Bass*
Rocco, jailer of the prison	*Bass*
Marcellina, his daughter	*Soprano*
Jaquino, assistant to Rocco	*Tenor*
Don Fernando, Prime Minister of Spain	*Bass*

Prisoners, soldiers, townspeople.

TIME: *Eighteenth Century.*
PLACE: *Seville, Spain.*

ACT ONE

SCENE ONE: *Courtyard of the prison fortress.*

Two years before the action of the opera begins, a Spanish nobleman named Florestan was illegally put into prison by Don Pizarro. No reasons for this imprisonment were given out and as Don Pizarro is the governor of the prison with autocratic powers, he has been able to keep Florestan there under cruelest conditions. Florestan's wife, Leonora, refuses to admit to herself the possibility that her husband may be dead, but believes instead that he is being kept in solitary confinement. In an effort to learn the truth and to rescue him if possible, Leonora dresses in men's clothes and succeeds in getting employment with the prison jailer, Rocco.

The first scene shows the gray stone walls of the prison on one side and the gatehouse on the other. This cheerful little house is the home of the jailer and it stands in the midst of the hard grimness of the prison like an oasis in

11

a desert. Rocco has a charming young daughter, Marcellina, and when the story opens she is busy ironing on a small table which has been placed just outside the door of the gatehouse.

She is not alone. Jaquino, a young assistant to her father, is anxiously asking her why she has been avoiding him lately and when is she finally going to say "Yes" and marry him—*"Jetzt, Schätzchen, jetzt sind wir allein"* ("At last, dear, we are alone"). The truth of the matter is that Marcellina has lost interest in Jaquino and is dreaming of her father's new assistant, the young man known as Fidelio. She sings a wistful melody, *"O wär' ich schon mit dir vereint"* ("O if I were already married"). Rocco enters from the main prison building and Jaquino is sent about his business.

Rocco inquires if Fidelio has returned yet and just as he does so there is a knock at the door. It is Fidelio, who has been doing some errands for Rocco and who delivers, among other things, some dispatches for the governor, Don Pizarro. The disguised Leonora makes a very handsome young man and it is easy to see how Marcellina has fallen in love with him and why the match is being encouraged by Marcellina's father, Rocco. Leonora is embarrassed by this situation, but she must keep up the pretense of being a man in order to carry out her mission.

Jaquino returns to the scene and the four people sing a quartet begun by Marcellina and joined by the others, one by one, *"Mir ist so wunderbar"* ("How wonderful to me"). Marcellina is blissfully in love, Leonora is deeply worried, Rocco is benevolent, and Jaquino is frankly jealous.

The young man, Fidelio, asks Rocco if he cannot be of greater assistance to him, and suggests that he might be taken along to the subterranean dungeons. Rocco replies that the prisoners of state are kept in these dungeons and he has strict orders that no one is to see them. The infatuated Marcellina is sure that the governor would not object to having such a fine young man as Fidelio assist her father in all his work. Rocco is willing to ask for Don Pizarro's permission, but he is sure that there is at least one dungeon which will be denied him. The prisoner there has been in solitary confinement for two years and is slowly dying of neglect and starvation. Leonora suspects that this unfortunate man is her husband and cries out that she would be only too happy to go with Rocco to this terrible place. Rocco smiles indulgently and promises that he will speak to Don Pizarro at the earliest possible moment.

SCENE TWO: *Same as Scene One.*

There is the sound of military music and Don Pizarro enters accompanied by a detachment of soldiers. He posts special guards on the ramparts and at the drawbridge and gives strict orders to be notified at once if anyone approaches the fortress. Rocco hands him the dispatches which Fidelio has brought from the city and, as he reads them, Pizarro's face darkens and he mutters to himself. The document which has distressed him is a notice that the prime minister is coming to inspect the prison, as he has been informed that certain political prisoners are being held there illegally. Pizarro knows that this refers to Florestan and he resolves at once to do away with him and hide the body before the minister arrives. He orders a captain to go to the watchtower with a trumpeter, and the moment the minister's carriage is seen approaching from Seville, the trumpeter is to sound a warning. In the aria, *"Ah, welch' ein Augenblick"* ("Ah, what a moment"), Pizarro exults in the fiendish delight he will experience in killing his old enemy, Florestan.

Pizarro turns to Rocco and hands him a purse filled with gold coins. "There will be more if you obey orders," he says. Rocco inquires what the orders are and Pizarro tells him that it is necessary, for reasons of state, that one of the political prisoners be killed. But Rocco refuses to take such orders, stoutly maintaining that he is a jailer, not a murderer. "Then I will kill him myself," cries Pizarro, but adds that Rocco at least must dig the grave. There is an empty cistern in the dungeon where Florestan lies and Pizarro orders Rocco to open this up to receive the dead body. Rocco is to hurry, as there is no time to lose, and Pizarro tells the jailer that he will follow him to the dungeon and meet him there in a few minutes.

Unknown to both Rocco and Pizarro, this entire conversation has been heard by Leonora and now she comes out of her hiding place after both men have left the scene and expresses her horror and fear in the aria, *"Abscheulicher! wo eilst du hin?"* ("Monstrous creature, what will you do?"). Her only hope is that her love for Florestan will give her courage and strength to meet whatever the future may bring.

As Leonora goes into the little garden which adjoins the gatehouse, Marcellina and Jaquino come into the courtyard and, after all the grim horror of the preceding scene, these two young people bring us a little comedy. Jaquino is still pleading with Marcellina to give up her dreams of the handsome Fidelio and come back to his faithful love, but she will have none of him.

Leonora returns from the garden with Rocco and she pleads with him to allow the prisoners to come out of their cells for a few minutes of sunlight and fresh air. Rocco is a kindly man at heart, and he finds it hard to refuse any request from the young man he has learned to admire so much, so he tells Fidelio and Jaquino they may unlock the cell doors and release the prisoners, while he goes off to ask the governor if his young assistant may accompany him in his gruesome errand to the underground dungeon where Florestan lies.

As the pale, dejected prisoners creep out of the prison door into the sunlit courtyard, shading their eyes from the unaccustomed glare, and staggering with weakness, they sing a very touching and beautiful "Prisoners' Chorus"— *"O welche Lust!"* ("Oh, what joy!").

Rocco returns to report that the governor has given his consent to having Fidelio accompany Rocco to the dungeon, and for good measure has also given his consent to the marriage of Fidelio and Marcellina. Rocco explains to Fidelio that the young man's duty will be to assist in preparing a grave for the prisoner who is to be killed. This is terrible news to Leonora, but she is prepared to go through any ordeal in the hope of rescuing her beloved Florestan.

Pizarro enters and flies into a rage at the sight of the prisoners in the courtyard and orders them to be returned to their cells immediately. Then he orders Rocco to take his tools and proceed at once to the dungeon, as there is no time to lose. This scene concludes with a magnificent chorus.

ACT TWO

SCENE ONE: *Florestan's dungeon.*

Florestan lies in chains in the darkness and silence. He despairs of his fate and tries to resign himself to death. In a beautiful melody, *"In des Lebens Frühlingstagen"* ("In the springtime of life"), he recalls his past life and the happiness of his marriage with Leonora. Yielding himself to fantasy, for a few moments, she seems to be with him, but the vision vanishes and he sinks back exhausted.

The door of the dungeon opens and Rocco and Fidelio creep cautiously down the stone steps at the back of the dungeon, lit only by a lantern which Rocco carries. With pickax and shovel, they go to work clearing away the rubble from the opening to the cistern. Leonora cannot get a good look at the prisoner, on account of the darkness, but when he calls to Rocco and begs for a drink of water, she recognizes his voice. It is Florestan!

The kindly Rocco gives him a drink of wine and after a few minutes of work blows a whistle which is the signal to Pizarro that the cistern is cleared and Florestan's grave is ready.

Pizarro enters and orders Rocco to send Fidelio away, but the faithful Fidelio refuses to leave. Now begins the very dramatic quartet. Florestan recognizes his old enemy Don Pizarro and, knowing all too well what has brought him to the dungeon, hails him as a murderer. Pizarro draws his dagger, but before he can plunge it into the defenseless body of his victim, the young man Fidelio springs between them and cries out "Before you kill him, you must kill me! I am his wife!" Pizarro tries to brush Leonora aside, but she draws a pistol and points it at him.

At this very moment, while Leonora and Pizarro confront each other, one with a dagger and the other with a pistol, a sound penetrates into the dungeon which changes the whole situation. It is the trumpet call from the watchtower announcing the arrival of the prime minister.

"God be praised!" cries Rocco. In baffled rage and fear Pizarro leaves the dungeon, and Rocco follows him. Leonora embraces her long-lost husband and assists him to rise. They sing a joyous duet, *"O namenlose Freude!"* ("Oh, joy inexpressible!"), as Leonora guides his faltering footsteps up the stone stairway to light and freedom.

SCENE TWO: *An open square before the fortress.*

In striking and dramatic contrast to the dark and gloomy dungeon is the sunlit square in front of the prison-fortress. Don Fernando, Prime Minister of Spain, and Don Pizarro, governor of the fortress, are seated on a dais overlooking the square where the townspeople have gathered to welcome their distinguished visitor. They hail him in a stirring chorus and in reply he says that he has come to bring justice to all.

Rocco leads in Leonora and Florestan and demands justice for them. Don Fernando is astonished to see his old friend Florestan, whom he believed dead. He demands an explanation and Rocco tells him the whole story. Pizarro attempts to interrupt to exonerate himself, but in vain. Fernando orders his arrest and he is led away, a prisoner in the fortress which he had ruled too brutally.

Rocco is delighted at this sudden turn of events and, although he has fancied Fidelio as a son-in-law, he consoles himself with the thought that Marcellina can always return to the faithful Jaquino. Don Fernando hands to Leonora the keys which will unlock Florestan's fetters and declares that none but she is worthy to strike off the last symbol of the injustice to which he has been subjected. The townspeople join in a happy chorus (*"Wer ein holdes Weib errungen"*), extolling the devoted wife and the triumph of faith and love over cruelty and wrong.

Norma

by VINCENZO BELLINI (1801-1835)

Four Acts. Libretto by Romani.
First produced in Milan, 1831.

Oroveso, Arch-Druid	*Bass*
Norma, High Priestess, his daughter	*Soprano*
Pollione, Roman proconsul	*Tenor*
Flavio, his friend	*Tenor*
Adalgisa, a temple virgin	*Contralto*
Clotilda, Norma's nurse	*Mezzo-soprano*

Druid priests and priestesses, temple virgins, Gallic soldiers, attendants, two young children of Norma.

TIME: *During the Roman occupation of Gaul, about 50 B.C.*
PLACE: *Gaul.*

ACT ONE

SCENE: *The sacred grove of the Druids.*

Under the Roman occupation the people are restless and rebellious, but they dare not commit any overt act until the Druids give the word. In the center of their sacred grove in the heart of the forest stands a huge oak tree and beneath it is a great stone altar. The branches of the oak tree are covered with mistletoe and the cutting of the mistletoe is a mystic ceremony connected with prophecy of the future.

It is night as a solemn procession approaches the sacred tree. Gallic warriors lead the procession, followed by the Druid priests. Last to come is Oroveso, the High Priest. Standing in the center of the clear space before the altar, Oroveso orders them to ascend the nearby hills and watch for the rise of the moon which is to be the signal for the cutting of the mistletoe. Before they go, they implore their god Irminsul to aid them in driving out the hated Roman legions. Near the altar hangs the great bronze shield of

Irminsul, the striking of which will be the signal for the ceremony.

When the grove is empty, two young Romans enter cautiously. They are Pollione, the Roman governor of the district, and his friend, Flavio. Flavio reminds his friend that Norma had warned them that they are forbidden to enter the grove sacred to the Druids and that such sacrilege would be punishable by death. In the dialogue between the two men, we learn that Pollione has been secretly married to Norma, the High Priestess of the Druids, for several years, and that they have two children. This marriage had been kept a close secret for, in marrying a foreigner, Norma had been false to her vows as a Druid priestess. Pollione tells his friend that he has lost his love for Norma and is now in love with Adalgisa, a young priestess of the temple. He knows that Norma's vengeance would be ruthless should she discover this fact and he recounts a dream he has had in which he and Adalgisa knelt side by side before an altar in Rome, when suddenly Adalgisa disappeared and a voice sounding through the temple declared that thus did Norma revenge herself.

The signal is now given that the moon is rising and the two young Romans escape from the sacred grove just as the Druids return to it, marching to the dignified measures of the well-known *"Religious March"*. When all are in their places, the High Priestess, Norma, enters, carrying a golden sickle and accompanied by her attendants.

Mounting the steps before the altar under the oak tree, she warns her people that the time for driving out the Roman conquerors has not come yet. The fate of Rome, she says, is in the hands of the gods and when the end of Roman power comes, it will come not from any outside force, but from weakness within. The moonlight is shining brightly on her and on the altar as she turns and cuts branches of the mistletoe and sings her great aria, praying for peace, *"Casta Diva"* ("Pure goddess").

At its conclusion she tells the people she will give them the signal when the time for rebellion comes, and the people cry out that the first to fall will be the pro-consul, Pollione. The crowd leaves the grove and for a few moments it is deserted and then the young priestess, Adalgisa, returns and kneels before the altar in prayer, imploring the gods to release her from her guilty love. Pollione enters and implores her to flee with him to Rome. At first she repulses him, but finally yields to his pleading and they embrace each other ardently. Adalgisa swears that she will go with him wherever he may go, no matter what their fate will be—*"Vieni in Roma"* ("Come to Rome"). He asks her to meet him at this very spot at the same time tomorrow night and they will escape together. The curtain falls as they sing passionately of their love.

ACT TWO

Scene: *Norma's dwelling.*

Norma enters with her two children and their nurse, Clotilda. Norma expresses her anxiety for the future of her children, for Pollione has been recalled to Rome and she fears that he will desert both her and the children, and she knows that the eventual discovery of her secret marriage will bring terrible retribution. She hears someone approaching and urges Clotilda to hide the children.

The newcomer is Adalgisa, who is in great distress of mind because of her falseness to her vows and the conflict in her life caused by her love for Pollione. Dropping to her knees before the High Priestess, she confesses that she has fallen in love and has resolved to leave the temple and flee with her lover to a distant land.

She begs for forgiveness, or else for strength to resist this guilty love. Norma recalls how her own vows have been broken and remembers the great secret happiness of the first years of her marriage, *"Ah! si, fa core e abbraccia"* ("Ah! be cheerful, weep not"). With great warmth and sympathy, she absolves Adalgisa from her religious vows and assures her of pardon. She asks Adalgisa who her lover is and Adalgisa replies, "A Roman." Just at that moment, Pollione stands before them. Innocently, Adalgisa exclaims, "Behold him!"

After a moment of shocked surprise, Norma is transformed. In a wild outburst, she denounces Pollione for his treachery to her and to their children. Then she turns to Adalgisa and points out that her lover is doubly guilty, deceiving both his own wife and the young girl. Adalgisa is at first bewildered and incredulous, but when she realizes the true situation, she assures Norma that her love for Pollione is dead and that she has given up all thought of fleeing with him.

Pollione begs Adalgisa not to desert him, but she eludes him and flings herself into the arms of Norma, begging for protection. Norma orders Pollione out of her sight, *"Vanne, sì, mi lascia, indegno"* ("Go, leave me, unworthy one"), but he defies her. Just as the scene reaches this climax, the booming of the great bronze shield of Irminsul is heard summoning the Druids to the temple. Norma still stands with her arms around Adalgisa as Pollione, in baffled fury, hurries away.

ACT THREE

SCENE: *Bedroom in the home of Norma.*

The two children lie asleep on a couch. Norma enters the room quietly, carrying a lamp. Setting the lamp on a table, she stands contemplating her children intently, and slowly draws a dagger from her bosom. "It is better for them to die than to live as slaves in Rome," she says sadly. She raises the dagger but cannot force herself to kill her own children and, as she stands irresolute, she utters a cry of anguish, and falls on her knees beside the bed sobbing.

The children waken and Norma summons the nurse, Clotilda, and orders her to bring Adalgisa to her. When the young girl enters, Norma asks her to take the children to their father, Pollione, in the Roman camp, and to confide them to his care. Adalgisa knows only too well that Norma is planning to take her own life and she begs her not to do so. She has resolved never to see Pollione again but she will go to him once more, not for the sake of the children or for her own sake, but to beg him to return to the woman who loves him and is the mother of his children.

But Norma is too crushed and heartbroken to be won over to this plan at once and for a time she gives way to despair. But Adalgisa pleads so earnestly and is so obviously sincere in her love for the High Priestess, that finally Norma gives her consent. The voices of the two women blend in a beautiful duet, *"Mira o Norma"* ("See, oh Norma").

ACT FOUR

SCENE ONE: *A rocky cavern near the sacred grove.*

The Gallic warriors, still eager to attack the Romans and drive them from the land, have gathered in one of their secret meeting places in the forest. Oroveso, the Arch-Druid, appears before them. "I bring you evil tidings," he says. Pollione has been recalled to Rome and the commander who has been appointed to be his successor is reputed to be even more cruel and tyrannical than Pollione.

The restless warriors inquire if Norma still counsels peace, and Oroveso replies that the High Priestess has given no sign. He assures them that he hates the Romans as much as they do, and advises them to keep up the appearance of weak submission to bondage until the proper moment comes. Then, with victory assured, they will rid themselves forever of the hated conquerors.

SCENE TWO: *The temple of Irminsul.*

Norma stands before the altar hopefully awaiting the return of Adalgisa from her mission to Pollione. But it is not Adalgisa who enters, but Clotilda, who comes in with the news that Adalgisa has failed in her efforts to persuade Pollione to return to Norma. Instead of yielding to her entreaties, Pollione has renewed his pleas to Adalgisa to flee with him and has even tried to force her to do so. Adalgisa has escaped and has taken refuge in the temple.

Her hopes of happiness shattered, almost in a frenzy of rage, Norma strikes the great bronze shield three times and the sound echoes through the temple and surrounding grove. In answer to the signal, a great crowd of people rush into the temple, priests, priestesses, and warriors, with Oroveso in their midst. When the Arch-Druid asks the meaning of the signal, Norma replies boldly that the hour of war has come.

A great shout goes up from the people who vow a terrible vengeance on their oppressors, *"Guerra! le Galliche selve!"* ("War to the oppressors"). Oroveso steps forward and calls attention to the fact that no sacrifice has been prepared for the altar, a necessary ceremony at the beginning of so great an adventure, but Norma replies grimly that a sacrifice will be ready in the proper time.

There is a commotion outside and Clotilda rushes in, crying out that the sacred grove has been desecrated by a Roman. Soldiers drag in Pollione. He shakes himself free from his captors and stands before the altar, arms folded, staring arrogantly at his enemies.

Oroveso takes up the sacrificial knife and advances toward the haughty Roman, but Norma seizes the knife from his hand and raises it over the defenseless Pollione. She pauses, and after a moment asks the people to leave, as she wishes to learn from the prisoner if he had any accomplices in gaining entrance to the temple.

When Norma and Pollione are alone, she tells him that if he will swear never to see Adalgisa again, she will grant him his freedom, *"In mia man alfin tu sei"* ("Under my power you are at last"). He refuses passionately and will not yield even when she threatens to kill his children. Though he will not renounce Adalgisa, he begs Norma to spare the children and offers his own life in exchange for theirs. Norma now declares that the gods demand a sacrifice and Adalgisa must be that sacrifice. Again Pollione offers himself as the victim, but Norma insists that by killing the woman he loves, she will inflict greater torture on him than he could experience in any other way.

Norma turns to the altar and ascends the steps and stands there like an avenging goddess. She summons the people and announces to them that the sacrificial victim has been chosen. "It is a priestess," she says, "a priestess who has been false to her vows." The crowd angrily demands the name of the false priestess and Pollione, thinking she is about to denounce Adalgisa, implores her not to speak.

"It is I," cries Norma. "I am the false priestess."

She takes the ceremonial wreath of flowers from her head and drops it to the ground as she orders the sacrificial pyre to be prepared. Then she turns to Pollione and tells him that she loves him still and will continue to love him beyond the grave. Deeply moved, Pollione replies that the veil has been lifted from his eyes, the fleeting infatuation with Adalgisa has gone forever and in its place is his deep and abiding love for Norma.

Oroveso and the Druids have listened to this scene in stunned silence. Now they beg Norma to rescind her judgment, thinking it must have been uttered in a moment of madness. But Norma insists that she is guilty beyond hope of pardon and implores her father to care for her orphaned children.

The sacrificial pyre is ready and Pollione begs to be allowed to share the atonement with Norma. In a grim chant, the Druids announce that this sacrifice will cleanse their temple of defilement. A black veil is thrown over Norma's head. She embraces her father, Oroveso, in a last farewell, *"Deh! non volerli vittime!"* ("O! let my children not be victims"). Then, arm in arm, Norma and Pollione walk slowly toward their doom as the priests chant a solemn dirge.

Carmen

by GEORGES BIZET (1838-1875)

Four Acts. Libretto by Meilhac and Halévy, based on novel by Mérimée.
First produced in Paris, 1875.

Carmen, a gypsy	*Mezzo-soprano*
Don José, a corporal	*Tenor*
Micaela, a peasant girl	*Soprano*
Escamillo, a toreador	*Baritone*
Morales, an officer	*Baritone*
Zuniga, a captain	*Bass*
Mercedes } gypsies	*Mezzo-soprano*
Frasquita	*Mezzo-soprano*
El Remendado } smugglers	*Tenor*
El Dancairo	*Baritone*

Cigarette-factory girls, dragoons, an innkeeper, smugglers, dancers.

TIME: *About 1820.*
PLACE: *In and near Seville.*

ACT ONE

SCENE: *A public square in Seville.*

On the right-hand side of the stage is a cigarette factory, on the left a guardhouse with a group of soldiers lounging in front of it. Passers-by throng the square and the scene is a brilliant one, with bright-colored Spanish costumes in the bright Spanish sunlight. Lieutenant Morales, one of the soldiers, notices a shy young girl crossing the square and approaches her gallantly. "I am looking for a certain corporal named Don José," she says. Morales tells her that Don José is not there, but will come in when the guard is changed. The young girl, whose name is Micaela, is too timid to accept his invitation to wait for Don José and she leaves.

Soon a bugle call sounds, signaling the changing of the guard, a delightful episode with a striking military march as the new guard marches in and a group of street urchins follows them mockingly. It is now noon and the factory girls, smoking cigarettes, come out for their midday recess —and a little flirtation with the soldiers—*"Chorus of the cigarette girls"*. Carmen, the most colorful personality of them all, comes last. She sings the familiar "Habanera"— *"L'amour est un oiseau rebelle"* ("Love is like a wood bird")—trying with great frankness (but no obvious success) to get the attention of Don José, who has come in with the new group of soldiers. The factory bell calls the girls back to work. As Carmen leaves, she tosses a flower at José. He is left alone and he picks up the flower and hides it in his uniform.

Now Micaela returns, bringing a letter from José's mother. He is delighted to see his childhood sweetheart and they sing a melodious duet, *"Parlez-moi de ma mère"* ("Tell me of my mother").

As Micaela leaves and Don José is thinking tenderly of his mother in his far-off native village, he is rudely interrupted by the sounds of a violent quarrel breaking out in the factory. The girls come running out to lay their troubles before Captain Zuniga, the officer in charge of the soldiers. Carmen, they say, has attacked one of the other girls and

Don José is sent into the factory to arrest her. A minute later he returns with Carmen who is in a defiant mood. "Tra la la," she sings mockingly. "You may cut me, burn me, I'll not say a word."

After considerable excitement, she is left alone in charge of Don José, with her hands tied behind her back. With a too-obvious air of innocence, she sings the enchanting "Seguidilla"—*"Près des ramparts de Séville"* ("Near to the walls of Seville")—a Spanish dance in ⅜ time, slyly suggesting that she and the young soldier meet outside the walls of Seville at the inn of a certain Lillas Pastia. Gradually, José falls under her spell and secretly unties her hands. And so, when Zuniga comes with the order to send her to prison, she is able to push Don José aside and make good her escape. Don José is immediately put under arrest, and we hear the laughter of Carmen's friends as the curtain falls.

ACT TWO

SCENE: *The Inn of Lillas Pastia on the outskirts of Seville.*

Soldiers, smugglers, and their girls are indulging in a jolly round of gypsy songs and dances, Pastia must close the inn for the night and the party is about to break up when Escamillo, a popular toreador, makes an impressive entrance and sings one of the most popular of all operatic arias, the *"Toreador Song"*. His eyes light on Carmen as the most attractive of the girls present, but when the party breaks up, she remains behind, awaiting Don José.

It is just two months since he was arrested for allowing her to escape, and his prison term has ended that very day. Before he comes, Carmen takes part in a delightfully high-spirited quintet with four companions, her friends Frasquita and Mercedes and two smugglers named El Dancairo and El Remendado. She agrees to try to persuade Don José to join them on their next smuggling expedition. Soon we hear Don José singing off-stage as he approaches the inn. Carmen is left alone to welcome her lover.

As he enters, singing a lilting melody, *"The Dragoon of Alcala"*, she takes up her castanets and dances gayly for him. But in the middle of her dance, the sound of a distant bugle is heard and Don José starts to leave to return to his regiment. Furious at what she considers Don José's faint-heartedness, she flies into a rage, throwing his cap and sabre at him scornfully. But he draws out the faded flower she tossed to him at their first meeting and tenderly and passionately sings the "Flower Song"—*"La fleur que tu m'avais jetté"* ("This flower you gave to me")—telling her how he treasured it throughout his two months in prison.

She is almost reconciled to him, when Captain Zuniga enters, hoping to carry on a flirtation with Carmen. He orders José back to the barracks. Furious with jealousy, the young dragoon cries "I will not go!" The two men draw their swords and a duel is about to begin when Carmen calls in the gypsies and Zuniga is disarmed.

Guilty of serious insubordination, Don José is afraid to return to the army and feels compelled to join the band of smugglers. The scene ends with a stirring chorus in praise of liberty and a free life.

ACT THREE

SCENE: *A wild mountain pass.*

The smugglers are picking their way over the rocky ground. Dancairo suggests that the party set down their boxes and bales and rest while he sends scouts ahead to see if it is safe to go on. Carmen and Don José are already quarreling. He is conscience-stricken about his new way of life, and she is a little tired of him.

Carmen's two friends, Frasquita and Mercedes, taking out their cards and beginning to tell their own fortunes, sing the charming duet, *"Et maintenant, parlez mes belles"* ("Now, pretty cards, tell us"). Carmen spreads her blanket on the ground and engages in the same pastime and finds in her cards only death. Time and again the cards repeat the same message—death. Then the three women unite in singing the famous Card Scene—*"Quant au douanier"* ("As for the guards, 'tis our affair").

As dawn turns to day, the gypsy band goes off toward the border, leaving Don José to guard the pass from a rocky height just off-stage. Micaela comes in looking for Don José and, very much frightened by the sinister aspect of the lonely place, prays for protection in one of the most beautiful of all soprano arias, *"Je dis que rien ne m'épou-vante"* ("I said naught should frighten me here").

Meantime, Don José sees someone climbing the mountain and fires a shot. It is not intended for Micaela (though naturally it frightens her into running away) but for another figure coming up the mountain pass—the toreador Escamillo. The toreador is looking for Carmen, and José's jealousy is at once aroused. Both men draw their knives and the fight is bitter, with Escamillo getting somewhat the worst of it, when the gypsies come running back and Carmen saves the toreador. Not the least upset by his narrow escape from death, Escamillo gaily invites everyone, and especially Carmen, to see his next performance in the bull ring in Seville, *"Et qui m'aime y viendra!"* ("They who love me will come").

As he leaves, the gypsies discover Micaela, who has been hiding nearby. She comes out to tell Don José that his mother is dying. Scornfully, Carmen tells him that he had better go home. Torn between jealousy and duty, Don José is about to leave when the toreador is heard singing the *"Toreador Song"* once more as he picks his way down the mountainside. Carmen shows her excitement. In a jealous rage, Don José prevents her from running after the toreador, furiously hurling her to the ground. And then José reluctantly leaves with Micaela. As the curtain slowly descends, the smuggler's march is heard as the gypsies prepare for departure.

ACT FOUR

SCENE: *Entrance to the bull ring in Seville.*

It is a bright sunny day and it seems as if the entire city has gathered there. Street vendors cry their wares, the brilliantly costumed throng strolls in and out, there is dancing and merriment, and then a procession of city officials, picadors, and other dignitaries crosses the stage and enters the arena.

Last of all comes Escamillo, the favorite hero of the day, and by his side in the open carriage sits Carmen dressed in all her holiday finery. They step from the carriage and before he goes into the arena they sing a tender love-duet, *"Si tu m'aimes, Carmen"* ("If thou lovest me, Carmen"), and Carmen assures him that she loves him and him alone.

Carmen is warned by Frasquita and Mercedes that Don José has been seen lurking about in the neighborhood. She is determined to end the quarrel with her erstwhile lover and waits outside while the others enter the bull ring. Soon Don José comes on to the stage, but a sadly changed Don José, bedraggled, haggard, and woebegone. He makes a desperate plea for Carmen to return to him. He has sacrificed everything for her, even his self-respect.

It is no use. Carmen is now heart and soul in love with Escamillo and she treats Don José with scorn. "All is over between us," she cries. Again and again we hear Escamillo being applauded in the arena, and Carmen, though she knows it may mean her death, throws José's ring away and insists on going past him into the arena to share her new lover's triumph.

Changed now from a heart-broken, pleading man to a jealous, furious one, he blocks her way into the arena. He threatens her, he draws his knife and, even as the crowd in the arena hails Escamillo's victory, he strikes. Carmen shrieks and falls dead at his feet as the crowd rushes out.

"I have killed her," cries Don José. "You may arrest me. O Carmen, my adored Carmen!" and he flings himself on her body as the curtain falls.

Peter Grimes

by BENJAMIN BRITTEN (1913–   )

Three Acts and a Prologue. Words by Montague Slater, derived from the poem of George Crabbe.
First produced in London, 1945.

Peter Grimes, a fisherman	*Tenor*
Boy, his apprentice	*Silent*
Ellen Orford, a widow, schoolmistress of the Borough	*Soprano*
Captain Balstrode, retired merchant skipper	*Baritone*
Auntie, landlady of "The Boar"	*Contralto*
Niece I **Niece II** } main attractions of "The Boar"	*Sopranos*
Robert Boles, fisherman and Methodist	*Tenor*
Swallow, a lawyer	*Bass*
Mrs. (Nabob) Sedley, a rentier widow of an East India Company's factor	*Soprano*
Rev. Horace Adams, the rector	*Tenor*
Ned Keene, apothecary and quack	*Baritone*
Dr. Crabbe	*Silent*
Hobson, carrier	*Bass*

Villagers

SCENE: *The Borough, a small fishing village on the East Coast of England.*
TIME: *About 1830.*

PROLOGUE

SCENE: *The Coroner's Court in Moot Hall.*

Peter Grimes is unpopular in the Borough—a man inclined to keep himself to himself; to work out his fierce pride in cruel treatment of any apprentice he must have to operate his fishing boat; and to creep away into the overturned boat that serves him and his current apprentice as home, ignoring what social life exists in the town's church and the town's tavern. The village has not paid too much attention to the cries of pain that come all too frequently from the hut. "Peter Grimes is at his exercise," the villagers

29

are wont to say, shrugging it off callously. But when one of the boys dies during a disastrous trip to London, ugly rumors get about. There is an inquest, and the word "murder" begins to be heard. The opera opens on this inquest in the Coroner's Court. Mr. Swallow, the local lawyer, also Mayor and Coroner, is presiding.

The temper of the spectators is menacing. Against the cross-examination which fails to prove that Peter is guilty of any crime except ambition, a chorus comments acidly: "When women gossip the result is someone doesn't sleep at night." At Swallow's verdict of accidental death, the Chorus does not approve: "But when the crowner sits upon it, Who can dare to fix the guilt?"

Swallow warns Peter not to get another apprentice, but to hire a grown man instead. Peter protests. Swallow suggests a woman to help look after the boy. Peter shows that the idea is agreeable, but says he must first stop people's mouths. In a frenzy of appeal, he sings: " 'Stand down,' you say. You wash your hands. The case goes on in people's minds. . . . Let me speak, let me stand trial . . . O let me thrust into their mouths the truth itself, the simple truth."

Constable Hobson tries to clear the court. The chorus is shouting its disapproval, but Swallow's dignified exit draws them after him. Peter is left alone with Ellen, the schoolmistress, his only friend in the Borough. In one of the rare lyrical moods of the opera, they sing a duet of hope and fear, joining in an expression of mutual trust: "Your voice out of the pain is like a hand that I can feel and know: Here is a friend." They walk off slowly as the curtain falls.

(The musical interlude here is properly the prelude to the opera, and forms the first of four such interludes, which are often played in concert under the title "Four Sea Pieces". They are highly expressive of the moods of the sea-coast, as well as of the characters of the opera.)

ACT ONE

SCENE ONE: *A street by the sea.*

The fishing boats are coming in, one by one, met by the women with baskets. Captain Balstrode, a retired merchant sea-captain, watches the proceedings and keeps an eye on the open sea through his telescope from time to time. "Sea horses" a long way out show that the wind is holding back the tide. If it veers, he says, they must watch for their lives.

As one character after another enters the scene—the hospitable Auntie, who stands in the doorway of her Inn; Boles, the Methodist fisherman who condemns her establishment and all who patronize it; the Rector, who makes his way in a series of melodious "good mornings"; Mrs. Sedley, the town gossip; and Ned Keene, the apothecary —the chorus of women and fishermen comment on the scene and people in the manner of a Greek chorus. Their language is poetic, set against the everyday speech of the villagers.

Peter tries to get help to bring in his boat, but no one will lend a hand. He must haul it in himself. Ned tells him that he has found an apprentice, a work-house boy. He must be fetched by Hobson, the carter. Hobson is reluctant; he has too much work and does not want the responsibility of minding the boy on the late ride back. Ellen volunteers to go along, to the disapproval of the crowd. She voices her stand in an aria, *"Let her among you without fault cast the first stone"*, and follows Hobson to his cart.

A little side play here reveals that Mrs. Sedley, so respectable on the surface, depends heavily on laudanum for a sleeping draught, and must meet Ned at the pub to get a fresh supply, although she protests at the indecorum of such a thing. Now the storm is ready to invade the oft-battered coast; and the choruses warn of its terrors and join in a plea to the elements: *"Oh tide that waits for no man, Spare our coasts"*. Some go to make their belongings secure; most decide to drown their apprehensions in The Boar's beery comfort. Peter is left alone with Balstrode, who rather sympathetically leads the lonely man on to bare his heart. Peter says that he is rooted in the Borough, no matter how unsympathetic the people are, with their "shut faces". In a passionate burst he tells Balstrode about the day the boy was killed: *"Picture what that day was like, that evil day"*. Then he confides his ambition: to make enough money to win over the Borough and to marry Ellen. He rejects Balstrode's advice to ask her now, money or no. His stubborn pride will not allow it. Balstrode enters the pub, and Peter sings, "What harbour shelters peace? . . . With her there'll be no quarrels." The wind rises as the curtain closes on his loneliness.

SCENE TWO: *Interior of The Boar.*

It is almost closing time in the crowded and convivial pub, and air is the cosier within for the raging storm without. Auntie closes the door with difficulty after Mrs. Sedley, who has come for her drug. Boles and some fishermen enter, bringing the wind with them and upsetting the room. The Nieces come downstairs in pretty panic. They behave like twins, as though each has only half a personality. Balstrode is rude to them, and Auntie angrily shouts at him: "Loud man, I never did have time for the sort of creature who spits in his wine. A joke's a joke and fun is fun, but say your grace and be polite. . . ." Her attention is diverted by Boles, who is drunk and paying court to the Nieces in a most un-Methodist fashion. Balstrode subdues him, and leads a chorus in a refrain that concludes: *"We'll live and let live and look—We keep our hands to ourselves."*

Ned brings news that the cliff has slid down, just by Grimes' hut. *"Talk of the devil,"* sings the chorus, for just then in comes Peter himself. Shunned by the others, he breaks into a soliloquy that, to the drunken, bawdy company, sounds more than half mad. *"Now the Great Bear and Pleiades . . . are drawing up the clouds of human grief. . . . Who can turn skies back and begin again?"* Boles' reaction is to cosh Peter over the head with a bottle. A fight is averted by Balstrode, who leads off in a sea chanty, a round, enormously complicated and requiring the attention of everybody: *"Old Joe has gone fishing".* Peter joins in, breaking the round with a macabre verse out of rhythm, but the others recover and repeat. At the climax, the door opens to admit Ellen, Hobson, and the boy, soaked and bedraggled. Peter takes the boy out again into the storm.

ACT TWO

SCENE ONE: *The same as in Act One. The street.*

It is a fine sunny morning some weeks later, and the Borough is at its Sunday worship. Ellen brings the boy to sit beside her on the breakwater, and knits as she talks to him. Her conversation is punctuated by verses of a hymn from within the church, and comes to a climax as she discovers that the boy has a bruise on his neck—Grimes' ill treatment has begun again in spite of her hopes. Peter comes to fetch the boy—there is work to be done even on Sunday—and Ellen pleads with him to let the child rest. The dialogue and the chorus' hymn form a responsive musical scheme that builds up until Peter in anger strikes Ellen. The neighbors have been watching from behind their doors and windows. Ned, Boles, and Auntie emerge and discuss the situation until the church congregation begins to trickle out.

Then it is the turn of the respectable people of the Borough. Between their hypocrisy and the scandal-mongering of Mrs. Sedley and the righteous inveighing of Boles, the crowd is incited to call on Grimes and demand an explanation. Led by the Rector and Swallow, they go off, singing *"Now is gossip put on trial".*

Auntie, the Nieces, and Ellen are left alone to sing a reflective trio—a trio it is, since the two Nieces sing as one—pondering on the ways of men, its refrain *"Shall we smile or shall we weep or wait quietly till they sleep?"*

SCENE TWO: *Grimes' hut.*

Grimes is preparing to go fishing, and prompts the frightened boy to get ready. In a long monologue, he tells of his hopes to "fish the sea dry and flood the market", then to marry Ellen. He changes his tune and sings *"In dreams I've built myself some kindlier home".* The boy watches him in fascinated horror, and his face reminds Peter of the other boy. Already he is becoming haunted. The crowd sings from far off, coming nearer by the moment: *"Bring the branding iron and knife, What's done now is done for life".* Peter turns and accuses the boy of gossiping. In his neurotic rage, the boy becomes a focal point for all his troubles. He thrusts him roughly out the door, and the boy screams as apparently he loses his footing on the eroded cliff. Peter goes out after him as the Rector enters by the street door. The mob is quieted by finding a neat hut, its occupants presumably out fishing. They disperse, all but Balstrode, who suspects that all is not well. He looks out the door by the cliff, and climbs down himself.

ACT THREE

SCENE ONE: *Same as in Act One.*

It is a summer evening, a few days later. A dance is in progress in Moot Hall, and we hear the polka and see the shadows of the dancers. The Boar is lit brightly, too. The stage is empty as the curtain rises, but soon one of the Nieces scampers across, pursued by Swallow. The other Niece soon joins them. Swallow sings a tipsy, sprawling tune, *"Assign your prettiness to me"*, and the Nieces reply that they feel safer together and that tête-à-têtes should always be "in threes". Both girls elude Swallow, who goes into the inn in disgust. Ned Keene now becomes their pursuer, and is about to follow them to the boats at the back of the scene when he is stopped by Mrs. Sedley. The music from the dance hall changes to a waltz. Mrs. Sedley is determined to place the charge of murder at Grimes' door. The boy has not been seen for two days. *"Murder most foul it is, Eerie I find it"*, she sings malignantly. Ned is bored and breaks away from her.

The music changes to a hornpipe as the Rector and Burgesses come from Moot Hall. The rector sings a sweet "good-night" to one and all, alternating with the chorus. The hornpipe fades out and Mrs. Sedley's sinister music begins, as that interfering lady prepares to eavesdrop again, this time on Ellen and Balstrode. Ellen has found the boy's jersey with her embroidered anchor on it, wet, down by the tide-mark. She sings an aria about it: *"Embroidery in childhood was a luxury of idleness"*, halting the progress of the tragedy for a moment. Grimes' only friends are now in despair for him. As they leave to search him out, the dance band strikes up a galop, which later is worked up into the music that accompanies the man-hunt for Grimes. Mrs. Sedley, of course, is the instigator for this. She demands that Swallow leave his carousing, points out Grimes' boat, deserted, gloats over the crime that is her hobby. Now the hunt is on. Voices call "Peter Grimes" from all over, eerily advancing and retreating. The fog comes in.

SCENE TWO: *Same as Scene One.*

Peter has returned to his boat, his only refuge. A distant foghorn pierces the gloom; occasionally a voice from the distance calls Peter's name, weirdly. Peter begins a long recitative, *"Steady. There you are. Nearly home. What is home?"* He remembers that the first boy died, just died; the other slipped and died. His speech becomes muddled, mixed with bits from former songs, things the townspeople have said, his own hopes, his helplessness. He roars back at the voices, now near at hand. At last Ellen and Balstrode find him, but it is too late. Ellen cannot save him; Balstrode has the only solution. "Sail out until you lose sight of Moot Hall," he counsels, "then sink the boat." Peter obeys. Balstrode tries to comfort Ellen, and he leads her off. The night advances.

Dawn comes at last to the Borough, and another day of fishing, gossiping, drinking, begins. Swallow reports that a coastguard has seen a boat sinking out to sea. No one knows whose it is. The Nieces begin to polish the brasses outside The Boar. The Chorus comments on the beginning of another day; the sea will always dominate this place:

> In ceaseless motion comes and goes the tide
> Flowing it fills the channel vast and wide
> Then back to sea with strong majestic sweep
> It rolls in ebb yet terrible and deep.

The curtain falls slowly.

Louise

by GUSTAVE CHARPENTIER (1860–   )

Four Acts. Libretto by Charpentier.
First produced in Paris, 1900.

Louise, a seamstress	*Soprano*
Julien, a poet	*Tenor*
The Father	*Bass*
The Mother	*Mezzo-soprano*
Noctambulist	*Tenor*

Workers, vendors, seamstresses, policemen, artists, citizens of Paris.

TIME: *About 1900*.
PLACE: *Paris*.

ACT ONE

SCENE: *The home of Louise.*

The curtain rises on the plainly furnished living-room of a Parisian working-class family. At the right-hand side of the room part of the kitchen can be seen. At the back is a large window opening onto a balcony, across from which is another balcony on an adjoining house. Standing on this neighboring balcony is a young man, the poet Julien. It is early evening in April and the light of the sunset illuminates the roofs of Paris which can be seen in the distance.

Julien sings a song of gaiety and freedom, a song in praise of the city of Paris and it is really a kind of serenade to his young neighbor, Louise, *"O coeur ami! O coeur promis"* ("O friendly heart! O promised heart!"). We see her cautiously open the window and reply to Julien, assuring him that she is alone. He reminds her that he had written to her father and has received no reply and that her parents have refused to allow them to meet. He has just written to her father again and tells her that if he receives no answer to his second letter, Louise must elope with him as she has promised. But Louise denies that she has ever promised to elope, and declares that she loves her parents too much to leave them without their consent. The two young lovers speak of their first awareness of each other and their few brief and secret meetings.

During this conversation, Louise's mother returns from her marketing and listens cynically to the rapture of the young lovers until she hears Julien refer to her as an "old witch," then she drags Louise away from the window, pushes her into the kitchen and slams the door. Julien laughs mockingly and goes back into his studio as the mother angrily shuts the window. Louise and her mother quarrel bitterly but when they hear the sound of footsteps coming slowly up the stairs, they suddenly become silent and busy themselves preparing supper.

The door opens and the father enters, holding in his hand Julien's second letter. He is dressed in humble working clothes and sinks wearily into a chair. After a moment he looks up at Louise and holds out his arms to her, and father and daughter embrace tenderly. He reads Julien's letter, but makes no comment. Supper is placed on the table and the little family sit down to eat. The mother complains bitterly that her husband has to work hard, year in and year out, while some good-for-nothings do not work at all but only write poems and make love. The father remarks quietly that it is true he works hard, but he finds real happiness in his home and family.

Supper over, the dishes are removed from the table and the father contentedly lights his pipe. Louise picks up Julien's letter and hands it to him. He reads it again and then tells his wife that perhaps they have been too hard on the young people. But the mother angrily retorts that if ever Julien enters the house she will leave it and in her outburst of temper, she slaps Louise. The father tells Louise that she is still too young and inexperienced to know what is best and that she must learn to forget Julien. The mother can be heard banging the pots and pans in the kitchen, while the father tries to console his weeping daughter, *"O mon enfant"* ("O my child").

In a few minutes, the mother returns to the living-room

and picks up her sewing basket. The father asks Louise
if she will read the evening paper to him. Sitting in the
lamplight by the bare table, she reads, "The spring season
is most brilliant. All Paris is gay." Her voice breaks. With
a sob, she buries her head in her arms as the curtain falls.

ACT TWO

Scene One: *A street in the Montmartre quarter of Paris.*

It is very early morning just outside the building where
Louise is employed as a seamstress. By the pale light of
the street lamps we can see a rag-picker, a street-sweeper,
a milk woman placing her milk-cans in a booth, a young
girl folding morning newspapers, various vegetable vendors, policemen and other participants in the drama of
Paris streets at night.

In striking contrast to their poverty a man in full evening
dress, covered with a long black cloak, strolls through the
street. When asked who he is, he answers that he is "The
Pleasure of Paris" and that his mission is to bring gaiety
and pleasure to those who have lost the joy of living. With
an arrogant gesture, he goes on his way, pushing rudely
against an old rag-picker, who falls to the ground. The
old man picks himself up, cursing the stranger who, he
says, is the scoundrel who years before had run away with
his daughter. One of the group, a junkman, remarks sadly
that that is the way of life and young people must have
their pleasures.

As it grows lighter, Julien appears with a group of his
bohemian friends. Julien speaks of his young love, Louise,
who works in a building near-by. With exaggerated comic
gestures, his friends strike up a serenade, *"Enfants de la
bohème"* ("Bohemian children"), to the surrounding windows. But they leave when Julien tells them that it is time
for Louise to appear. After they have gone, Julien hides
himself and in a few moments Louise appears, chaperoned
by her mother. Other young seamstresses enter the building and when she is assured that Louise is safe, the mother
departs.

When she is out of sight, Julien rushes into the building
and brings Louise out with him. A long duet follows, in

which the girl is frightened and reluctant, but her lover argues with great eloquence. Louise, he says, must not allow her "golden youth" to be imprisoned. She is a woman now, not a child any longer and she has a will as strong as her parents' and has an equal right to happiness. More than half persuaded, despite her love for her father, she stammers out a half-promise, then embraces him and rushes back into the sewing-room. The disappointed Julien stands for a moment looking at the window where she works, then sadly walks away. An old-clothes man comes slowly down the street, calling his wares and in the distance we hear, softly and far-away, the street-cries of Paris.

SCENE TWO: *Inside the workshop.*

The room is crowded with seamstresses, young and old, who keep up a lively chatter as they work. From time to time we hear the whirring sound of sewing-machines. A young apprentice keeps bobbing around, amusing the workers with playful little tricks, while the forewoman passes from girl to girl to supervise their work.

Louise takes no part in the merry chatter and sits alone, sewing. After a while the other girls notice her silence and begin to tease her and accuse her of being in love. Louise hotly denies this, but the others pay no attention. The talk is now all of love and Louise is becoming more and more uncomfortable.

Suddenly from the street outside we hear the sound of several musical instruments and then the sound of voices singing. It is Julien and his friends who have returned to serenade Louise with the charming air, *"Dans la cité lointaine"* ("In the far-away city"). The sewing girls are delighted and leave their work and rush to the windows. But they soon become bored and begin to mock the serenaders. Some pretend to faint with emotion and the little apprentice throws odds and ends of remnants out of the window. Louise has remained at her work-table, becoming more and more excited. Suddenly she rises to her feet, dropping her work. She tells the other girls she is ill. They help her with her wraps and she hurries out. The others wonder what can be wrong with her. They rush to the windows again and see her going off with Julien, the serenader. Amid peals of laughter, the curtain falls.

ACT THREE

SCENE: *A hill-top in Montmartre*.

Julien and Louise are living together in a little cottage with a garden overlooking the city of Paris. The young lovers are in the garden and as twilight falls, Louise sings of the great happiness that love has brought her—the famous aria, *"Depuis le jour"* ("Since the day I gave myself").

As darkness falls and the lights of Paris appear one by one in the background, they sing a passionate duet of love and of Paris, "The marvelous city," as Julien calls it, declaring that his love for Louise and his love for Paris are one and the same. In an ecstasy they embrace and go slowly into the house.

Then come their friends, the citizens of Montmartre, to decorate the little dwelling with lanterns, festoons, and flags. Quickly the scene is filled with a merry throng, some carrying torches and all singing the praises of love and of Paris. Julien and Louise appear at the door of the cottage to receive the homage of their neighbors. In the midst of the crowd the Noctambulist appears—"The Pleasure of Paris"—now dressed in a bright-colored masquerade costume with jester's cap and bells as "King of the Fools." He sings again of gaiety and pleasure, and in a ceremony of mock solemnity Louise is crowned "Muse of Montmartre."

All join in a brilliant chorus praising youth and joy. Suddenly the merry-making ceases abruptly. At the entrance to the garden appears the dark and tragic figure of Louise's mother. The crowd shrinks back in awe as she enters the garden. Before the sad silent figure the crowd slowly disappears and Louise, terror-stricken, throws her arms around Julien and clings to him tightly.

Quietly, sadly, the mother tells Julien she does not come as an enemy. She and her husband have accepted the loss of their only child. But now the father is very ill—only a great joy can save his life. A rag-picker, wandering by, sings of a father who lost his daughter in the city. Quietly impressed, Julien asks whether the mother will let Louise return if she goes to visit her father and the mother promises. With great reluctance, Louise agrees to go with her mother back into the city. One last embrace between the lovers and the curtain falls.

ACT FOUR

SCENE: *Same as Act One.*

Louise sits sewing by the open window. The mother is at work in the kitchen, while the father sits dejectedly by the table. He is broken by sorrow and by illness. His wife attempts to cheer him, pointing out among other things that they now have a much better view of the city since Julien's house and terrace next door have been torn down.

But the father refuses to be comforted and indulges in a bitter soliloquy, *"Bête de somme que je suis"* ("Beast of burden that I am"), in which he says that the lot of the working-man is hard enough in itself but is made even more difficult to bear by the selfish ingratitude of his children for whom he has sacrificed so much. Louise knows that this is meant for her and she is even more distressed when her father curses the man who has robbed him of his only joy in life.

The mother calls Louise into the kitchen to help with the work there, but the old quarrel breaks out again. Louise returns to the living-room to say good-night to her father. As she bends over to kiss him, he draws her down on his lap and puts his arm around her, singing softly an old lullaby which he had sung to her as a child, *"Reste, repose-toi,"* ("Rest thee and slumber"). Speaking to her as to a child, he suggests that she stay with her parents now and forever.

Louise becomes angry and as her father tries to describe the probable disaster which will eventually come to her, she struggles to her feet and declares that her parents can never win her back by denying her the love and freedom which are rightfully hers.

More and more passionately her excitement rises and she sings to Paris itself to come and aid her. Angrily the father closes the window, only to have his daughter sing brazenly of her love and call frantically for Julien. Her father, in a paroxysm of anger, is about to strike his daugh-

ter, but instead he opens the door with a dramatic gesture
and bids her go—go to the gay city of Paris.

Louise at first is too frightened to do anything but elude
his angry attack and then finally she runs to the door. At
the height of his emotion, the father seizes a chair and hurls
it after his fleeing daughter. Even the mother is shocked
now. Her husband calls after his daughter and sorrow
suddenly overcomes him. He stumbles through the door
after Louise and calls to her again. But there is no answer.
He staggers back into the room and stands for a moment,
weak and exhausted. Then he turns to the window, shakes
his fist at the city and in a pent-up flood of anger and
despair, he cries "O Paris" as the curtain falls.

Pelléas et Mélisande

by CLAUDE DEBUSSY (1862–1918)

Five Acts. Libretto based on Maeterlinck's play.
First produced in Paris, 1902.

Mélisande	*Soprano*
Goland, grandson of King Arkel	*Baritone*
Pelléas, half-brother of Golaud	*Tenor*
Geneviève, mother of Golaud and Pelléas	*Contralto*
Arkel, King of Allemonde	*Bass*
Yniold, young son of Golaud	*Mezzo-soprano*
A physician	*Bass*

Servants, chorus of sailors.

TIME: *The Middle Ages.*
PLACE: *The Kingdom of Allemonde.*

ACT ONE

SCENE ONE: *A forest.*

The setting is a gloomy old castle by the sea, in an
imaginary country. Deep in some legendary forest, Golaud, grandson of the aged King Arkel, is lost far from
home, while hunting.

There, in the woods, beside a fountain, he finds a child-like girl with long blonde hair. She answers his questions in haunted, incomplete phrases. She cannot tell who she is or where she came from, but says her name is Mélisande. Strangely fascinated by this elfin creature out of the unknown, Golaud mutters that he, too, is lost, and he leads her away as the curtain falls.

SCENE TWO: *A room in the castle.*

It is six months later and Golaud's mother, Geneviève, is reading a letter from him to his grandfather, the old King Arkel, *"Voici ce qu'il écrit a son frère, Pelléas"* ("It is thus that he writes to his brother, Pelléas"). The letter is about meeting Mélisande in the forest and how, though he has learned nothing about her past, he has married her. Golaud thinks he may not be welcome at home with his strange bride. Therefore, if he is forgiven, Pelléas, his younger brother, is to place a lamp in the tower of the castle so that Golaud may see it from his ship. If the lamp is not there, he will sail away, never to return. The wise old king says that it is not for ordinary mortals to interfere with destiny and to let Golaud come home.

SCENE THREE: *The garden of the castle.*

On a terrace outside the castle, overlooking the sea, Mélisande is complaining to Geneviève about the darkness of the forests about the castle—*"Il fait sombre dans le jardin"* ("In the garden here it is dark"). Everywhere in this place it is too dark for this child of light. Pelléas joins them and they speak of a storm that is brewing. Night begins to fall and Geneviève leaves Pelléas and Mélisande alone. "I am leaving, perhaps tomorrow," says Pelléas. And Mélisande asks, "Oh—why are you going away?" And so the curtain falls with this bare suggestion of the tragedy that is to follow.

ACT TWO

SCENE ONE: *A fountain in the park surrounding the castle.*

It is noon, and Pelléas and Mélisande, who have been strolling in the park, sit down to rest on the edge of the marble basin. Mélisande, in child-like fashion, begins to play with her wedding ring, tossing it up into the air and catching it. But she does it once too often, and she misses it, and it falls into the well. "Oh, we shall never find it again!" she cries. "What are we going to tell Golaud?" *"La vérité, la vérité"* ("The truth, the truth"), says Pelléas. But Golaud never learns the truth, for Mélisande is much too afraid of him.

SCENE TWO: *A room in the castle.*

Golaud is in bed, for he was thrown from his horse at the very moment that Mélisande's ring fell into the fountain. Mélisande stands beside the bed and he asks in a kindly fashion why she weeps so much. Has anyone been unkind to her? Does she wish to leave him? "No," says Mélisande. It is only the gloomy place that bothers her—where one sees the sun so seldom.

Taking her hands in his, Golaud discovers the absence of the ring. He is greatly upset, and Mélisande tells him she lost it in the grotto by the seashore. Well, then, says Golaud, she must go and search for it at once, even before it is completely dark.

SCENE THREE: *A grotto in the seashore.*

Through the darkness, Pelléas and Mélisande pick their way timidly to the entrance of the mysterious cave. Suddenly the moon comes out from behind the clouds, and in the foreground three old men are seen asleep at the entrance of the cave. "It is because there is a famine in the land," explains Pelléas; but Mélisande is now terribly frightened, and wishes to run away. "Let us go," she says. "We can return another day."

ACT THREE

SCENE ONE: *A tower of the castle.*

Mélisande stands in the window of a tower in the castle combing her beautiful long blonde hair. Pelléas passes by below, and the moonlit night plays on their emotions. "Give me your hand," begs Pelléas, "for I must leave tomorrow."

And Mélisande reaches her hand to him and, leaning over farther out of the window, her hair falls on the head of Pelléas. He winds it about his neck—and a strangely quiet and intense love-duet follows. And there Golaud, the husband of Mélisande and the brother of Pelléas, find them. "Don't you know how late it is?" he says. "It is almost midnight." And laughing nervously, he adds, "What children you are, what children!"

SCENE TWO: *The vaults of the castle.*

Golaud has taken Pelléas down to the dank, dark caverns which underlie the castle. Golaud's hands tremble in this suffocating, evil place, as he points out how easy it would be to fall into the abyss. But he never says that some such fate might be in store for a man who loves his wife, even though that man were his brother. He never says it, but the suggestion is there.

SCENE THREE: *A terrace before the castle.*

Golaud and Pelléas emerge from the dark caverns underneath the castle. Pelléas expresses his relief at coming up into the fresh air again, and points out that children are going down to the shore to bathe, while within the castle tower he can see Mélisande and his mother together. Golaud warns him that he must not spend so much time with Mélisande.

SCENE FOUR: *Terrace in front of Mélisande's tower—same as Scene One.*

Golaud is on the terrace with his little son Yniold, the child of an earlier marriage. Golaud questions him about Pelléas and Mélisande. But all he can learn is that they are often together, that they talk of Golaud, and that they weep and are afraid. Suddenly, Mélisande's window lights up. Golaud raises the child so that he can look into the room. And the innocent boy reports to the tortured, miserable man that Pelléas and Mélisande are in there together, saying nothing, only staring at the light. Then the child says he is afraid and begs to be let down—so Golaud has again learned nothing, but he goes out, deeply disturbed.

ACT FOUR

SCENE ONE: *A room in the castle.*

Pelléas and Mélisande meet briefly in a room in the castle, and Pelléas tells Mélisande that he will leave the next day and Mélisande will never see him again. They arrange to meet for the last time that night in the park. They separate guiltily, and a few moments later Arkel, the old king, comes in with Mélisande and speaks comfortingly to her about a bright future.

But Golaud comes in, in a very strange and angry mood. He brushes Mélisande aside, commands her to bring him his sword, puts it away again and questions Mélisande darkly. He speaks about the apparent innocence of Mélisande, an innocence that seems to hide secrets. He works himself up into an angry passion, forces Mélisande to her knees, seizes her brutally by the hair, and forces her from right to left in so bitter and cruel a fashion that King Arkel interrupts with the cry of "Golaud!"

And now Golaud assumes a calm dignity he does not feel. "You shall do as you like," he says. "I am too old. I shall just wait." And he leaves them. But poor Mélisande, speaking for the first time, says, *"Il ne m'aime plus . . . je ne suis pas heureuse"* ("He loves me no longer . . . I am not happy").

SCENE TWO: *A fountain in the park.*

That night in the park beside the fountain, Pelléas and Mélisande meet for the last time. Again Pelléas tells her he must leave. Does she not know why? It is because he loves her. "I love you too," she murmurs simply. It is their first and only avowal of love, and it is spoken with lowered voices. But it is only a very brief happiness they know. For they must disregard the lateness of the hour, their danger, the sound of the castle gates closing—and finally the sense that Golaud is in the garden, too, watching them. But here he is, in the semidarkness, with drawn sword. Deliberately, they do not look his way—they embrace—and Golaud rushes upon Pelléas and kills him. Mélisande, terror-stricken, runs away from the scene, as Golaud, without ever speaking a word, grimly follows after her.

ACT FIVE

SCENE: *A room in the castle.*

Mélisande lies dying in her bed, and a physician is telling Golaud that it was not the slight wound he gave her which is causing her death. Golaud, however, refuses to be comforted. Remorsefully, he drags himself to the foot of her bed and asks to be left alone with her. Then he questions her. Did she love Pelléas? "Yes," she answers, "where is he?" "Was it a guilty love?" "No," says Mélisande—why should he ask? But Golaud cannot believe her and tortures himself with doubt till the others return. Mélisande is now feeling cold—she thinks winter is approaching and she dislikes the cold, she says. King Arkel puts her new-born infant into her arms, but Mélisande is now too weak to hold it. Six women servants file slowly into the room and kneel beside the bed. The physician says quietly that Mélisande is dead. Golaud sobs in anguish and the old king picks up the new-born infant and carries it from the room saying sadly to Golaud, "It is her turn to live now."

Lucia di Lammermoor

by GAETANO DONIZETTI (1797–1848)

Three Acts. Libretto by Commarano, based on Scott's *Bride of Lammermoor*.
First produced in Naples, 1835.

Lord Enrico Ashton	*Baritone*
Lucia, his sister	*Soprano*
Sir Edgardo of Ravenswood	*Tenor*
Raimondo, chaplain of Lammermoor	*Bass*
Normando, Captain of the Lammermoor guard	*Tenor*
Lord Arturo Bucklaw	*Tenor*
Alisa, Lucia's companion	*Mezzo-soprano*

TIME: *About* 1700.
PLACE: *Scotland.*

ACT ONE

SCENE ONE: *Grounds near the castle of Ravenswood*.

The two noble families of Lammermoor and Ravenswood have been deadly enemies for many years. Edgardo of Ravenswood is the sole survivor of his family. His father has been killed and he has been dispossessed of his ancestral castle. But the fortunes of the Lammermoor family have not prospered. In the first scene, Enrico Ashton, head of the Lammermoor family, discusses with his captain of the guard, Normando, and his old chaplain and tutor, Raimondo, the uncertainty of his future. He has not only lost his fortune but is out of favor at court. The only solution of his problem is for his only sister, Lucia, to marry a man who has both riches and influence in the royal court of Scotland. Such a man is Lord Arturo Eucklaw.

But Lucia has refused to marry Lord Arturo. The old chaplain, Raimondo, suggests to Enrico that Lucia cannot think of love as she is in mourning for her mother. But Normando scornfully remarks that he has reason to believe Lucia has a lover whom she meets in secret. Enrico asks if he knows the man and Normando says he thinks it is none other than the family enemy, Edgardo of Ravenswood— *"Cruda, funesta"* ("Each nerve with fury"). He and his men have been searching the grounds looking for him, but have only had brief glimpses of him. "She must be forced to wed Lord Arturo," declares Enrico angrily.

SCENE TWO: *A park near the castle*.

Lucia and her companion, Alisa, have come to the fountain in the park which is the place of her secret meetings with Edgardo of Ravenswood. Lucia is full of foreboding and tells Alisa that the fountain was the scene of a murder in days long ago, and that the spot is haunted by the ghost of the maiden who was stabbed there by her treacherous sweetheart. Lucia tells her that she herself has seen the apparition, who warned her of an unhappy ending to her own love affair with Edgardo— *"Regnava nel silenzio"* ("Silence reigned over all").

But in another aria, Lucia says that when Edgardo

comes all these dark forebodings will vanish—*"Quando rapito in estasi"* ("If he were here, what ecstasy").

Edgardo enters and Alisa withdraws. Edgardo says sadly that this must be their last meeting as he must leave Scotland at once on a political errand to France. Although he has sworn by his father's tomb an oath of vengeance, he proposes to go at once to Enrico Ashton to ask for Lucia's hand in marriage, but Lucia persuades him that this is hopeless. Edgardo is torn between his love for Lucia and his hatred for her brother, Enrico, and agrees to keep their love a secret.

The two lovers exchange rings and pledge eternal faith and the scene closes with the beautiful duet, *"Veranno a te sull' aure"* ("When twilight falls").

ACT TWO

SCENE ONE: *A room in Lammermoor Castle.*

Edgardo has now been in France for several months and Enrico, Lucia's brother, has intercepted all his letters to her. This we learn from a brief dialogue at the beginning of the scene between Enrico and Normando. Normando gives Enrico a forged letter designed to convince Lucia that Edgardo has been unfaithful to his vows of eternal love for her. Lord Arturo Bucklaw, Enrico's candidate for Lucia's hand, is expected that very day.

When Lucia comes in, Enrico tries to win her with a show of kindness and appeals to her family pride, but all she will do is to tell him of her despair—*"Il pallor funesto"* ("See these cheeks"). And so Enrico plays his trump card, showing her the forged letter. Now her hopes are completely shattered and at that moment we hear off-stage the sound of Lord Arturo's arrival at the castle. Enrico tells his sister that unless she marries Lord Arturo the family will be ruined, for not only has he lost his fortune but he has committed treasonable acts against the king, and Lord Arturo is the only one powerful enough at court to win his pardon—*"Soffriva nel pianto"* ("My sufferings").

Enrico goes out to greet his guest and Lucia, brokenhearted at her lover's faithlessness, sadly tells the kindly old chaplain, Raimondo, that she will marry Lord Arturo.

SCENE TWO: *Great hall of the castle*.

This scene is the real climax of the opera. In the great hall of the Castle of Lammermoor (the home of the Ashton family) the wedding guests sing the festive *"Bridal Chorus"*. Lord Arturo, resplendently dressed in white, makes an impressive entrance and greets his future brother-in-law in stately terms. The bride then enters accompanied by her maids-in-waiting. But her face is pale and haggard and she is weeping. Lord Enrico endeavors to reassure the bridegroom by telling him that Lucia is still mourning for their dead mother, but of course the real cause of her grief is her belief that her lover has been faithless to her.

Insistently urged on by her brother, she at last signs the marriage register, but with deep misgiving. Even as she does so, a noise is heard at the back of the hall and Edgardo of Ravenswood, returned from France, makes his way in, together with a few followers. At a glance he takes in the situation, believing Lucia to have willingly been a part of the wedding ceremonies.

Now comes the thrilling and dramatic sextette sung by Edgardo, Enrico, the bridegroom, Arturo, the old family chaplain, Raimondo, Alisa, and Lucia herself in which they all express their various emotions. The tenor (Edgardo) sings the famous melody, *"Chi mi frena in tal momento?"* ("What restrains me at this moment?"). In spite of his bitter disillusionment, and his hatred of her family, Edgardo realizes that he still loves her; Lucia is bewildered and filled with despair; Enrico's heart is touched by the tragedy he has brought into his sister's life; Alisa, Raimondo, and the others all express sympathy for Lucia and all these various emotions are blended together in this great ensemble.

Enrico orders Edgardo to leave the castle—*"Esci, fuggi"* ("Fly from here"). Swords are drawn and only the intervention of Raimondo prevents bloodshed. Edgardo turns to Lucia and asks if she signed the marriage and when she admits it, he denounces her, gives her back her ring and demands his from her. Hardly conscious of what she is doing, Lucia draws the ring from her finger and then falls in a faint. With the entire company threatening him, Edgardo angrily makes his way out of the castle of Lammermoor.

ACT THREE

SCENE ONE: *Great hall of the castle.*

It is the night of the wedding of Lord Arturo Bucklaw and the unwilling Lucia of Lammermoor. The guests are still celebrating, though the bride and groom have left the hall. Suddenly Raimondo, the chaplain, appears at the head of the great staircase and in horror-struck tones gives a fearful report: he heard a cry in the bridal chamber, he forced the door to it, and there he saw the body of Arturo lying on the floor, with Lucia, completely crazed, standing over him, blood still dripping from the weapon she used; and with utter innocence, she turned to Raimondo and asked where her bridegroom could be.

And now, a moment later, deathly white in her night-robes, Lucia herself appears at the head of the stairs, dagger in hand. This is the world-famous "Mad Scene"— *"Ardon gl'incensi"* ("The burning tapers"). As she sings this great aria, Lucia slowly descends the broad stairway and the wedding guests make way before her, gazing at her with horror and pity. Lucia imagines she is once more with her true love, Edgardo; once more she imagines he discovers her being married to another. "Do not curse me!" she cries; once more she wishes for death to bring an end of her heart-break. It is a most effective scene both visually and musically. There stands the unfortunate bride, completely oblivious of the assembled wedding guests, of her brother and the chaplain, who stand aghast at what their plotting has brought to Lucia. At the end of the aria, Lucia collapses and is carried away by her attendants. Enrico is overwhelmed with remorse at this terrible outcome of his plan.

SCENE TWO: *A cemetery near the castle.*

Out in the graveyard, Edgardo lingers among the tombs of his own ancestors, longing for nothing but death now that Lucia has married another. Soon there will be a new tomb in the family graveyard—*"Fra poco a me ricovero"* ("Only a little while until I shall be there")—and it will be his. In the distance, he can see lights gleaming from the windows of the castle of Lammermoor and he imagines the gaity of the wedding festivities.

But in a few minutes, a group of people come from the castle and they are full of sadness and not gaiety—*"Fur le nozze"* ("This unhappy, fatal marriage"). They tell Edgardo of the unhappy Lucia who has lost her mind and is dying. Even in death, they say, she is calling for Edgardo.

This is the first he has heard of what has happened in the last scene, but even as he learns of her faithfulness, a bell tolls announcing Lucia's death. Raimondo enters to announce the end, and Edgardo sings his last farewell—*"Tu che a Dio spiegasti l'ali"* ("Thou hast spread thy wings to Heaven"). In Heaven, he says, they shall once more be reunited. He draws a dagger and, before Raimondo can stop him, he plunges it into his own breast.

Don Pasquale

by GAETANO DONIZETTI (1797–1848)

Three Acts. Libretto by Donizetti and Ruffini, based on Cammarano's "Ser Marc'Antonio."
First produced in Paris, 1843.

Don Pasquale, a wealthy bachelor	*Bass*
Ernesto, his nephew	*Tenor*
Dr. Malatesta, his friend	*Baritone*
Norina, a young widow	*Soprano*

A notary, major-domo, servants.

TIME: *Early Nineteenth Century.*
PLACE: *Rome.*

ACT ONE

SCENE ONE: *A room in the luxurious home of Don Pasquale.*

Don Pasquale, a wealthy middle-aged bachelor, is anxiously awaiting the arrival of his friend, Dr. Malatesta. Don Pasquale is much displeased with his young nephew and heir, Ernesto, because Ernesto has refused to marry as his uncle wished. To show his displeasure, Don Pasquale is planning that he, himself, will get married and thus cut off the rebellious young nephew. And this in spite of the fact that the Don is old, fat, and far from a romantic figure. When Dr. Malatesta arrives, he is full of enthusiasm about the bride-to-be whom he has selected for the Don. "She is as lovely as an angel," he says. And adds, for good measure, that she is his own sister. Don Pasquale is greatly pleased and urges Malatesta to bring the lady to see him at once. After Malatesta has left on this errand, Ernesto enters and is astonished and dismayed when his uncle makes the startling announcement of his own proposed marriage. This is bad news for Ernesto, and he is particularly distressed because it is apparently his friend Dr. Malatesta who has arranged it all.

SCENE TWO: *Norina's garden.*

As the curtain rises we see the charming widow, Norina, in the garden of her home reading a romance. Norina laughs at the idea that *she* can learn anything about romance from the pages of a book. We now learn that Norina is the reason why Ernesto has refused to marry the lady of his uncle's choice, for the two young people are very much in love. Though Don Pasquale has never seen the charming Norina, he refuses to sanction the match. A servant brings Norina a letter from Ernesto telling her the sad news that he is about to be disinherited by his uncle in favor of a new young bride, and that Ernesto in despair is planning to leave Rome that very day.

Dr. Malatesta comes in and tells her not to worry about Ernesto. He, Dr. Malatesta, has a plan which will solve the whole problem, and when he has explained it to Ernesto, all will be well. Don Pasquale is determined to marry and is trusting Dr. Malatesta to select the bride; Malatesta has selected Norina herself. But it is not to be a real marriage—the notary who will sign the papers will not be a real notary—the whole thing will be a trick. Pasquale knows that Malatesta has a young sister still in convent school, and Norina will be introduced as that sister, a sweet and innocent little creature who will fascinate the old

Don with her shy and winsome charm. But once the mock ceremony has been accomplished, the blushing young bride will suddenly turn into a demanding and extravagant woman who will so bedevil Don Pasquale that he will be willing to do anything to get rid of her.

Norina is delighted with the scheme but wonders if Ernesto will approve of it. Malatesta assures her that the whole thing is gotten up for Ernesto's benefit, and he and Norina have a merry time practising the airs and graces by which she expects to bewitch the fatuous old Don Pasquale.

ACT TWO

SCENE: *Don Pasquale's drawing-room.*

Ernesto, who does not know of the plot to discomfit his selfish old uncle, is lamenting his fate. Three misfortunes have befallen him—the cruel treatment of his uncle, the treachery of his friend, Dr. Malatesta, and, above all, the loss of his beloved Norina.

Ernesto leaves the room abruptly as the Don appears, magnificent in the velvet coat and lace ruffles he has put on for his wedding day. He gives orders that no one is to be admitted except Dr. Malatesta and his companion. In a moment, Malatesta enters leading a shy and hesitant Norina, heavily veiled. Don Pasquale at once expresses his approval of her graceful figure and wonders if her face is equally attractive. Dr. Malatesta declares that she would never think of unveiling her face in front of a man. Perhaps, later, after they are better acquainted. The Don asks her if she likes gay company and going to the theatre, and she replies shyly that she never had any gay company in the convent, and as for the theatre she has never been to one. The somewhat miserly Don is delighted with this, and again begs her to remove her veil. This time, Malatesta permits her to do so, and Don Pasquale is overcome at the sight of such beauty. He can hardly wait for the marriage ceremony, and asks Malatesta if the fair young lady is willing to take him as her husband. After some hesitation, Norina consents. The false notary is brought in and; with much legal verbiage, Don Pasquale dictates the terms of the marriage contract by which he gives half of his fortune to his wife and gives her full power over the household.

Just then, Ernesto comes in and is horrified to recognize his beloved Norina apparently being married to his cruel uncle. Before he can blurt out his astonishment and rage, he is persuaded by frantic gestures and whisperings to remain silent and even to act as a witness to the marriage contract. Dr. Malatesta whispers to him to be patient and assures him that the whole thing is for his benefit. Poor Ernesto is bewildered and suspicious, but signs the document as a witness.

No sooner has this been done than Norina abandons her pretended timidity. She refuses to embrace her new husband, and Ernesto is moved to laughter. This infuriates the Don, who orders him from the house. But Norina refuses to let him go. As the Don is so much older than she is, she says that she will require a young companion and she is engaging Ernesto for that position. She orders all the servants to be brought before her; and, when only a major-domo and two servants appear, she exclaims that such a small staff is ridiculous. She tells the major-domo that his salary will be doubled and orders him to engage twenty-four new servants, all of them young and handsome.

While Don Pasquale groans and moans in anguish, she orders two new carriages and ten horses, eight of them for the carriage, two for the saddle. New furniture for the entire house must be purchased at once. There are a few other things to be done, but they can wait. In the meantime, she wishes to have dinner that very evening with fifty guests.

"This cannot be!" cries Don Pasquale, choking with rage. "Oh yes, it can be," she replies. "I am mistress here."

ACT THREE

SCENE: *Same as Act Two.*

The room where the mock marriage ceremony took place is now piled high with a confused mass of bonnets, shawls, shoes, dresses, and other evidences of feminine luxury and extravagance. Don Pasquale, frantic and distracted, sits at a desk piled high with bills, while more tradespeople and servants rush in and out of the room with more purchases of the insatiable Norina.

Then Norina herself comes in dressed to go to the theatre. "You shall not go!" cries the Don, but she calls him an insolent fellow and slaps his face. She reminds him that he is an old man, and advises him to go to bed early and to take care of his health. At this, Don Pasquale declares that he cannot live with such a woman and threatens to divorce her, a threat which, of course, has no effect on Norina.

As she leaves the room, she drops a letter apparently by accident. Pasquale picks it up and is dismayed to find that it is a request from an admirer to meet Norina that evening behind the garden wall. This upsets the Don so violently that he declares that he is really ill and sends a servant for Dr. Malatesta.

He staggers from the room, and a group of servants begin trying to get some order out of the confusion. They speak of the endless comings and goings in the house, of the wild extravagance of the new mistress, and of the obvious quarrel of Pasquale and his bride.

The servants leave the room as Dr. Malatesta and Ernesto come in. They are discussing just how to handle the next move in the plot—the rendezvous in the garden when they hear Pasquale returning, and Ernesto hurriedly leaves the room.

Don Pasquale gives the doctor a long and agonized recital of his woes and says it would have been better for him to have given his consent to Ernesto's marriage rather than go through all this torture. As a fitting climax, he hands Malatesta the letter which Norina has dropped, indicating that she is about to take a lover. Dr. Malatesta pretends to be shocked and proposes that he and the Don, accompanied by servants, will surround the guilty pair and promptly take them to court. Pasquale is delighted with the idea of such a revenge on the young woman who has made his life unbearable.

SCENE TWO: *The garden of Don Pasquale's home.*

It is evening and the scene is the garden set for the lovers' rendezvous. As the curtain rises, we hear Ernesto singing his serenade, *"Com'e gentile, la notte a mezzo April"* ("How soft the air of the April night"). Norina cautiously opens the garden gate, admitting her lover. There is a brief love duet, but soon they hear Don Pasquale and Dr. Malatesta approaching. As has been arranged, Ernesto slips away in one direction and Norina in the other. When Pasquale catches up with Norina, he is astonished to find her alone and demands to know where her lover is hiding. But she declares that she has no lover, and that no one is in the garden but herself. Pasquale searches the shrubbery but can find no one. Angrily, he orders Norina to leave his house, but she pertly reminds him that the house is hers.

Dr. Malatesta now takes charge. He tells Norina that Don Pasquale has changed his mind, and has decided to give his consent to the marriage of his nephew Ernesto to the widow Norina. "That woman!" cries Norina in scorn. "I will not have her in the house. I will leave it myself first!" Pasquale is delighted to hear this, but Norina adds that before leaving she must be convinced that Ernesto and Norina are really married. Malatesta sends a servant to the house to bring out Ernesto; and when the young man appears, Malatesta tells him that his uncle has given his consent to the marriage, and will settle on him an annual income of four thousand crowns. Pasquale agrees to this and requests that Norina be sent for at once. "But this lady *is* Norina," says Malatesta.

It is then explained to the bewildered Don Pasquale that the wedding was a mock wedding, that Malatesta's supposed sister and Norina were one and the same person, and that his misfortune is the result of a mischievous scheme on behalf of two young lovers. The old man is so happy to extricate himself from his troubles that he sends his nephew and Norina away with his blessing.

Porgy and Bess*

by GEORGE GERSHWIN (1898–1937)

Three Acts. Libretto by DuBose Heyward (founded on the play, *Porgy*, by Dorothy and DuBose Heyward). Lyrics by DuBose Heyward and Ira Gershwin.
First produced in New York, 1935.

In the order of appearance

Clara, Jake's wife	*Soprano*
Mingo	*Tenor*
Sportin' Life, a dope peddler	*Tenor*
Serena, Robbins' wife	*Soprano*
Jake, a fisherman	*Baritone*
Robbins	*Tenor*
Jim, a cotton picker	*Baritone*
Peter, the Honeyman	*Tenor*
Lily, the Strawberry Woman	*Mezzo-soprano*
Maria, keeper of the cook-shop	*Contralto*
Porgy, a cripple	*Baritone*
Crown, a tough stevedore	*Baritone*
Annie	*Mezzo-soprano*
Bess, Crown's girl	*Soprano*
Undertaker	*Baritone*
Frazier, a "lawyer"	*Baritone*
Crab Man	*Tenor*

Mr. Archdale, a white man
Policeman
Coroner } *Speaking parts*
Detective
A Small Boy

Residents of Catfish Row.

PLACE: *Charleston, South Carolina.*
TIME: *The recent past.*

ACT ONE

SCENE ONE: *Catfish Row, a summer evening.*

Catfish Row, a tumbledown Negro quarter on the waterfront of Charleston, South Carolina, has seen better days, but now it is the home of Gullah (so-called perhaps because of their slave origin in West Africa) fishermen, stevedores, and drifters. *"Summertime, and the livin' is easy"*, sings Clara, a fisherman's wife, as a lullaby to her baby, setting the mood for the evening. The nightly dice game begins and Robbins, a stevedore, joins in despite his wife Serena's protests. Jim and Jake and the ensemble tell the world what they think of the opposite sex in *"A Woman Is a Sometime Thing"*.

Heralded by the honeyman's call, Porgy, the crippled beggar who makes his rounds in a little cart drawn by his pet goat, makes his entrance with *"They Pass By Singing"*. He joins the game to build up the money he has collected during the day. Also in the play are Crown, the bad man of the community, egged on by his woman, Bess, who is scorned by the respectable females, and Sportin' Life, a dope peddler from New York. He and Porgy share one emotion: a desire for Bess, though the way they express it is as different as day and night. The game continues to the accompaniment of a *"Crap Game Fugue"*, and excitement reaches its pitch as Crown, drunk and more than a little crazy on a pinch of Sportin' Life's "happy dust", kills Robbins after a quarrel. Everyone scatters indoors as a policeman's whistle sounds. Crown hurries off to hide in the jungle of Kittiwah Island across the bay. Porgy takes Bess into his little hut after she has been refused by the other inhabitants.

SCENE TWO: *Robbins' house, night.*

Robbins' corpse lies at home and the neighbors come in to say farewell and contribute a mite to the burial expenses. They sing "Gone, Gone, Gone" and "Overflow", expressing their sorrow and wrath. Serena, the widow, keens out her grief in *"My Man's Gone Now"*.

A white man enters, a detective, and the assemblage falls protectively, secretly silent. He tells Serena that Robbins must be buried the next day, or his body will be turned over to medical students for dissection. He takes away with him as a material witness Peter the Honeyman, and by accusing him gets the others to admit Crown's guilt. The undertaker agrees to bury Robbins, although the collection has reached only eighteen dollars. Bess leads the ensemble in the spiritual, "Leavin' fo' de Promis' Lan' ".

SCENE THREE: *Catfish Row, a month later.*

The fishermen are getting the nets ready for the next day. With Jim and Jake they sing *"It Takes a Long Pull"*, a rowing song. Porgy comes out from his little house. He is a thoroughly happy man. Bess has come to live with him, and he feels like singing the whole day long. He crystallizes his emotion in the banjo song, *"I Got Plenty O' Nuttin"*, then joins Bess, the lawyer, and the ensemble as they discuss Bess' divorce from Crown. Frazier will charge only a dollar if there are no complications. However, Bess was never really married to Crown, so Frazier says it will be fifty cents extra to change Bess from "Woman to Lady".

Sportin' Life, hankering after Bess, offers her some "happy dust", but she turns on him, and with Maria and the others says she hates his "Struttin' Style". She gladly runs to Porgy and they blend their voices and hearts in the duet, *"Bess, You Is My Woman Now."* Against her better judgment, she decides to go to the annual picnic of the "Repent Saith the Lord Lodge" on Kittiwah Island. The crowd gathers and sings a picnic song, "Oh, I Can't Sit Down." They ramble off, and Porgy is left alone.

ACT TWO

SCENE ONE: *Kittiwah Island, evening of the same day.*

Sportin' Life is up to his old tricks, trying to debauch the innocent picnic. He sings "I Ain't Got No Shame", and follows it with a skeptical review of Biblical history, *"It Ain't Necessarily So"*. Serena restores order and the picnickers depart. Bess is last to go. From the thicket Crown suddenly appears, and in spite of her protest, "What You Want with Bess?" he pulls her into the jungle. The old emotion is too strong for her, and she yields.

SCENE TWO: *Catfish Row, before dawn a week later.*

The fishermen go off to the Blackfish Banks. Bess has returned from the island delirious, and Porgy is in despair. Serena prays for her, singing *"Time and Time Again"*, and tells Porgy that Doctor Jesus will take the case and Bess will soon be well. The Strawberry Woman and the Crabman utter their traditional street cries as they vend their wares. Bess recovers, and in shame and fear, promises Porgy never to leave him, singing, *"I Loves You, Porgy"*. He sings with her. Their peace is shattered by hurricane warnings. The wind rises.

SCENE THREE: *Serena's room, the following dawn.*

The Catfish Row neighbors are in Serena's room, singing hymns and spirituals, "Oh de Lawd Shake de Heaven", when Crown breaks in. He has swum all the way from the island in the storm. Now he wants Bess. He sings *"A Red-Headed Woman"*, mocks at everyone, blasphemes, and curses. Clara looks out the window in a lull, and cries out that her husband's boat has capsized. She gives her baby to Bess, and rushes out. Crown follows her. The act ends as everyone sings "Oh Doctor Jesus," imploring help once again.

ACT THREE

SCENE ONE: *Catfish Row, the next night.*

Bess tends Clara's baby, while Porgy watches from his window. The neighbors comfort the distracted mother: "Clara Don't You Be Downhearted". Sportin' Life, glad to make mischief, foretells trouble between Crown and Porgy over Bess. Crown, indeed, is on the scene in a moment, making for Porgy's door. The crippled beggar surprises him, turning the enormous strength of his arms to the struggle, plunging a knife into Crown's body, and then strangling him to death. Now in truth Bess has her man—Porgy.

SCENE TWO: *Next morning.*

There is no trace of the incident of the night before when the white men come. No one knows anything. Still, the Coroner is allowed to see Porgy, and takes him away as an identifying witness. Now Sportin' Life gets his chance. He tells Bess that Porgy has gone for good. *"There's a Boat That's Leavin' for New York"*, he sing to her. She allows herself to be persuaded. A pinch of "happy dust" does the rest, and Bess is off to New York.

SCENE THREE: *A week later.*

Porgy returns home, a free man. The whole of Catfish Row is overjoyed, and receives his presents with love. But one person is missing. The bright red dress he bought for Bess will never be worn. As he enters his door, he sees a bird of ill omen, and sings his fear of the *"Buzzard"*. (This song, originally in the first act, has been transferred and is now used here instead.) The fear was well-founded. "Where's My Bess?" he asks all the neighbors. Sorrowfully, Maria and Serena tell him the truth in a trio answering his questions. But Porgy is not to be held down for long. He fetches his goat-cart and, in a burst of sublime faith, starts off to find Bess. *"I'm On My Way"*, he sings triumphantly, with the chorus joining in, as the curtain falls.

Andrea Chénier

by UMBERTO GIORDANO (1867–1948)

Four Acts. Libretto by Luigi Illica.
First produced in Milan, 1896.

Andrea Chénier	*Tenor*
Charles Gérard	*Baritone*
Madeleine de Coigny	*Soprano*
Countess de Coigny, her mother	*Mezzo-soprano*
Bersi, Madeleine's maid	*Mezzo-soprano*
Chevalier de Fléville	*Baritone*
The Abbé	*Tenor*
Incredibile, a spy	*Tenor*

(A popular nickname for unprincipled adventurers and spies who lived by their wits during the unsettled times of the Revolution)

Roucher, a friend of Chénier's	*Bass*
Major-domo	*Baritone*
Mathieu, a waiter	*Baritone*
Madelon, an old woman	*Mezzo-soprano*
Schmidt, jailer at St. Lazare prison	*Baritone*

Aristocrats, citizens of Paris, soldiers, servants, dancers, peasants, prisoners, members of the Revolutionary Tribunal.

TIME: *Just before the French Revolution and during the Reign of Terror.*

PLACE: *A château in the country and in Paris.*

ACT ONE

SCENE: *Ballroom in the château of the Countess de Coigny.*

Directed by a major-domo, a group of servants is preparing the room for a ball, moving furniture, dusting bric-a-brac, and bringing in potted plants and flowers. Among them is a young man named Charles Gérard, whose mind has been stirred by some of the revolutionary literature he has been reading and who is already more than half in rebellion against the menial duties he has to perform. One of the older servants enters the room, carrying a flower-stand which is too heavy for him. It is Gérard's father, who has been in the service of the Coigny family all his life. His son, Charles, takes the flower-stand from his trembling hands and urges him to rest. The old man leaves; and Charles, looking around the luxurious room, thinks bitterly of the contrast between all this wealth and extravagance and the miserable lot of the poor villagers and peasants of the neighborhood.

He resumes the respectful manner of a servant as the Countess and her daughter, Madeleine and the latter's maid, Bersi, enter. The Countess looks over the room to see that all is in readiness for the ball, and asks Gérard several times if the musicians and the ballet dancers have arrived yet. Gérard assures her patiently that everything is in order, and the Countess leaves after telling her daughter it is time to dress for the party. Madeleine complains at all the discomforts she must endure in the elaborate fashionable costume of the day. When her mother returns in a few minutes the young woman declares that she will wear a simple white dress and, as her only adornment, a red rose in her hair.

Madeleine and Bersi leave the room. The guests begin to arrive, and greet their hostess with a good deal of chattering and fluttering. Among the guests is the Chevalier de Fléville, a foppish old man, who introduces his two young companions, Signor Fiorinelli, an Italian musician, and Andrea Chénier, a young poet. Quite a commotion is stirred up by the arrival of the Abbé, and all crowd around him to learn the latest news from Paris, from which he has just returned. He tells them that the news is not at all good—

the revolutionary spirit is spreading, the crowds in the streets are getting out of hand, and the whole situation is deplorable.

Fléville interrupts this conversation to say that, after all, these political events are of no real importance, while the ballet which is about to be performed is something quite worth-while. The ballet which follows is a dainty bit of color about shepherds and shepherdesses, and is politely applauded. The Countess, wishing to keep her guests entertained, asks Chénier if he will not recite one of his poems. He declines with cold politeness, but Madeleine renews the request and asks for something about "love". (She has made a bet with some of her companions that she will make him speak of love.) Chénier bows and tells her that poetry is as elusive as love itself. Madeleine and her friends laugh heartily at this and declare that she has won her bet because he has spoken of love.

Chénier, stung by their laughter, says that he will indeed tell her about love. He sings of the love of nature, *"Un di all' azzurro spazio"* ("One day through azure skies"), and of divine love, which is desecrated by the mercenary priests who collect money from those who come to pray, but decline to help the beggars who come to the door of the church. In spite of murmurs of disapproval from his auditors, he goes on to speak of the hopeless struggle of the workers and peasants against the greed of the nobility and church. Coming closer to Madeleine, he tells her that he had at first thought he had seen an expression of love and compassion in her eyes, but now he knows it is nothing but mockery.

By this time, the listeners are highly indignant and express their annoyance at this brash young man in no uncertain terms. Madeleine, however, is embarrassed and quietly and humbly begs Chénier's pardon. The Countess is afraid that her party will be ruined, and she hastily calls for the musicians to begin the gavotte; but before they can do so, there is a commotion outside. Suddenly, the door is flung open by Gérard who, in mockery of a pompous major-domo, bows low and announces "His Lordship, Misery". As he does so, a group of ragged beggars crowd into the room crying piteously for alms.

Angrily the Countess orders Gérard to drive out these

creatures and go with them himself. But it is Gérard who has let them in, and he shouts that he will no longer live in this house of selfish extravagance while millions are starving. Other servants enter the room, among them the elder Gérard. The younger man tears off the flunky's coat which his father wears, throws it on the floor, and declares that never again will his father have to bow obsequiously before those who have no human sympathy in their hearts.

The other servants push the beggars, with Gérard and his father, out of the room, and Andrea Chénier follows them. The Countess quickly recovers her poise after this embarrassing episode, and once more signals the musicians to begin the gavotte. As the curtain falls the guests are dancing as if nothing had happened.

ACT TWO

SCENE: *Outside the Café Hottot in Paris.*

Several years have passed since the Countess's ball in Act One. The Revolution, which was then just an unpleasant possibility, is now an accomplished fact and has reached the extreme of fanaticism known as "The Reign of Terror". At a table in front of a cafe sit Bersi, Madeleine's former maid, and Incredibile, a spy of the Terrorists. She tells him that she is a real child of the Revolution, that she glories in the death of the aristocrats, but Incredibile jots down in his notebook that she is under suspicion.

At another table sits Andrea Chénier. His friend, Roucher, approaches him and advises him to leave the city as he has lost favor with those in power. But Chénier declares that he will not leave, as he has been receiving love letters from an unknown woman. She is his destiny, he feels, and he will not leave until he has found her.

There is the sound of shouting in the street as Robespierre, supreme autocrat of the Terror, passes by, accompanied by the other heroes of the moment, including Gérard who pauses in front of the cafe. The spy, Incredibile, offers to locate anyone he is looking for; whereupon, Gérard launches into a glowing description of Madeleine. Incredibile assures him that he will meet her that very evening.

It is growing darker. Bersi returns to inform Chénier

that he must not leave, as a lady is coming in a few minutes to seek his aid, a lady known as "Speranza". It is Madeleine, heavily veiled, who enters. She raises her veil and is recognized by Chénier, but at the same moment is also recognized by the spy, Incredible, who is lurking in the shadows nearby. The spy hurries away to inform Gérard, while Madeleine confesses that she is the unknown writer of the letters which have kept Chénier in Paris. She knows that he is out of favor with those in power and she, as an aristocrat, is also in danger.

Although she has forsaken her aristocratic friends and has taken up the cause of the people, she knows that this will be of no avail once her identity is known. In the shadow of death, they declare their love for one another.

It is quite dark now. Madeleine and Chénier are about to leave, when suddenly a figure appears out of the darkness, crying out Madeleine's name. It is Gérard. But Roucher also appears, and Chénier pushes Madeleine into his arms and shouts to him to escape with her. Both Chénier and Gérard draw their swords. The duel is a very brief one, and Gérard falls to the pavement. As Chénier bends over him they recognize each other for the first time. Gérard, believing himself mortally wounded, urges Chénier to flee as his name is on the death-list of the Terrorists. Chénier hurries away just as a group of gendarmes enter, brought in by the spy, Incredibile. As he falls into unconsciousness, Gérard murmurs that he has no idea who his assailant was.

ACT THREE

Scene: *The Revolutionary Tribunal.*

Gérard, still weak from the wound which he received in the duel with Chénier, enters the courtroom and is received with acclamation by the crowd. In a stirring speech, he urges them to give their all, even their jewels and trinkets, to the cause of France, which is beset on all sides by enemies. Aroused by his eloquence, many of the crowd go to a large urn which stands in a corner of the room and drop into it their contributions. Madelon, a blind old woman, gives all that she has by sending her young grandson, whose father has already been killed in the Revolution, to serve in the army.

The spy, Incredibile, comes up to Gérard and tells him the net is closing in on Chénier, who will undoubtedly be arrested in a few hours. Even as he says this, a newsboy's shout is heard from the street outside, announcing the arrest of Andrea Chénier. Incredibile reminds Gérard that once Chénier is in custody it will be easy to catch Madeleine, as she will step right into the trap. Gérard, urged by the spy to write out Chénier's indictment, sits down at a table and picks up a pen to do so. However, after writing a few words he is overcome with remorse and shame, realizing that in order to win the lady he loves, he is about to condemn his friend to death—the friend whose verses first aroused in him the idealistic feeling for humanity which made him a revolutionary. The bitter struggle which is going on in his mind and heart is vividly reflected in the aria, *"Nemico della patria?"* ("Enemy of the fatherland?").

Selfishness triumphs for he cannot give up the thought of Madeleine; he finishes the indictment and signs it. Madeleine is brought in, and Gérard tells her that he has caused Chénier's arrest because of his love for her. With mounting ardor he tells her that he has loved her ever since she was a child and he served as a lackey in her mother's château. At first Madeleine is horrified; she cries that she will rush out into the street and give herself up to the mob before she will submit to him. Sadly she recalls the night when the château was attacked by a mob and burned, and her mother died in the flames, *"La Mamma morta"* ("The Dead Mother"). Now the only thing which makes her life worth living is her love for Andrea Chénier; and, suddenly changing her mood, she offers herself to Gérard if he can save Chénier's life.

But it is too late. The enemies of Chénier have had his trial brought forward and he is led into the court to be tried at once. The judges take their places and the indictment of Chénier is read. He is accused of having written against the revolution. Chénier shouts a denial, but is told that he is not to be allowed to answer the indictment. Gérard rises and demands that Chénier be heard and the court reluctantly gives him permission to speak.

Chénier makes an impassioned plea in his own defence, telling how his pen had always been at the service of justice and humanity, and always opposed to tyranny and hypocrisy. When the judges call for witnesses, Gérard comes forward and declares that the whole indictment is a lie, that he wrote it himself, inspired by personal jealousy and hate. The crowd in the courtroom is thirsting for blood and shout that Gérard has been bribed. But Gérard denounces the whole proceeding as unjust and tyrannical; he shouts that instead of condemning Chénier to death, they should hail him as a hero. Embracing Chénier, he manages to whisper in his ear that Madeleine is in the courtroom.

The judges retire to consider the verdict, and Chénier searches the courtroom anxiously until he sees Madeleine. Just to have seen her once again, he says, is all he has longed for, and now he will die gladly. The judges return and the verdict is announced—death. Chénier is led away as Madeleine cries out his name despairingly.

ACT FOUR

Scene: *Courtyard of St. Lazare Prison.*

Andrea Chénier is awaiting death at the guillotine and his friend, Roucher, has come to pay him a last visit. Even in this last moment of farewell, the two friends are not talking. Chénier is writing at a table, and Roucher sits silently beside him. The jailer, Schmidt, comes in to tell Roucher his time is up, but Roucher hands him a small bribe and asks him not to interrupt the poet.

Finally Chénier lays down his pen. He has finished his last poem, a kind of poetic last will and testament. In a beautiful aria, *"Come un bel di di Maggio"* ("As a beautiful day in May"), he compares his life to a beautiful day in spring, full of goodness and beauty and the joy of living, inspired by the Muse of Poetry, but now drawing toward darkness and death.

His friend Roucher embraces him in a last goodbye and leaves the prison as Chénier is led back to his cell. And now there is another caller. It is Madeleine, who is received respectfully by the jailer as she is accompanied by Gérard, who is still a member of the ruling party, in spite of his outburst at the trial of Chénier. Another bribe is passed and the jailer agrees to let Madeleine take the place of a condemned woman named Idia Legray.

Gérard leaves, still marvelling at a love which is stronger

than death. Chénier is brought in, and he and Madeleine have time only for a brief but ecstatic embrace declaring that they will be united in death. The jailer enters with the guard and calls out the name of Andrea Chénier and Idia Legray. One last kiss, and Madeleine and Chénier, hand in hand, turn and walk calmly to their death.

Orfeo ed Euridice

by CHRISTOPH WILLIBALD VON GLUCK (1714–1787)

Three Acts. Libretto by Ramieri de Calzabigi.
First produced in Vienna, 1762.

Orfeo	*Contralto*
Euridice	*Soprano*
Amor, god of love	*Soprano*
A Blessed Spirit	*Soprano*

Nymphs, shepherds, shepherdesses, demons, furies, Blessed Spirits, attendants, ballet.

TIME: *Mythological.*
PLACE: *Ancient Greece and the Underworld.*

ACT ONE

SCENE: *The Tomb of Euridice.*

Orfeo, the great legendary musician of antiquity, is mourning the untimely death of his beloved wife, Euridice. He has laid aside his lyre—the magical lyre with which he charmed not only human beings but even the rocks and trees. Orfeo's music was more than human; it was, in truth, divine, for he was the son of Apollo, god of music, and of Calliope, muse of epic poetry.

Now he sits songless and silent beside the tomb of Euridice, set in a grove of cypress trees. Shepherds, shepherdesses, and nymphs place garlands of flowers on the tomb, while they sing a chorus of sorrow and sadness. After a time, Orfeo rouses himself from his brooding grief and asks to be left alone. Circling the tomb once more in a solemn procession, his companions leave. In bitter lamentation Orfeo expresses his despair, *"Chiamo il mio ben cosi"* ("I call to my loved one").

In mounting excitement, he rages against the gods for their cruelty and, finally defying them, declares that he will go to the Underworld to seek Euridice. Suddenly a voice speaks to him, and he turns to see Amor, the god of love. Amor tells him that the gods have heard his lamentations and prayers and have decided to grant him his request. He is to be permitted to do what no other mortal has ever done—to enter the abode of the dead and to return to the world of the living with his wife, Euridice. But this great boon is to be granted on one condition: he must not gaze upon the face of his beloved until they have returned safely; if he does so, she will be lost to him forever.

Orfeo knows that this condition will be hard to fulfill, but he is eager to begin the dangerous mission. Amor exhorts him to be courageous and confident, and tells him to take his lyre which with its magic power will be his strongest weapon against whatever dangers may befall him. Orfeo sets out on his journey as the curtain falls.

ACT TWO

SCENE ONE: *Entrance to the Underworld.*

The gateway to the world of the dead is guarded by terrible creatures—the Furies who frighten away any mortals who dare to come near. The sound of harp arpeggios arouses them and they angrily demand to know who is approaching. In a moment, Orfeo stands on a promontory looking down into the abyss. Dancing wildly, the Furies describe the horrors that await him in the infernal regions—Cerberus, the three-headed watchdog and, worst of all, the avenging Eumenides, with snake-locks, bringing punishment for every human misdeed.

Orfeo waits calmly until their fury dies down, and then he strikes his lyre and in moving tones describes to them his unbearable grief over the loss of Euridice, begging them to let him pass. At first they refuse to do so, but Orfeo sings again more passionately and, at length, they are so moved by the power of his music that they grant him passageway through the portals of the Underworld. Still writhing and twisting in a terrifying dance, they present a horrid spectacle, but Orfeo, holding his lyre, unmoved by their threatening gestures, walks steadfastly through them into the world beyond.

SCENE TWO: *The Elysian Fields.*

In striking contrast to the dark abode of the Furies, the Elysian Fields are bright with sunlight and clear air. This is the home of the Blessed, those mortals who have passed through the gates of death to dwell in eternal peace and serenity. A group of these Blessed Ones move in a slow and dreamlike dance to music of ineffable purity and grace. One Happy Spirit sings of the joy which is theirs, all sorrows of earth forgotten, *"E quest' asilo ameno"* ("All are happy in this abode").

Into this scene of immortal peace comes Orfeo, the mortal. He exclaims in wonder at the unearthly beauty of the scene, and from a distance come voices which tell him that his Euridice is near. Accompanied by a group of the Blessed Ones, Euridice approaches. Her face is heavily veiled. With a great effort, Orfeo masters his excitement and takes her hand. When the veil is lifted from Euridice's face, Orfeo resolutely turns his eyes away and leads her gently by the hand as they begin their strange and fearsome journey back to the land of the living.

ACT THREE

SCENE ONE: *On the way to the land of the living.*

A weird unearthly light pervades the scene. Orfeo and Euridice enter. He is still holding her hand and leading her with averted face. She cannot understand this and reproaches him for his coldness and indifference. Orfeo answers evasively and tells her she must have faith in him until they escape from these deathlike regions. She begs him for just one loving glance to reassure her; and when he will not turn his head, she exclaims that she will go no further. It were better to return to the unbroken trancelike happiness of the Elysian Fields.

At length, Orfeo can resist her no longer. He turns and embraces her and instantly she collapses lifelessly in his arms. And now Orfeo is desperate with redoubled grief and remorse. "How can I live without Euridice?" he cries, in one of the most famous arias in all opera, *"Che faro senza Euridice"*.

Rather than live without Euridice, he will join her in death. He draws his dagger and is about to plunge it into his breast when Amor, the god of love, appears once more and stays his hand. He tells Orfeo that the gods are impressed with his faithfulness and courage and decree that he has suffered enough. Euridice is to be allowed to return to earth with him.

Life returns to the lifeless figure of Euridice, and she rises from the ground. She and Orfeo embrace each other fervently. Orfeo declares that hence forth he will devote himself to the worship of Amor, god of love. Hand in hand, he and Euridice continue on their journey.

SCENE TWO: *The Temple of Love.*

In a beautiful garden, flanked on either side by stately cypress trees, stands the altar of Amor, god of love. A crowd of his disciples await his coming and in a moment he appears leading the reunited lovers, Orfeo and Euridice. All join in singing of the power of love to overcome distrust and to heal the wounded heart. A series of stately dances is performed before the altar as Orfeo and Euridice are crowned with garlands of flowers. The final chorus is a great paean of praise to Amor and the triumph of true love, even over death itself.

Faust

by CHARLES GOUNOD (1818–1893)

Four Acts. Libretto by Barbier and Carré, based on Goethe's
Faust.
First produced in Paris, 1859.

Faust	*Tenor*
Mephistopheles	*Bass*
Marguerite	*Soprano*
Valentine, her brother	*Baritone*
Siebel, a youth	*Mezzo-soprano*
Martha, neighbor of Marguerite	*Contralto*

Soldiers, students, villagers, dancers.

TIME: *Sixteenth Century.*
PLACE: *A small town in Germany.*

ACT ONE

SCENE ONE: *The study of Doctor Faustus, a philosopher
and scientist.*

The room is full of books and manuscripts, and the old
philosopher, Faust, with a long white beard, has been por-
ing over his books all night long. He is tired of life and
longs for death—*"En vain j'intérroge"* ("In vain I question"). His lifetime of study has taught him nothing of the
real meaning of life. He lifts a cup of poison to his lips, but
pauses when he hears a gay chorus of youths and maidens
outside his window greeting the beautiful Easter dawn.

Made still more bitter by the happiness of others, he calls
on the powers of darkness to come to his aid. He is surprised when his call is answered. Mephistopheles, a gallant,
splendidly dressed Devil, appears in the fireplace and offers
Faust whatever he wants. "Youth and pleasure are what I
want," cries Faust, and Mephistopheles causes a lovely
vision of the fair young Marguerite to appear at the back
of the old philosopher's cell.

Faust is impressed by the supernatural powers of the Prince of Darkness. Mephistopheles offers him a contract —on earth the Devil will be his servant, but in the afterworld, Faust's soul will belong to the Evil One. Faust agrees, the Devil produces a magic potion, Faust drinks it and is miraculously transformed into a handsome young man. Then, repeating Faust's song of pleasure and youth, *"A moi les plaisirs"* ("To me these pleasures"), the two rush out and the curtain descends.

SCENE TWO: *Market place of a small town.*

It is a festival day, and everyone is making merry, singing and dancing. Marguerite's brother, Valentine, brings a note of seriousness to the occasion. He is a soldier and about to go off to the wars, and in the famous aria, *"Avant de quitter ces lieux"* ("Before leaving this place"), he tells of the fears he has on leaving his home and his young sister.

Marguerite's village swain, the youthful Siebel, and several others reassure him and then a song is called for. A young fellow named Wagner starts singing, *"Un rat plus poltron que brave"* ("The song of the rat"), when a splendidly dressed stranger appears and interrupts him. It is Mephistopheles and he says he will sing a better song. It is the vigorous irreverent tune known as *"Le veau d'or"* ("The calf of gold"), and all the men join in the chorus heartily.

Mephistopheles further entertains the company by telling fortunes (all of them bad) and causing wine to flow magically from the signboard hanging outside the inn door. He even proposes a toast to Marguerite, but that is too much for Valentine, who challenges him with his sword. But Valentine's sword mysteriously breaks in two, and now they all know with whom they have to deal. Led by Valentine, the men reverse their swords making the sign of the cross and the Devil cringes in fear and loathing as they sing the impressive *"Chorale of the Swords"*, backing away step by step from the Evil One.

Soon, however, a little dance orchestra appears on the stage—a waltz is struck up and everyone starts dancing. In the midst of this, Marguerite crosses the stage and is met by Faust who offers her his arm. Gently, modestly, she declines the offer and passes on, but Faust has fallen head over heels in love—*"O belle enfant! Je t'aime!"* ("O beautiful child! I love you!"). And so, with everyone taking up the dance once more the first act ends on a note of gaiety.

ACT TWO

SCENE: *The garden of Marguerite's home.*

Part of the house appears at one side of the garden and in the background can be seen the tower of a church. The garden is full of flowers including a large rose bush in the center. This is the famous "Garden Scene". When the curtain rises after a short Prelude, we hear at once the "Flower Song"—*"Faites-lui mes aveux"* ("Gentle flowers of spring"), in which Marguerite's young admirer, Siebel, picks and arranges for his adored one a pretty bouquet. After Siebel has left his flowers at Marguerite's door, Faust and Mephistopheles enter and a few minutes later Faust sings his aria, *"Salut! demeure chaste et pure"* ("Hail thou dwelling pure and lowly").

Now Mephistopheles returns after a few moments' absence with a far grander present for Marguerite than poor Siebel's flowers. It is a casket of jewels and he places it beneath the flowers.

Faust and Mephistopheles now retire and Marguerite enters the quiet garden. She sits down at her spinning wheel and begins to work as she sings *"The Ballad of the King of Thulé"*, pausing now and then to turn over in her mind the meeting with the handsome and wealthy young stranger, Faust. But soon she espies Siebel's offering and underneath it the casket of jewels.

In an outburst of innocent delight, she bedecks herself with the jewels, singing the brilliant aria known as the "Jewel Song"—*"Je ris de me voir"* ("Saints above, what lovely jewels"). Soon a gossipy neighbor, Martha, drops in and Mephistopheles and Faust return. Mephistopheles makes mock love to Martha, thus taking her attention away from the two young people.

And then as night begins to fall, we hear Mephistopheles in his invocation to night, *"O nuit, entends sur eux ton ombre"* ("O Night, draw thy curtain"), in which he calls on the night to encourage the love of Faust and Marguerite.

The lovers wander through the garden in the soft summer night and we hear the beautiful love duet, *"Laisse moi contempler ton visage"* ("Let me gaze"). Marguerite, overwhelmed by this new experience, bids Faust goodnight and goes into the house to be alone with her thoughts.

Her sweetness and innocence have won Faust's respect, and he is about to leave when Mephistopheles taunts him with cowardice. At that moment, we hear Marguerite sing, from her open window, of her ecstasy in her new-found love—*"Il m'aime!"* ("He loves me!") Rushing back, Faust climbs to the window and as the two lovers embrace, Mephistopheles howls his delight with a great sardonic laugh. His plot has succeeded.

ACT THREE

SCENE ONE: *Interior of the church.*

Marguerite, who has been deserted by Faust, comes to pray to God for comfort. But the evil figure of the Devil appears behind her and mockingly bids her remember the days of innocence. "Pray no more," he says. "You shall never be forgiven." Off-stage, we hear the choir intoning the solemn *"Dies Irae"* ("Day of Wrath, Day of Judgment").

From another direction, we hear a chorus of demons and, with Marguerite's voice rising in prayer and Mephistopheles telling her that her soul is lost, the scene rises to a passionate climax. With a dreadful cry, Marguerite faints and the congregation, coming out, finds her there and carries her away as the brief but highly dramatic scene closes.

SCENE TWO: *A square outside Marguerite's house.*

Military music is heard off-stage as the villagers gather. The soldiers are returning from the wars with Valentine at their head. We hear the familiar and rousing *"Soldiers' Chorus"* as the men are greeted by their wives and sweethearts. With a band on the stage playing the tune, they march off again, leaving Valentine to ask Siebel about Marguerite. Siebel replies evasively and, troubled in his mind, Valentine enters his own home. Now Faust and Mephistopheles come into the square and the Devil sings a cruel, mocking serenade to Marguerite, *"Vous qui faites l'endormie"* ("You who pretend to sleep"), accompanying himself on his guitar and ending with evil, sneering laughter.

This brings Valentine out with drawn sword. He angrily breaks Mephistopheles' guitar, challenges the betrayer of his sister and, during the martial trio that follows, throws away the holy charm which Marguerite gave him to guard his life.

And so, in the duel that follows, Mephistopheles successfully guides Faust's sword straight to the heart of Valentine. The Evil One hurries his protegé off with him and leaves the dying soldier lying on the ground as the villagers gather. Valentine curses his sister as the cause of his death and, with the awestruck citizens kneeling in a brief prayer, Marguerite throws herself on the body of her brother, virtually out of her mind with grief and terror.

ACT FOUR

Scene: *A prison cell.*

Marguerite, in prison garb, lies asleep on a pallet of straw. Her mind has succumbed to the horrors she has endured and in her madness she has slain her child. She has been convicted of murder and condemned to hang this very morning. But Mephistopheles has drugged the jailer and stolen his keys and now he and Faust enter the cell determined to rescue her. Mephistopheles departs almost at once to fetch horses so that the two lovers may escape.

Faust sadly contemplates the stricken girl. She hears his voice, awakens, and for a brief while she is happy once more. Her mind wanders back to their first meeting, and we hear again the music of their greeting at the fair, then a reminiscence of the waltz and the love duet in the garden. But the spell is shattered by the entrance of Mephistopheles, who urges them to hurry away.

In the dim light of the prison cell she recognizes the Evil One and shrinks away, crying "The Demon, the Demon!" She knows but one defense from him—prayer. She sinks to her knees and prays as Mephistopheles and Faust urge her to hurry away. In this great final trio, Marguerite's voice mounts upward toward heaven, *"Anges purs, anges radieux"* ("Angels pure, angels radiant"), and this time her prayer is answered.

Marguerite sinks dying to the floor as a great chorus of angels sings the *"Hymn of Redemption"*. In the back of the cell, we see a vision of the angels carrying Marguerite's soul to heaven while Mephistopheles, shuddering, draws Faust away from the holy scene he cannot endure to behold.

Romeo and Juliet

by CHARLES GOUNOD (1818–1893)

Five Acts. Libretto by Barbier and Carré, based on Shakespeare's play.
First produced in Paris, 1867.

Count Capulet	*Bass*
Juliet, his daughter	*Soprano*
Romeo, a Montague	*Tenor*
Mercutio, his friend	*Baritone*
Friar Laurence	*Bass*
Tybalt, nephew of Count Capulet	*Tenor*
Count Paris	*Baritone*
Gertrude, Juliet's nurse	*Mezzo-soprano*
Gregorio, a Capulet retainer	*Baritone*
Stefano, page to Romeo	*Mezzo-soprano*
Duke of Verona	*Bass*
Benvolio, a Montague retainer	*Tenor*

Ladies and gentlemen, servants.

TIME: *Fourteenth Century.*
PLACE: *Verona, Italy.*

ACT ONE

SCENE: *Ballroom of the Capulet palace.*

The opera begins with a Prologue. After a brief orchestral introduction, the curtain rises on a darkened stage where we dimly make out the entire cast of the opera. They

Purchaser _____ Order No. _____

Date entered _____ Date _____

Author _____

Book _____

Publisher & address _____

Purchaser's Name: _____
(vertically please) _____

sing of the feud between the two noble houses, the Montagues and the Capulets, and of the tragic love of young Romeo and Juliet.

The curtain falls after this brief Prologue and rises again almost immediately on the first act. The scene is a brilliant one. It is the ballroom in the palace of the Capulets where a masked ball is in progress in celebration of young Juliet's birthday. At the beginning of the act we learn that Juliet is to be betrothed to a young nobleman named Count Paris.

Among the guests we find Romeo, son of the Montagues and deadly enemy of the Capulets, accompanied by his friend Mercutio and others. These daring young men have come to the ball trusting to their masks to conceal their identity. Romeo says that he is troubled by a dream he has had and Mercutio says it was undoubtedly a message from Queen Mab, a fairy queen who plants dreams and illusions in the minds of men. This is the "Ballad of Queen Mab"— *"Mab, la reine des mensonges"* ("Mab, the queen of dreams").

In spite of his feeling of impending trouble, Romeo lingers on in the home of his enemies as he is fascinated by the youth and beauty of the fair Juliet. She sings of her joy in living in the famous waltz song, *"Je veux vivre"* ("I would live in dreams of youth").

Romeo addresses Juliet as *"Ange adorable"* ("Adorable angel") and the beginning of their love is revealed in a delightful duet, which is interrupted by the entrance of Juliet's cousin, Tybalt. Romeo leaves the room after a moment, Tybalt realizes that the young man is Romeo, the enemy of the Capulet family. He rushes out angrily, swearing he will kill the rash intruder. Romeo returns with his friends, followed by Tybalt with drawn sword, but bloodshed is avoided by the intervention of Juliet's father who does not want to have the festivities spoiled, and Romeo and his friends depart.

ACT TWO

SCENE: *Garden of the Capulets.*

The curtain rises on a lovely night scene showing the garden surrounding Capulet's house, with a balcony and a window leading to Juliet's apartment. The ball is over and the guests are leaving, but Romeo lingers in the garden, hoping to catch a glimpse once more of the fair Juliet. In the distance we hear the voice of Mercutio and his other friends calling for him to join them, but he pays no heed. Under the balcony he sings a serenade, *"Ah, lève-toi, soleil"* ("Arise O sun!"). Juliet appears on the balcony. "Wherefore art thou Romeo?" she says sadly. "Deny thy name or I'll foreswear my own."

Just then a group of Capulet retainers comes in, and Romeo hastily hides. They are searching the garden because they suspect that one of the hated Montagues is hiding there, but they find no one. Gertrude, Juliet's nurse, inquires as to the unseemly commotion and promises them her help in looking for the intruder. Then she scolds Juliet for being up so late and urges her to come to bed. After a few moments, Juliet reappears on the balcony. Romeo has emerged from his hiding place, and they resume their love duet, *"O nuit divine"* ("O night divine"). Romeo pleads with Juliet to stay a little longer and the act closes with the beautiful farewell duet by the young lovers, *"Ah! ne fuis pas encore"* ("Ah, go not yet"). "Be sweet thy rest," sings Romeo. "May the breezes of night bear my kiss to thee."

ACT THREE

SCENE ONE: *Friar Laurence's cell.*

The good Friar Laurence is surprised by a visit from Romeo, who tells him of his love for Juliet. The friar cries out in amazement at the idea that a Montague could love a Capulet. He agrees to lend his aid to the match, saying that he hopes the hatred which has existed between the families for so many years will be quenched by this love.

Soon Juliet arrives with her nurse, Gertrude, and while Gertrude keeps watch, the two lovers are married by the friar, who blesses their union and prays for peace between the houses of Montague and Capulet in a beautiful air, *"Dieu, qui fis l'homme à ton image"* ("God who madest man in Thine own image"). The scene closes with a quartet sung by the two lovers, the nurse and the friar, who join in a prayer of gratitude to God who has blessed their love.

SCENE TWO: *Public square in front of the Capulet palace.*

Romeo's young page, Stefano, is singing an impertinent song, *"Que fais-tu, blanche tourterelle"* ("Dainty dove, what are you doing"), in which he warns the Capulets in slightly veiled language that their beloved Juliet may one day fly away. This brings out an angry group of Capulet retainers, led by one Gregorio, who recognizes Stefano as one of the disturbers they were hunting for in the garden a few night ago. Hot words follow and Stefano and Gregorio engage in a duel.

Suddenly Romeo's good friend, Mercutio, comes on the scene and accuses Gregorio of drawing his sword on a mere child, with the insulting remark that that is just what might be expected of the house of Capulet. Others arrive on the scene, including Juliet's cousin, Tybalt, who denounced Romeo in the ballroom scene in the first act.

Then Romeo appears and when he sees Mercutio and Tybalt draw their swords, he tries to stop them. Insults follow but Romeo, thinking of Juliet, will not allow himself to be drawn into a duel with her kinsman. But Mercutio hurls the insult that Romeo has prudently left unsaid. He and Tybalt attack each other and Mercutio falls, mortally wounded. Romeo can no longer refrain from avenging his friend and fatally wounds Tybalt, who falls into the arms of Count Capulet as the nobleman comes upon the scene.

Suddenly the bystanders cry, "The Duke! The Duke!" and the Duke of Verona appears with his retinue. Capulet cries out for "justice", meaning revenge, denouncing Romeo as the murderer of Tybalt. When the Duke learns the cause of the trouble, he pronounces judgment—that Romeo be banished from Verona. Romeo cries out against this unhappy day of woe, and vows that he will see Juliet once more before he leaves. The Capulets renew their vows of hatred against the Montagues, crying out "Peace? No, never, never" and the curtain falls.

ACT FOUR

SCENE: *Juliet's chamber.*

It is night. By the light of a torch, we see Juliet reclining on a couch with Romeo at her feet. He has again found a way into Capulet's house, this time at imminent risk of death. The lovers are spending a few treasured moments in a tender farewell before Romeo goes into exile. They sing an impassioned duet, *"Nuit d'hyménée"* ("O consecrated night—sweet night of love"). At the end Romeo sadly tells her that he hears the morning lark, but Juliet insists it is the nightingale. But lark or nightingale, the lovers must part, and Romeo departs as he has come, by the balcony.

Hardly has Romeo gone when the nurse Gertrude runs in to warn Juliet that Capulet and Friar Laurence are coming—and they enter immediately. Juliet's father, not knowing of her secret marriage to Romeo, tells her that he is speeding the arrangements of her wedding to Count Paris, and neither Juliet or the friar dare tell him that she is already wed to Romeo.

Juliet and the friar are left alone. She begs him to help her and shows him a dagger hidden in her breast with which she says she will destroy herself if forced to marry Count Paris. The friar tells her of a drug which will make her appear as if dead. He promises her that he will bring her husband to her and when she awakens from her drugged sleep, they can escape together.

When the kind priest leaves, Capulet comes in with Count Paris. Juliet drinks the potion and sinks, as if dead, to the floor as the curtain falls on this tragic scene.

ACT FIVE

SCENE: *Tomb of the Capulets.*

There is a solemn orchestral prelude reflecting the peace of the tomb where Juliet lies in deathly silence, her face pale as marble, for she is still in her trance. Through the darkness and silence Romeo steals softly and gazes sadly at his bride. The messenger sent by Friar Laurence to tell him of the plan has failed to reach him and Romeo does not know that Juliet's apparently lifeless body is only in a drugged sleep. After a few moments, he lifts a phial of poison to his lips and drinks it.

Hardly has he done so, when to his amazement Juliet stirs and begins to shake off her lethargy. Romeo stares at her as if stunned. Gently she breathes his name. Romeo cries, *"Juliette est vivante!"* ("Juliet is alive!") The two lovers embrace and Juliet begs Romeo to take her away to safety and happiness.

Then Romeo realizes his horrible mistake and he confesses to her that, thinking her dead, he has already taken poison. They have only a brief moment to say farewell in this the last of their love-duets, *"Console-toi, pauvre âme"* ("Yield not to sorrow"). Romeo slips from her arms and falls to the ground. Juliet picks up the empty phial and upbraids him for taking every drop, leaving none for her. Then, remembering the dagger hidden in her breast, she stabs herself and they die in each other's arms praying that heaven will grant them peace.

Hänsel and Gretel

by ENGELBERT HUMPERDINCK (1854–1921)

Three Acts. Libretto by Humperdinck's sister, Adelheid, based on Grimm's fairy tale.

First produced in Weimar, 1893.

Hänsel	*Mezzo-soprano*
Gretel	*Soprano*
Peter, their father	*Baritone*
Gertrude, their mother	*Mezzo-soprano*
The Sandman	*Soprano*
The Dawn Fairy	*Soprano*
The Witch	*Mezzo-soprano*

Angels, children.

TIME: *Imaginary time of fairy tales.*
PLACE: *Germany.*

ACT ONE

SCENE ONE: *Home of Peter and Gertrude.*

The first scene is in the interior of a very humble little house on the edge of the woods. It is the home of Peter, a broom-maker, his wife, Gertrude, and their two children, Hänsel and Gretel. Father and mother have gone to market, leaving the two children with work to do—Hänsel making brooms and Gretel knitting. But, as children will, they spend their time playing. Gretel singing a merry little nursery song, *"Suzy, little Suzy"*, about how the geese have to go barefoot because the cobbler can't make them shoes. Hänsel adds a verse of his own and soon they grow more boisterous and begin to dance—*"With your foot you tap, tap, tap—With your hands you clap, clap, clap."*

In the midst of their frolic, their mother returns, cross and tired. She has not made a penny for all her work and there is nothing in the house to eat except a pitcher of milk. She is annoyed with the idle children and turns on them angrily. In giving them a push she accidentally knocks over the milk pitcher.

It is the last straw! She sends the children out into the wood to gather strawberries, sinks down onto a chair, and praying heaven to send food for her family, falls asleep. Soon, we hear a rollicking voice outside the house, *"Ra-la-la-la, Hunger is the best of cooks."* It is Peter, the children's father who has had the good luck to sell all his brooms and has come home with a basket full of food.

"But where are the children?" he asks, and Gertrude tells him of the broken pitcher and how she has sent them out to pick strawberries. "Don't you know there is a wicked old witch who lives in the forest?" cries Peter in alarm. "At midnight she rides out on her broomstick hunting for little children. By day she bakes them into cookies in her magic oven so that she can eat them." Both parents are terrified at this prospect and determine to find the youngsters at once.

SCENE TWO: *A forest glade.*

The curtain is lowered for a few minutes and we hear the orchestral interlude, *"The Witch's Ride"*, and when the curtain rises again we are under the trees of the great forest just before sunset. Gretel sits on a grassy hummock weaving a garland of flowers and singing an old nursery rhyme, *"There stands a little man in the wood all alone."* Hänsel comes running in, his basket full of berries. A cuckoo calls softly through the forest and the children try to imitate him.

It is growing dark, Hänsel cannot find the path out of the forest, the shadows deepen, and will-o'-the wisps flicker through the bushes. The children are terrified as they realize they must spend the night in the forest. They sink down together on the grassy hummock, and a gentle little man dressed in gray draws near and sings soothingly to them as he sprinkles their eyes with sand from a little bag he carries. It is the Sandman, singing, *"Then from the starry sphere above."*

He slips quietly away, and brother and sister kneel together and sing their evening prayer: *"When at night I go to sleep, fourteen angels watch do keep."* Holding each other closely, they fall asleep. It is now quite dark.

Suddenly, a brilliant light shines through the trees, and we behold a vision of white-robed angels standing on a celestial stairway leading up through the trees to heaven itself.

One by one the angels descend silently and group themselves around the sleeping children. The Sandman's song gives way to the theme of the *"Children's Prayer"* which rises to a mighty climax from the trumpets and trombones and then dies away as the curtain falls slowly.

ACT TWO

Scene: *Same as previous scene.*

The first light of dawn is creeping into the dark forest where the children are still asleep. The Dawn Fairy comes in and sprinkles them with drops of dew shaken from a bluebell. The children awaken in a happy mood, and gleefully imitate the warbling birds. Gretel tells of dreaming about angels, but the celestial stairway and the angels have disappeared, and the children now discover something which they had not seen before. It is a fantastic little house.

made of gingerbread, trimmed with candy and surrounded by a fence of cookies.

Hänsel approaches timidly and breaks off a bit of cake from the wall. A shrill voice from inside the house calls out, *"Nibble, nibble, mousekin, who's nibbling at my housekin?"* The children are frightened at first, but they are hungry and soon are nibbling again. Thus they do not see the wicked old witch stealing up behind them until she has thrown a rope around Hänsel's neck.

The children try to run away but she stops them in their tracks by a magic wand. There is a little cage at one side of the yard and she claps Hänsel into it and slams the door. "I'll eat Gretel first," she says. "She's so nice and plump, but Hänsel is scrawny and needs fattening up."

She is a fearful looking creature, with sharp chin and nose like a bird's beak, and a mop of disorderly gray hair. She heaps up a fresh fire under the oven near the cage and then mounting a broom-stick, as a mysterious darkness descends over the wood, she flies through the air to the music of *"The Witch's Ride"* which was heard as the interlude in the first act. In a few moments she returns to earth and daylight returns also, as mysteriously as it had disappeared.

She sends Gretel into the house to get some raisins and almonds to feed to Hänsel. Returning with the goodies from the house, Gretel finds a juniper branch, just like the magic one the witch carries. Perhaps she too can work a spell. "Hocus pocus," she whispers and waves the branch. Hänsel, magically released, creeps out of the cage and hides behind his sister.

The witch beckons Gretel to the oven. "Come here, child, and see if the gingerbread is ready. Just stand on tiptoe and look inside." Gretel pretends not to understand. "Show me what you mean," she says slyly. As the witch opens the door and peers into the oven, the children spring on her from behind, shove her in, and lock the door. *"Hurrah!"* cry the children. *"The wicked witch is dead."* And they waltz about gaily. Suddenly there is a loud explosion.

The oven has blown up and falls in ruins and the gingerbread house collapses and the cookie fence disappears and in its place stand a score of children who have been bewitched. Another wave of Gretel's magic wand and they are restored to life. Joyously, they form a ring and dance around Hänsel and Gretel, singing, *"The witch's might is broken quite."*

And then Peter and Gertrude appear, and children and parents embrace each other happily. Two boys go to the ruins of the oven and bring out a large cookie which they find in the ashes. It is the old witch herself, browned to a turn. The opera closes with all singing a "Hymn of Thanksgiving"—*"When in direst need we stand, God will offer us His hand."*

I Pagliacci

(The Strolling Players)

by RUGGIERO LEONCAVALLO (1858–1919)

Two Acts. Text by Leoncavallo.
First produced in Milan, 1892.

Canio		*Tenor*
Nedda, his wife		*Soprano*
Tonio	Strolling players	*Baritone*
Beppe		*Tenor*
Silvio, a villager		*Baritone*

Peasants and villagers.

TIME: *About 1870.*
PLACE: *Montalbo, Italy.*

ACT ONE

SCENE: *An open space near the village.*

There is an orchestral introduction in which several melodies are presented which are used later in the opera. Suddenly in the midst of the prelude, the curtains part and a man in a clown's costume slips out and steps to the footlights. "Ladies and gentlemen," he says, bowing, "pardon me if I appear alone, I am the Prologue." Then he goes on in a very beautiful baritone aria, *"Si può? Signore! Signori!"* ("A word—allow me! Ladies and gentlemen!"), to inform the audience that whereas it used to be the custom for the "Prologue" to assure the audience that the story they were about to witness was fiction and the various characters merely actors, in this case he wishes them to know that actors, too, are human beings and are moved by real and deep emotions. "Our hearts are just like yours, beating with passion, with gladness and sorrow. So now, let us begin, up with the curtain!"

The curtain rises and we see the strolling players make their effective entrance to the village—all done very theatrically. A portable theatre has been set up and is to be seen at the right. We hear a crude and slightly out of tune trumpet sound a few flourishes and there is the booming of a bass drum. A donkey appears, drawing a brightly painted cart in which sits Nedda, the leading lady, while Canio, the leading man, bangs away on the big bass drum and announces the performance that evening at seven o'clock.

It is the day of the Feast of the Assumption and the villagers are gaily dressed and in a holiday mood. But there is a hint that all is not well within the players' company. Tonio, the clown, tries to assist Nedda down from the cart and receives a box on the ear from Canio, who in real life is Nedda's husband. Someone suggests they all go to the tavern and have a drink, but Tonio refuses to go, saying he has to take care of the donkey. When one of the villagers jestingly hints that perhaps he wants to remain behind to make love to Nedda, Canio gives him a black look and threateningly says that while such a situation might happen in a play on the stage, if it happened in real life, the ending of the story would be quite different.

And now the sound of church bells summons worshipers to the vesper service. The villagers sing a beautiful *"Chorus of the Bells"* and many of them stroll off toward the church. The voices fade into the distance and Nedda is left alone to brood over the jealous fire she has seen in Canio's eyes. But the beauty of the summer afternoon and the song of the birds soon drive away her gloomy thoughts and, looking up into the sky, she sings the happy *"Ballatella"* ("Ye happy birds, flying in freedom").

There, outside the little portable stage on which they are to act that evening, Tonio, the hunchback clown, approaches Nedda and tries ludicrously but earnestly to make love to her. Nedda only laughs at him and when he persists, strikes him with a whip. Tonio goes off muttering vengeance, the opportunity for which comes all too soon.

Silvio, a young and handsome villager whom Nedda had met on previous visits, now enters by a secret pathway. They have fallen in love with each other and at the end of a long and rapturous duet, *"Silvio! a quest'ora. . . . che imprudenza"* ("Silvio! What madness at this hour"), she agrees to elope with him that night. Tonio spies on the two lovers for a few minutes and then runs off to the tavern to bring back the jealous husband, Canio. They return just in time to hear Nedda call a loving farewell "Tonight and forever" to Silvio, who escapes unrecognized by Canio. Furious with jealousy, Canio demands to know his rival's name and when Nedda refuses to give it, threatens her with a knife. She is saved just in time by Beppe, another member of the troupe, who reminds his master that the show must go on that night.

Left alone Canio sings his great aria, *"Vesti la giubba"* ("Put on the costume and make-up"), in which he sings of the actor's cruel necessity of going on with the show even though his heart may be breaking—*"Ridi, Pagliaccio"* ("Laugh, clown, laugh"). Sobbing bitterly, he staggers into the little theatre as the curtain falls.

ACT TWO

SCENE: *Same as Act One.*

It is evening and the villagers are assembling to witness the play. Beppe blows the little trumpet and Tonio beats the big drum, just to add to the excitement of the occasion. The audience seat themselves on low benches in front of the little portable stage and some of them sit on the ground. An air of eager anticipation pervades the scene. Nedda passes through the audience, collecting the admission money. As she does so, Silvio manages to speak to her to remind her of their rendezvous for that night and she replies that she will be there.

A bell rings in the little theatre and Nedda, Beppe, and

Tonio go behind the scenes. In a moment the curtain rises on this play-within-a-play. Nedda, dressed as Columbine, is seated at a table and is awaiting the return of her husband, Pagliaccio, who is to be played by her real-life husband, Canio. As she waits, someone behind the scenes sings a serenade to her, *"O Colombina, il tenero fide Arlecchin"* ("O Columbine, your faithful Harlequin awaits you").

As the serenade is finished, in comes Tonio, who in the play is called Taddeo, the servant. He brings a basket containing a chicken which he has purchased at the market. As in real life, Tonio ("Taddeo") begins to make ardent love to Nedda and, as in real life, she ridicules him. She goes to the window and makes a sign to someone outside and in comes Harlequin (who in real life is Beppe). Harlequin gives Taddeo a kick and tells him to be off, and then Columbine and Harlequin (who has brought a bottle of wine) sit down at the table for a gay little supper party. Harlequin gives Columbine a small bottle containing a sleeping potion which she is to give her husband so that the two lovers can elope. Just at that moment, Taddeo rushes in and exclaims excitedly that Pagliaccio is approaching. Harlequin escapes through the window by which he entered and Pagliaccio comes in just in time to hear his wife's parting words, the very words which Canio had heard Nedda say to Silvio that very afternoon, "Tonight and forever".

The resemblance to real life is almost too much for poor Canio, who has difficulty in going on with his part. He follows the lines of the play by accusing his wife of infidelity and demanding to know the name of her lover and Nedda responds with the lines of the play, denying everything.

Finally, Canio can stand no more. Giving up all pretense at acting his comic role, he wipes the makeup off his face and shouts, *"Pagliaccio non son"* ("Now I am Punchinello no more!")—and the crowd, misunderstanding, applauds him for his very convincing acting. Nedda tries to go on with the lines of the play; but Canio, becoming more and more desperate as he demands to know her lover's name, finally pulls out his knife (again just as he had done in real life)—and this time he plunges it into her back.

Dying, Nedda calls upon Silvio for help and, rushing up, he too meets the avenging knife of the wronged husband.

Standing in horror at his own deed before the crowd Canio announces in a broken voice, *"La commedia è finita"* ("The comedy is over"). And the curtain falls as the orchestra thunders out the heart-breaking climax of his great aria, *"Ridi Pagliaccio"* ("Laugh, clown, laugh").

Cavalleria Rusticana

(Rustic Chivalry)

by PIETRO MASCAGNI (1863–1945)

One Act. Libretto by Targioni-Tozzetti and Menasci, based on story by Verga.
First produced in Rome, 1890.

Santuzza, a beautiful peasant girl	*Soprano*
Turiddu, a young soldier	*Tenor*
Lucia, mother of Turiddu	*Contralto*
Alfio, a village teamster	*Baritone*
Lola, wife of Alfio	*Mezzo-soprano*

Villagers and peasants.

TIME: *Nineteenth Century.*
PLACE: *A Sicilian village.*

SCENE: *Open square in a Sicilian village.*

There is an orchestral prelude in which we hear the principal melodies to be used later in depicting this tale of violent passions—love, jealousy, and revenge. The prelude is suddenly interrupted and we hear a tenor voice singing behind the curtain to a guitar-like accompaniment. This is the "Siciliana"—*"O Lola, bianca come fior de spino"* ("O Lola, fair as flowers")—a serenade by the young soldier, Turiddu, to his beloved Lola.

When the curtain goes up, it is Easter morning in a small Sicilian village. On the left of the stage is the inn kept by Lucia, Turiddu's mother, and on the right is the church. Villagers are passing by singing a happy melodious chorus.

Soon Santuzza hurries in to ask Lucia where her son Turiddu may be. "Not yet returned from a trip to the next town to purchase wine," says Lucia, who does not know he has already been seen in the town early in the morning.

Presently we hear the cracking of a whip, and the popular teamster of the town, Alfio, accompanied by his many friends, sings a rollicking tune in praise of his trade, *"Il cavallo scalpita"* ("Gaily goes the tramping horse").

And now through the open doors of the church we hear the solemn tones of the organ and we hear the beautiful *"Easter Hymn"* sung by the villagers, some inside and some outside the church. Among those remaining outside is Santuzza, and we learn that she has been excommunicated and cannot enter the church, but she kneels outside the church and joins in the singing.

When the hymn is ended and all the villagers have gone inside the church, Santuzza signals to Lucia to remain behind and she tells her in the aria, *"Voi lo sapete"* ("Well do you know, good mother"), how Turiddu has betrayed her. She reminds Lucia that Turiddu was engaged to Lola before he went away to serve in the army and that while he was gone Lola had married Alfio. On his return from the army, Turiddu had turned to Santuzza. They were lovers, she says, but Turiddu seduced her. He has taken up again with his former sweetheart, Lola, wife of Alfio. That explains why he returned secretly during the night from his trip to the neighboring town to buy wine.

Lucia, deeply shocked to hear this about her son, goes into the church, promising Santuzza she will pray for her. Santuzza is left alone for a moment, and then she sees Turiddu crossing the square. She accuses him of being false to her and he responds angrily.

In the middle of their violent quarrel, Lola, the cause of it all, enters singing a gay little tune that contrasts strangely with the angry tones of Santuzza and Turiddu. When Lola has entered the church (after coquettishly tossing Turiddu the rose she has been wearing), the quarrel reaches a violent pitch. Turiddu refuses to make up with Santuzza, throws her off roughly so that she falls to the ground, and then follows Lola into the church. Just then Alfio comes by, and Santuzza, mad with jealousy, tells him of the affair between his wife and Turiddu, *"Oh! Il Signore vi manda"* ("God has sent you, neighbor Alfio").

Alfio goes off vowing vengeance. Santuzza, overcome with remorse goes after him, realizing too late the hatred she has aroused. The stage is empty now, after the stormy passions of this dramatic scene, we hear the serene and peaceful strains of the famous *"Intermezzo"*.

The services over, Turiddu invites all the villagers to drink at his mother's tavern, and we hear the spirited drinking song, the "Brindisi"—*"Viva il vino spumeggiante"* ("Hail the red wine richly flowing"). But Alfio will have none of his enemy's wine, and Turiddu promptly challenges him to a duel. The challenge is accepted, and while Alfio goes off to the orchard where the duel is to take place, Turiddu bids a last despairing farewell to his mother (*"Addio alla madre"*), begging her to take care of Santuzza in case he should not return. Realizing his own guilt, he rushes off to his doom. A minute later we hear a horrified voice exclaim, "Turiddu has been murdered!" Santuzza falls fainting to the ground as the curtain drops quickly.

Manon

by JULES MASSENET (1842–1912)

Five Acts. Libretto by Meilhac and Gille, based on Abbé Prévost's novel.
First produced in Paris, 1884.

Lescaut, a member of the Royal Guard	*Baritone*
Manon Lescaut, his young cousin	*Soprano*
Chevalier des Grieux	*Tenor*
Count des Grieux, his father	*Bass*
De Brétigny, a nobleman	*Baritone*
Guillot Morfontain, Minister of France	*Bass*

An innkeeper, actresses, porters, servants, townspeople, travelers, vendors, gamblers, croupier, a sergeant.

TIME: *1721.*
PLACE: *Amiens, Paris, on the road to Le Havre.*

ACT ONE

SCENE: *Courtyard of an inn at Amiens.*

A crowd of people has gathered in the courtyard to await the arrival of the stage-coach which is due any minute now. On one side of the yard is a pavilion for serving refreshments and from this partially enclosed spot we occasionally hear the merrymaking of two noblemen, one middle-aged and the other young, who are having dinner with three gaily dressed young women.

The older man is an important member of the government named Guillot and the younger man is an aristocrat named de Brétigny. In the crowd is an officer in the bright-colored uniform of the Royal Guard. This is Lescaut who is to meet his young cousin Manon, a passenger on the stage-coach.

The coach arrives and with it Manon, a pretty, good-hearted, but somewhat light-headed young lady, who is making her first journey away from home on her way to a convent—*"Je suis encore tout étourdie"* ("I am still a simple maiden"). Lescaut has never met his young cousin before and is delighted to discover how pretty and unsophisticated she is. He goes off to find her luggage and while he is away, Guillot comes out from the pavilion.

To him any pretty girl is legitimate prey and he immediately begins to make love to Manon. His gay companions in the pavilion call him back to them, but before he goes he tells Manon that he has ordered a carriage and he invites her to accompany him. Just at that moment, Lescaut returns and Guillot leaves in some confusion. Lescaut warns Manon that Guillot is an old roué and tells her she must have nothing to do with him. He has some duties to perform, he says, and leaves her alone again, after admonishing her not to stir from the spot and not to speak to strangers.

Manon waits demurely in the courtyard, envying the three girls who seem to be having such a good time in the pavilion, and regretting the fact that soon she will be shut away from the world and its pleasures in the quiet walls of a convent.

And now, a young, handsome and aristocratic young

man, the Chevalier des Grieux, enters the courtyard. It is a case of love at first sight and when Guillot's coachman appears and says the carriage is at Manon's disposal, the temptation is too great to resist. The two young people hasten off to the carriage to go to Paris together just as Lescaut returns, *"Nous vivrons à Paris"* ("We to Paris will go"). Guillot also comes in and both men are mystified and angry at the disappearance of Manon. The innkeeper explains that the two young people have just left by carriage and the crowd laughs at the old roué, who is by this time terribly angry and vows vengeance on both Manon and her fool of a cousin, Lescaut.

ACT TWO

SCENE: *Des Grieux's apartment in Paris.*

Manon is blissfully happy with her new-found lover, the Chevalier des Grieux, in his Paris apartment. Des Grieux is writing a letter to his father asking permission to marry Manon, and delightedly she reads over his shoulder the glowing description of herself.

They are interrupted by a servant who announces two callers, Manon's cousin, Lescaut, and the nobleman de Brétigny, who has been sending Manon flowers. Pompously and angrily Lescaut demands satisfaction from des Grieux for the injury against his family's honor. Des Grieux soon pacifies him, however, by showing him the letter to his father, indicating that his intentions are most honorable.

While des Grieux and Lescaut are so engaged, de Brétigny takes Manon aside and tells her that des Grieux's father, the Count, will disinherit his son if he marries Manon. Furthermore, he tells her, the Count is planning to have his son kidnapped from her that very evening. If she truly loves des Grieux, says de Brétigny, she will not warn him and be the cause of his ruin, but will rely on de Brétigny's own generosity when her lover is gone. When the two visitors have politely left, des Grieux goes out to mail his letter while Manon sings a touching farewell to the little table where they had supped together *"Adieu, notre petite table"* ("Farewell, our little table").

On his return to the room des Grieux sings a beautiful aria, full of serene happiness, in which he tells her of his dream of a cottage in the country where the two young lovers can live happily, *"En fermant les yeux"* ("With fancy's eye I saw").

Suddenly there is a knock at the door. With a last vain impulse, Manon begs her lover to stay at her side, but he opens the door, there is the sound of a struggle, des Grieux is captured and carried off by the kidnappers of whom she has been warned. Manon, left alone, utters a heart-broken cry, *"Mon pauvre chevalier"* ("My poor chevalier"), as she realizes that her brief happiness is over.

ACT THREE

Scene One: *Cours La Reine, Paris.*

The brilliantly decorated square is alive with people buying and selling and having a good time—among them Manon's cousin Lescaut, the three young ladies we met in Act One at the inn at Amiens, and their companion Guillot, who had vowed vengeance on Manon and des Grieux.

Presently Manon comes in with de Brétigny, who is her lover now that des Grieux is gone. She is apparently quite happy and light-hearted again, the belle of the town, and she sings a gay song with a gavotte-like air, which gives her present philosophy of life, in effect: "Gather ye rose-buds while ye may."

Then the Count des Grieux enters—our hero's stern and aristocratic parent—and Manon overhears him tell de Brétigny that the young Chevalier has entered the seminary of St. Sulpice. Manon finds an excuse to talk to the old man alone, and discovers, through artful questioning, that young des Grieux still loves her. As the curtain falls, she orders her cousin Lescaut to get her carriage for she is going off post-haste to the church of St. Sulpice.

Scene Two: *Seminary of St. Sulpice.*

Des Grieux, in the seminary, is about to become a priest. We hear first a group of ladies admiring a sermon the young man has just preached as well as his modest and manly behavior. The elderly Count des Grieux comes to visit his son to dissuade him from entering the church. The young man, however, is steadfast in his purpose, and when his disappointed father has left, he eloquently tells us the reason: he is joining the church in order to forget Manon. "*Ah! fuyez, douce image*" ("Ah! depart, sweet vision"), he sings, in one of the great arias of the opera.

Scarcely has he left the stage when the "sweet vision" herself—Manon—comes in and asks for des Grieux. While the porter goes to call him she hears the choir singing offstage and utters a short prayer herself. Des Grieux enters and tries at first to harden his heart against the temptation she represents, but he cannot resist her tears and entreaties to come to her once more. In a long and moving duet, he slowly weakens. With a final cry of, "*Ah, viens, Manon, je t'aime*" ("Ah, come, Manon, I love you"), he deserts the church and they rush through the door together.

ACT FOUR

SCENE: *Hôtel de Transylvanie, a gambling house in Paris.*

Manon and des Grieux, once more united, come to a sumptuous and elegant gambling hall, where a brilliant and lively session is in progress. Manon, brightly clad and bejeweled, urges des Grieux to try his luck; and though he is at first reluctant to gamble, he lets himself be persuaded to accept the challenge given him by, of all people, Guillot, the old roué whom Manon jilted at Amiens, and who vowed vengeance. While they play for a thousand crowns a hand, Manon voices her philosophy of life once more: "*La jeunesse passe, la beauté s'efface, Que tous nos désirs soient pour les plaisirs*" ("Youth passes and beauty fades, So let's worry about nothing but pleasure").

Meantime des Grieux has been having scandalously good luck, and Guillot rises in a rage to accuse him of cheating. The young chevalier hotly denies the unfounded charge, but Guillot storms from the room to return shortly with officers of the law, who arrest both des Grieux and Manon on his charge of cheating. Des Grieux is about to resist, but his father, the Count, also appears, and orders the officers to do their duty. Under his breath, the Count tells his son that his influence will shortly liberate him. Des Grieux would still resist, but the officers drag out both him and the despairing Manon, as the curtain falls.

ACT FIVE

SCENE: *A road near Le Havre.*

Time has passed, and Manon has been convicted and sentenced to be deported to a penal colony; while des Grieux, of course, has been set free through the influence of his father, the Count.

Des Grieux has enlisted the support of Lescaut in a desperate scheme to rescue Manon with a group of hired desperados. When the curtain rises, however, Lescaut tells him that they have all deserted. There is one chance left—bribery. Des Grieux gives Lescaut all the money he has and Lescaut is successful in his conniving. For when the sorry troop of prisoners and their guards pass, Manon comes last and with a single guard, whom Lescaut gets aside with a nice fat tip.

But the Manon that des Grieux greets with delirious joy is not the old gay, carefree Manon. She is already sick unto death and though she recognizes her lover, she cannot respond to his entreaties to escape. Slowly her mind wanders, slowly she sinks to the ground.

With her lover's arms once more about her, she dies there on the road, uttering the last pathetic line of the opera: *"Et c'est là l'histoire de Manon"* ("And this is the story of Manon"). Heartbroken, des Grieux falls on her body as the curtain slowly descends.

The Medium

by GIAN-CARLO MENOTTI (1911–   )

Two Acts. Libretto by Gian-Carlo Menotti.
First produced in New York, 1946. Revised and produced in
New York, 1947.

Mme. Flora (Baba), a medium	*Contralto*
Monica, her daughter	*Soprano*
Toby, a mute	*Dancer*
Mrs. Gobineau ⎫	*Soprano*
Mr. Gobineau ⎬ clients	*Baritone*
Mrs. Nolan ⎭	*Mezzo-soprano*

TIME: *The present.*
PLACE: *U.S.A.*

ACT ONE

SCENE: *Mme. Flora's parlor.*

Mme. Flora practices her trade in a squalid room on the
outskirts of a big city. She is, as the composer has said, a
woman "caught between two worlds, a world of reality she
cannot wholly comprehend and a supernatural world in
which she cannot believe. She has no scruples about
cheating her clients until something happens which she
herself has not prepared. This insignificant incident shat-
ters her self-assurance and drives her almost insane with
rage."

As the tragedy opens, its chief character is absent.
Monica, her daughter, play-acts in front of a mirror, singing a song about a queen who has lost her golden spindle.
Suddenly in the mirror she notices Toby, the mute, who
is improvising a gaudy costume for himself out of bits and
pieces he takes from an open trunk. Monica scolds him,
for Baba will be furious if she comes home and finds him
messing with her belongings; besides, nothing is ready for

the séance. Then, struck by his beauty, she sings to him, while he dances his reply. They are frozen as Mme. Flora enters, coming only partially up the stairs. She reviles Toby, but is pacified by Monica, who begins to get ready for the séance by putting on a long white dress. Toby arranges the puppet theater in the corner, showing its mechanism behind the white curtain. He tests one lever that raises the table and another that lowers the lamp, then hides himself in the small aperture while Monica runs off stage. They are ready.

The three clients appear on the stairs. The Gobineaus have been resorting to Baba's spurious help for two years to keep "in touch" with their infant son, who had drowned in a fountain. Mrs. Nolan is a newcomer; her daughter has recently died.

As the séance begins, Monica appears in a faint blue light, singing *"Mother, Mother, are you there?"* Mrs. Nolan is convinced that it is her daughter, although Monica asks about a gold locket she cannot remember. She rushes towards the ghostly figure, which immediately disappears. Now Monica laughs obligingly for the Gobineaus, who expect nothing else as a manifestation of their son. The séance is almost over when something unforeseen occurs.

Baba starts up in alarm. A cold hand has brushed her throat. Almost hysterically she demands to know who touched her. The gullible clients reassure her: why be afraid of the dead? The clients depart, leaving Baba shaking all over from terror. She takes a drink, then draws the curtain to reveal Toby. She drags him out of the cabinet, and begins to beat him, accusing him of being the ghostly presence. Monica's protests fall on deaf ears, until at last Baba's rage spends itself. Monica draws her away, and Baba lies down with her head in Monica's lap. Monica can always soothe her mother by singing a song about a black swan. *"O black swan, where is my lover gone?"* she sings, while Toby accompanies on the tambourine. Baba joins in the last verse until suddenly she hears voices—someone is calling "Mother, Mother, are you there?" and laughing eerily. But only Baba hears. She will not be convinced that nothing is there. As Monica sings a few phrases of a cradle song, Baba prays. A child's laughter is heard and Baba hides her head in Monica's lap in terror.

ACT TWO

SCENE: *Same as before, evening, a few days later.*

Toby gives a puppet performance for Monica, then they play a game that begins lightly but turns into a love scene, with Monica singing for Toby and answering him in her own right, while he mimes. They reach a pitch of emotion broken by Toby's tears, just as the door slams below. Baba is home. Monica runs to her room, and Toby crouches in the corner. Baba carries a bottle from which it is evident she has been drinking freely. She calls Toby to her and with simulated gentleness reminds him of all she has done for him—taken him from the streets, fed him, given him a place to sleep. Now, will he tell her—did he touch her throat? As he doesn't show any indication of answering, her rage mounts and she goes for her whip. Unmercifully she flogs him until the ringing of the doorbell brings her to her senses.

It is the faithful trio, wanting another séance. Baba repulses them, tells them never to come back. Everything she has done was a trick—"Monica, show them." But no matter how brutal the revelations, the believers still believe. They will not go until Baba chases them out, screaming, "You fools!" Toby must go too. Monica pleads, but it is no use. Toby is sent away. Monica runs to her room, and Baba turns the key on her.

Now, brooding and drinking, she faces her terror alone. Her hysterical laughter dies into silence, and she sleeps soddenly.

Toby creeps in, tries Monica's door and finds it locked. Baba stirs in her sleep and the bottle falls. Toby hides behind the couch, then tries Monica's door once more. He goes to the trunk, begins to rummage in the silks, and lets the lid slam. This wakes Baba. Toby hides quickly behind the curtain of the puppet theater.

Baba calls out: "Who's there?" In her fear, half dazed, she pulls a revolver out of the table drawer. "I'll shoot!"

The curtain moves. Baba screams and fires at it several times. For a few seconds, everything is completely still. Then very slowly a red spot appears on the white curtain and runs down the length of it.

"I've killed the ghost!" Baba screams.

Toby's hands appear at the sides of the curtain, clutching it. The rod breaks under his weight and he falls, shrouded in the curtain.

Monica pounds at the door from within and Baba goes slowly to unlock it. Monica calls faintly for help, and runs downstairs. The door slams.

Baba, in a hoarse whisper, still questions: "Was it you?"

Amahl and the Night Visitors

by GIAN-CARLO MENOTTI (1911–   )

One Act. Libretto by Gian-Carlo Menotti. First produced on NBC Television, 1951. First stage production, New York, 1952.

Amahl, a crippled boy	*Boy soprano*
His Mother	*Soprano*
Kaspar	*Tenor*
Melchior	*Baritone*
Balthazar	*Bass*
Page	*Baritone*

Shepherds.

TIME: *The Year of the Birth of Christ.*
PLACE: *The road to Bethlehem.*

SCENE: *The cottage of Amahl and his mother, within and without.*

Under a brilliant, star-filled sky, Amahl plays his pipe. His mother calls him in, but he pleads with her to let him stay a little longer. Reluctantly he obeys at last, but he is loath to leave the glorious night—there is a star in the sky "as large as a window." His mother impatiently scolds him for telling lies, and in spite of his protests, puts him to bed. They will have to go begging soon, she says, there is nothing to eat in the house and no firewood. "What good beggars we'll be!" Amahl responds cheerfully. They lie down, he on his hard pallet, she on a bench.

From far off, the procession of the Kings is heard. On their way to worship the new-born babe, Melchior brings gold, Balthazar an urn of incense, Kaspar a chalice of myrrh. Their Page knocks at the cottage door. Amahl's mother sends him to see who it is.

"Mother, come with me. I want to be sure that you see what I see!" exclaims the excited child. "Well?" "It is a King!" Twice she sends him back in exasperation, and each time another King is added, until she must see for herself. Then, humbled, she offers what poor hospitality she can, and goes for firewood.

Amahl loses no time. "Are you a real King?" he asks Melchior. "And is your blood royal? What's the difference?"

"No difference."

"What's the good of having it, then?" he wonders. He asks about Kaspar's parrot. "Does it bite?"

Kaspar silently holds up a bandaged finger. Kaspar is a little deaf and all questions must be repeated. "What's that?" and Amahl points to a little chest Kaspar keeps beside him.

"This is my box, this is my box, I never travel without my box!" Kaspar sings, showing the bedazzled boy that in the top drawer are beads, and in the next precious stones, and—ah! in the last, licorice. "Have some!" he offers.

The mother returns and scolds Amahl for bothering the distinguished visitors, then sends him off to summon the shepherds. She wonders at the mission of the Kings.

"Have you seen a child the color of wheat, the color of dawn?" Melchior asks her. Yes, she has, but it is her own child she thinks of. Always he comes first.

The shepherds approach timidly. All they have is fruits and grains and simple gifts, but they are welcome, and they dance for the visitors, shy at first but with increasing boisterousness. The little hut rings with their merriment. At last the Kings plead weariness, and the throng withdraws. As the mother bids them farewell, Amahl approaches Kaspar.

"Do you have in your box anything that would cure a

crippled boy?" he asks hopefully, thinking of how dependent he is on his crutch.

But Kaspar's uncomprehending "Hey?" discourages him, and he turns away.

The Kings sleep on their bench. Guarding the gold, the Page dozes. The mother eyes the gleaming metal greedily— *"All that gold! Do they know?"* What it would buy for a little boy! Cautiously she creeps nearer. Just one piece. Just two.

But she is caught. The Page cries out, and the Kings wake. Amahl beats the Page bitterly with his two little fists, shouting "Don't you dare hurt my mother!" until he collapses in exhaustion.

"Woman, you may keep the gold," says Melchior. "The king we seek does not need it. His kingdom is built on love."

Hearing of the true nature of this king, the Mother repents and longs to send an offering as well. But she has nothing.

"Mother, I can send my crutch," quavers Amahl from the corner. Then he stands, holding the wooden support in his two hands. Stumbling, he takes a step, two steps. He is walking!

It is a Christmas miracle! All the Kings are anxious to touch the blessed boy, and the Page too, but Amahl refuses *him* until his mother remonstrates. At last it is decided that Amahl must go in person to present his gift, and after a tender farewell between mother and son, the cheerful boy follows the procession up the hill, piping a merry tune.

L'Amore Dei Tre Re

(The Love of Three Kings)

by ITALO MONTEMEZZI (1875-1952)

Three Acts. Libretto by Benelli.
First produced in Milan, 1913.

Archibaldo, King of Altura	*Bass*
Manfredo, his son	*Baritone*
Fiora, Manfredo's wife	*Soprano*
Avito, former Prince of Altura	*Tenor*
Flaminio, a servant	*Tenor*

People of Altura.

TIME: *Tenth Century, forty years after a barbarian invasion led by Archibaldo.*
PLACE: *A remote castle in Italy.*

ACT ONE

SCENE: *A hall in the Castle of Archibaldo.*

It is just before dawn and the great hall of the castle, with its vaulted ceiling and gleaming mosaics can be seen but dimly in the darkness. Two arched doorways open onto a terrace, on which a lighted lantern stands. Archibaldo, the blind old king of Altura is led in by Flaminio, one of the castle guards. He is restless and cannot sleep, hoping for the return of his son, Manfredo. Even after all these years the Alturans are not completely conquered and Manfredo is on a campaign against them in the mountain country. Flaminio reminds the old king that he himself is an Alturan and has remained in the service of the invader only for the sake of peace. And it was for the sake of peace that the Princess Fiora married Manfredo, for she had been betrothed to the Alturan Prince Avito.

There is no sign of Manfredo, and Archibaldo bids Flaminio extinguish the signal light. As he does so, the sound of a flute floats up from the valley and Flaminio hurries the king back to his room. Hardly has he done so when another door leading to the hall opens and Avito comes out cautiously, looking about to see that he is not observed. He is followed by Fiora, who begs him to linger a little longer. She assures him that the door to Archibaldo's room is tightly shut and asks that he kiss her— *"Dammi le labbre"* ("Give me thy lips"). The lovers embrace and sing a duet of passionate intensity. There is another signal from the flute outside. It is growing light and Avito observes with dismay that the signal lantern has been put out, and he knows that someone has been on the terrace. As Avito hurries away across the terrace, the door of Archibaldo's room opens and the old king calls to Fiora. "I know you are there," he says. "I can hear you breathing and I heard you talking to someone. Who was it?"

"I was talking to myself," she replies. "I could not sleep for thinking of my husband Manfredo and came out on the terrace to watch for his return."

"Do not lie to me," cries Archibaldo angrily and orders her to her room as trumpet calls outside herald the coming of Manfredo. He and his father greet each other affectionately and Manfredo speaks of his great happiness in returning to his home and to his young wife, *"O padre mio"* ("O my father").

Fiora comes out of her room and greets him, concealing her real feelings with words of welcome. "I came out on the terrace before dawn to look for you," she says. "Is it not so, father?" Archibaldo would not hurt his son and has to admit that she was, indeed, on the terrace before dawn. Manfredo, embracing Fiora tenderly, leads her back into her room. The old king is left alone. He raises his hands to heaven and exclaims, "O God, since Thou hast taken away mine eyes, let me be truly blind!"

ACT TWO

SCENE: *A terrace of the castle.*

It is late afternoon and Manfredo is bidding Fiora a most affectionate farewell, *"Dimmi, Fiora, perchè ti veggo ancora"* ("Tell me, Fiora, why do I leave you again"). From the courtyard of the castle comes the sound of trumpets and Manfredo says with sorrow that in a few minutes he will be on his way down the valley. He begs Fiora to watch from the battlement which surrounds the high terrace on which they stand and to wave her scarf so that it will be the last thing he sees as he goes away. Fiora, pitying the man she cannot love, promises him she will do as he asks.

Manfredo departs and Fiora climbs the stone stairway leading to the battlement. As she stands looking over the wall, she hears her name called and turns to see Avito dressed as one of the guards. She begs him to leave and to leave forever. Manfredo's kindness and devotion have touched her heart and she is unwilling to continue her guilty affair with Avito. They are interrupted by a servant who brings Fiora a casket containing a long white scarf, sent to her by Manfredo.

She returns to the battlement wall and waves the scarf slowly. Avito ascends the steps and stands below her. He reaches up to touch the scarf in her hand, but she forbids him to touch it. "You may kiss the hem of my garment," she says. "I embroidered it myself."

He seizes her mantle and covers it with kisses. She turns to him slowly and he draws her down, half-fainting, into his arms, *"Ho sete! Ho sete!"* ("I thirst! I thirst!"). They are so lost in ecstasy that they do not hear the approach of Archibaldo and Flaminio and are startled when the old king calls, "Fiora!" Avito draws his dagger and rushes toward the blind man, but Flaminio intercepts him and Fiora, in great distress, signals to him to escape. He does so silently and when Archibaldo asks "Who is there?" Flaminio answers truthfully "No one." But he reports that Manfredo has turned his horse and is returning to the castle. Archibaldo orders him to go and greet his master.

Left alone with Fiora, Archibaldo demands to know who her lover is. She denies that she has a lover, and he grows more angry with each denial. He seizes her by the throat as she cowers on a bench before him, and she finally admits that she has a lover and that she loves him truly and not Manfredo, but she refuses to give his name, even though it may cost her her life. In his rage and fury, Archibaldo's fingers tighten on her throat and almost before he realizes what he is doing, she is dead.

Manfredo rushes in frantically. He saw Fiora and her waving scarf as he began his journey down the valley and then after a while he could see them no longer and, full of anxiety, returned to the castle to learn what happened. He is horrified as he sees his father standing before the dead body of his wife. Archibaldo despairingly begs Manfredo for his sword so that he too may die. "I have slain her," he says, "because she was as impure as she was fair."

Broken-heartedly, Manfredo asks the name of her lover but Archibaldo tells him that he does not know as, being blind, he could not see him. Archibaldo will not let him look at Fiora, saying that he must not see the marks of his fingers on her throat. "Lead the way," he says. "I will follow the sound of your footsteps." As Manfredo slowly and sorrowfully leaves the terrace, Archibaldo lifts the body of Fiora to his shoulders and follows his son.

ACT THREE

Scene: *The crypt in the chapel of the castle.*

The white-clad body of Fiora lies in the crypt and from the chapel above we hear the chanting of the choir. A group of the people of Altura, men and women, stand respectfully with bent heads about the bier and mourn their lovely princess. Some of them grow angry and demand that her cruel murder be avenged, but their anger subsides and they slowly depart as the bell tolls its solemn requiem.

When they have gone, Avito enters the crypt to bid a last farewell to his beloved Fiora. Overwhelmed with the agony of his grief, he bends above her lifeless body and kisses her on the lips—*"Fiora! E silenzio"* ("Fiora! She is silent"). He starts up abruptly and realizes that his body is shaken with a terrible sensation. He suddenly knows that he is dying and rejoices in the knowledge. As he staggers toward the door, he is met by Manfredo who tells him that Archibaldo has spread a deadly poison on Fiora's lips in the hope that just what has happened would take place and that they would discover the identity of Fiora's lover.

But Manfredo can find no satisfaction in knowing at

last the name of the man Fiora had loved. He can only regret that she could not have loved him instead. He gently lowers Avito's body to the floor and marvels that he can find in himself no hatred for his rival. In an abandonment of grief, he throws himself on the body of Fiora and he too presses his lips against hers. As the poison begins to take effect, Archibaldo enters and rejoices that they have found the guilty man. But when he hears the dying voice of his own son, the old man cries out in agony and despair.

Boris Godunov

by MODEST MOUSSORGSKY (1835–1881)

Four Acts. Based on drama by Pushkin.
First produced in St. Petersburg, 1874.

Boris Godunov	*Bass*
Gregory, a novice, later called Dmitri	*Tenor*
Pimen, a monk and historian	*Bass*
Prince Shuisky, a royal councillor	*Tenor*
Missail } Mendicant friars	*Tenor*
Varlaam }	*Bass*
Marina Mnishek, a Polish noblewoman	*Mezzo-soprano*
Xenia, daughter of Boris	*Soprano*
Feodor, son of Boris	*Mezzo-soprano*
Rangoni, a Jesuit priest	*Bass*
Hostess of the Inn	*Mezzo-soprano*
The Simpleton	*Tenor*

Russian people, soldiers, guards, boyars, pilgrims, children.

TIME: *1598–1605.*
PLACE: *Russia and Poland.*

ACT ONE

SCENE ONE: *Courtyard in front of the Novodievichy monastery in Moscow.*

The young Czar Feodor, son of Ivan the Terrible, has just died, and as there is no heir in the direct line of succession it is necessary to choose a czar. Boris Godunov, who has been regent for the young Feodor, is secretly plotting to have himself made czar, but wishes to make it appear that he does so in response to public demand. He has retired to the monastery and has refused an offer of the throne, but has ordered the police to round up a crowd of people and force them to demand that he take the crown. A group of pilgrims comes in chanting (*Great is Your Glory*), and they distribute sacred amulets to the crowd, thus giving the impression that it is God's will that Boris become czar. A speaker appears at the entrance of the monastery and tells the crowd that Russia is doomed unless Boris can be persuaded to take the throne, and the people, urged on by the brutal police, kneel in prayer.

SCENE TWO: *A monk's cell in the Chudov monastery.*

The old monk, Pimen, is writing a history of Russia. He tells a young novice, Gregory, that he is too old to finish it and begs the young man to do so (*"Pimen's Narrative"*). He has reached the point in his story where Dmitri, the younger brother of the Czar Feodor, had been murdered at the instigation of Boris Godunov, who aspired to become czar himself. If the boy Dmitri had lived, says the old man, he would have been czar of Russia now and just Gregory's age. Thus is implanted an idea in the mind of this ambitious young man as he cries, "Here in this lonely cell is the avenger of a murdered child!"

SCENE THREE: *A square before the Kremlin in Moscow* (Coronation Scene).

We hear the clash and clangor of bells and the mounting zeal of the crowd in their now genuine enthusiasm over the new czar. A brilliant procession crosses the stage as the people sing, *"Glory to Russia, glory to Czar Boris"*. At last Boris himself comes on clad in his magnificent coronation regalia and accompanied by his daughter, Xenia, and his young son, Feodor. The music dies down as he speaks to the assemblage, quietly, even sadly. He says that he feels sorrow over having had to accede to their wishes that he become czar. Actually, he secretly feels the pangs of conscience for the crime that brought him to this moment. He blesses the crowd with becoming humbleness and dignity, and then enters the Cathedral of the Archangels as the procession moves on. With bells pealing loudly, the crowd takes up the jubilant *"Coronation Chorus"* and at its close, Boris appears again on the steps of the cathedral.

ACT TWO

SCENE ONE: *An inn near the Lithuanian border.*

As the curtain goes up, we hear the innkeeper, a simple peasant woman, singing a folk song as she busies herself about the place. Pretty soon a couple of jolly mendicant friars, Missail and Varlaam, come in and ask for wine and begin to drink it in huge quantities. Slipping in quietly behind them comes Gregory, the young priest we met in the first act. He is no longer a priest, for he has escaped from the monastery, gotten himself some fine clothes, and now hopes to raise an army against Czar Boris by himself posing as young Dmitri, the rightful heir, whom Boris is supposed to have murdered.

With a bottle in his hand, Varlaam sings a boisterous drinking song, *"Once upon a time in the city of Kazan"*. As both friars babble drunkenly, Gregory asks the innkeeper the shortest road to the frontier. He is about to slip away when a loud knock is heard at the door of the inn. The police enter seeking the renegade monk. They have with them a warrant for his arrest, but as they cannot read, Gregory obligingly offers to do it for them. As he does so, he makes up the description of the culprit to fit the drunken Varlaam. Varlaam now angrily rouses himself from his stupor and with difficulty spells out the real description of the fugitive which, of course, fits Gregory exactly. Gregory, however, has foreseen this. As he is about to be seized, he brandishes a knife and makes his escape by way of the window, shoving a table in the way of the others. Falling over themselves, they try to follow him, but it is obvious that their incompetence is going to permit him to make good his escape.

SCENE TWO: *Private apartments of the Czar in the Kremlin.*

The two children of Boris are sitting with their nurse. The boy, Feodor, is studying a book on geography, but the girl, Xenia, sings sadly of the death of her betrothed. Boris enters and advises his daughter to seek the companionship of her friends of her own age, and she and the nurse leave the room.

Boris talks with his son and commends him for his diligence in study, for some day he will be czar and will need both knowledge and wisdom. Then the czar muses sadly on his own unhappiness. He has been czar for five years now, but has not found any satisfaction in achieving power (*"I have attained the highest power!"*). There has been a famine in Russia, there are constantly plots and quarrels among the nobles, and, worst of all, his conscience is never at peace and he is haunted by visions of the murdered boy, Dmitri. A terrible sense of guilt is destroying his reason (*"I am suffocating"*).

Soon a courtier comes to tell of more troubles. He is followed by Prince Shuisky, a tricky and untrustworthy member of the court. Shuisky begins the *"Duologue"* with Boris, telling him of the rebellion that Gregory has organized, posing as the rightful heir, Dmitri. "Can Dmitri have been raised from the dead?" cries the czar. Trembling before his wrath, Shuisky, who himself had supervised the crime, rehearses the bloody details until Boris can stand it no longer. He shakes Shuisky by the collar, dismisses him and falls prey to a frightful attack of conscience. Imagining that he sees the ghost of Dmitri bathed in blood, he falls on his knees in an agony of remorse and prayer as the curtain falls.

ACT THREE

SCENE ONE: *A lady's boudoir in a castle in Poland.*

It is here that Gregory, posing as the rightful Czar Dmitri, is organizing his rebellion against Boris. Marina Mnishek, a haughty Polish noblewoman who is both vain and beautiful, sits before a dressing table preparing for an evening party with the aid of some maids-in-waiting. Saying she is tired of the rhythms of the polonaise and mazurka, she tells them to sing her songs of Polish warriors (*"Nay, Marina asks not songs of love"*). Dismissing her attendants, Marina dreams of wearing the crown of Russia, for she and the false Dmitri have met and she realizes that the young pretender to the Russian throne is in love with her. Rangoni, a Jesuit priest, now comes into the room. In a powerful scene he impresses her with the importance of making Dmitri offer not only marriage, but the espousal of the cause of the Roman Catholic Church, as opposed to the Orthodox Greek Church, the official church of the Russian empire. Marina protests at first that this is too grave an assignment for her, but Rangoni holds up a small cross that he carries with him and Marina, terrified for the moment, accedes to Rangoni's demands.

SCENE TWO: *A fountain in the garden of Marina's castle.*

Dmitri has been promised a meeting with Marina in the moonlit garden, and he is excitedly anticipating it as he sings of his love for her. Presently, we hear the strains of a polonaise, and Dmitri retires. The party of Polish noblemen and women now come in and dance and sing the brilliant polonaise, Marina leading them all on the arm of a middle-aged gentleman. When the party has once more retired to the castle, Dmitri comes out. He is unhappy, for he believes Marina has promised herself to the Polish nobleman with whom she has been dancing.

But she herself presently comes out into the garden alone, as she has promised to do, and meets him at the fountain. Like the skillful court lady she is, she plays upon the young man's emotions and the music becomes passionately romantic as she throws herself at his feet and calls him her hero. Their voices join in a beautiful *love duet*. Dmitri takes her up in his arms as the priest, Rangoni, passes by at the back of the stage, rubbing his hands with satisfaction at the way his plans are succeeding.

ACT FOUR

SCENE ONE: *A snow-covered clearing in the forest of Kromy near Moscow.*

A large crowd of peasants is taunting and beating a nobleman who has fallen into their hands, for they regard all the upper classes—the boyars—as evil, and Boris as the worst of all. The village idiot comes in wearing a kitchen pot as a tin helmet, and sings, *"In the moonlight the cats are crying."* A group of urchins teases him and steals the one piece of small change—a kopeck—that he has left. Wailing, he goes off stage, as the priests Varlaam and Missail come in cursing the rule of Boris and urging the crowd to support Dmitri (*"Dark is the sun and dark the moon"*). Two Jesuit priests are also victims of the crowd's ill humor, when the scene is interrupted by the arrival of soldiers. They are Dmitri's soldiers, and he himself finally comes in on horseback. Thus the nobleman is rescued and so are the priests, while the crowd enthusiastically follows him, singing, *"Glory! Glory to Dmitri Ivanovitch!"* The stage is now empty, save for the one sad figure—that of the poor simpleton, who, in *"The Idiot's Lament"*, bewails the state of Russia.

Scene Two: *Council Chamber in the Kremlin.*

A meeting is in progress and the men are making threats as to what they will do when they catch the pretender, the false Dmitri and his followers. Prince Shuisky is visibly disturbed in mind, for he has seen Boris in his secret agony of conscience, imagining that he has beheld the ghost of young Dmitri. Shuisky describes this scene in minute detail to the fascinated courtiers.

Boris himself suddenly enters and interrupts this narrative. Shuisky begs him to give audience to a wise old man and Boris consents. This old man turns out to be Brother Pimen, the ancient chronicler, whom we met in the first act in a cell with Gregory.

Now, he tells a mysterious tale of a blind old shepherd who heard a voice in his dreams—a voice that cried that he was the slain Dmitri, and that the shepherd should go to pray at his tomb, for he was now an angel who could perform miracles. The blind old shepherd did go to pray at the tomb of Dmitri—and lo! he miraculously regained his sight! Boris, who now believes that his young victim has become an angel, is so deeply moved by the old monk's story that he gives an agonized cry (*"I need air. Scarce can I draw a breath"*), and then almost faints. He quickly dismisses the council and calls for his son, Feodor. Solemnly the Czar admonishes his son to rule wisely and justly after him, to defend the holy religion of Russia (*"Farewell, my son, I am dying"*).

Off-stage a mournful bell tolls and we hear a chorus from the next room praying for the soul of Boris. And now, in the early throes of death, he gathers his strength and begins to pray, when the noblemen file in once more. Boris struggles to his feet, forces himself up to his full height, points regally to his son and cries, "There is your czar!" And with an appeal to heaven for mercy, he falls to the foot of the throne, dead.

The Marriage of Figaro

(Le Nozze di Figaro)

by WOLFGANG AMADEUS MOZART (1756–1791)

Four Acts. Libretto by da Ponte, based on comedy by Beaumarchais.
First produced in Vienna, 1786.

Count Almaviva	*Baritone*
Countess Almaviva	*Soprano*
Figaro, Almaviva's valet	*Baritone*
Susanna, the Countess's maid and fiancée of Figaro	*Soprano*
Cherubino, page to the Count	*Soprano*
Barberina, the gardener's daughter	*Soprano*
Dr. Bartolo	*Bass*
Marcellina, Bartolo's housekeeper	*Soprano*
Don Basilio, a music teacher	*Tenor*
Don Curzio, a lawyer	*Tenor*
Antonio, a gardener	*Bass*

TIME: *Early Eighteenth Century.*
PLACE: *Home of Count Almaviva, near Seville, Spain.*

ACT ONE

SCENE: *A room in the house of Count Almaviva.*

Several years have elapsed since the marriage of Count Almaviva and his beloved Rosina. Figaro, the former barber of Seville, is now the count's valet and is engaged to marry the Countess's personal maid, Susanna. The room which is to be occupied by the young couple is between the room of the Count and that of his Countess. Figaro calls attention to how convenient this will be as neither he nor Susanna will have far to go to answer a call. But Susanna points out that it might be equally inconvenient, especially if used as a bedroom.

She then reveals that the Count has been trying to flirt with her, as is, after all, his right as the lord and master. She goes into the Countess's room and Figaro gives way to his jealousy in the aria, *"Se vuol ballare"* ("If you wish to dance"), in which he declares that if that is the way the Count wants to dance, he, Figaro, will have something to say about it.

When Figaro has left the room, Dr. Bartolo enters—an elderly physician who bears Figaro a grudge and, with him is his housekeeper, Marcellina, a middle-aged woman. It seems that some time ago Figaro borrowed money from Marcellina and signed a contract to the effect that if he failed to repay the money he would marry Marcellina. She and Dr. Bartolo are trying to trap Figaro into the marriage. After Dr. Bartolo has sworn vengeance on Figaro, he departs and Susanna returns. She and Marcellina exchange barbed insults and Marcellina leaves in a rage.

And now in comes the youthful page-boy, Cherubino, who has just discovered how much fun it is to be in love, and so he loves virtually every female character in the opera, including Barberina, the gardener's daughter, whom we have not met yet.

Cherubino describes his emotions to the amused Susanna in the lovely melody, *"Non so più"* ("I know not what I am doing"). Actually Cherubino has no business being in that room and the entrance of the Count forces him to hide behind a big chair. There he overhears the Count trying to arrange a rendezvous in the garden with Susanna.

As he does so, Basilio, the music-master, enters, and then the Count also seeks refuge behind the big chair, as Cherubino slips around to the front of the chair and curls up on the seat which Susanna covers with a cloak. Basilio, a busybody, begins to gossip about the Countess and Cherubino. Angrily the Count steps forward and a moment later discovers Cherubino under the cloak. Things begin to look a little serious in our gay comedy, when Figaro enters leading a group of peasants who sing a song of flattery to the Count. Considerably mollified, the Count forgives Cherubino his youthful errors of taste, but he decides to send him away as an ensign in a distant regiment. Cherubino is unhappy about this, but there's nothing he can do and the act ends as Figaro sings a jolly, teasing military farewell, *"Non più andrai"* ("No longer will you flutter"), to the young nuisance.

ACT TWO

SCENE: *The Countess's apartment.*

The Countess is mourning over the passing of first love as she sings the beautiful aria, *"Porgi, Amor"* ("Love, thou holy impulse"). The Count apparently has been casting eyes in other directions, and so the Countess is quite ready to fall in with a plot against him which has been concocted by her maid, Susanna, and Susanna's fiancé, Figaro.

Figaro has penned an anonymous letter to the Count informing him that the Countess has a rendezvous in the garden with another man. Furthermore, Susanna is to agree to meet the Count himself in the garden the same night— an appointment that is to be kept by the page-boy Cherubino dressed as a girl. And now, Cherubino enters and sings an aria, *"Voi che sapete"* ("What is this feeling?"), about the sweet melancholy that love brings with it.

Cherubino now tries on one of Susanna's dresses, which he is to wear at the rendezvous in the garden that evening. Both Susanna and the Countess are amused at his airs and graces and declare that he will make a charming young woman.

There is a knock at the door and the Count demands to be admitted. Cherubino hides in the dressing room and locks the door. Susanna runs into the next room, while the Countess unlocks the apartment door and admits the Count. He has Figaro's letter and immediately wants to know why the door was locked. Before the Countess can answer, there is the noise of a chair being overturned in the dressing-room. The Countess explains that it is only Susanna, trying on her wedding gown. The Count orders Susanna to come out, but the Countess orders her to stay inside. When the Count discovers that the dressing-room door is locked also, he is more angry than ever and declares that he will get some tools and open it by force. He orders the Countess to come with him for the tools and, as they leave, he locks the apartment door from the outside.

Now Susanna comes out of her hiding-place in the next room and Cherubino comes out of the dressing-room.

When Susanna explains that the apartment door is locked and he cannot escape that way, Cherubino jumps out of the window into the garden below and Susanna hides in the dressing-room in his place. And so it happens that when the Count finally forces the door open both he and the Countess are surprised to find not Cherubino but Susanna in hiding. The Count quickly concludes that he is the victim of a joke and is almost penitent about his flirtation with Susanna, when a half-drunken gardener enters the room and complains that someone has jumped from the window right into his flower-bed. Figaro has opportunely turned up and, grasping the situation, announces that it was *he* who jumped from the window. When the gardener produces Cherubino's army commission (which he dropped), the quick-witted Figaro boldly claims that he was taking it into town to have it properly sealed.

Safely out of that dilemma, Figaro is plumped into another when Bartolo, Basilio, and Marcellina enter, demanding that Figaro keep his contract to marry the unattractive housekeeper. The Count agrees to look into the legal aspects of the question, and the act ends as everyone expresses his or her own emotions about the extremely complex state of affairs.

ACT THREE

SCENE: *A hall in Count Almaviva's house.*

Count Almaviva is not quite convinced that his wife is innocent and that Figaro's behavior has been entirely above board, but Susanna mollifies him in a pretty little duet, *"Crudel! perchè finora"* ("Too long have you deceived me"), and promises to meet him in the garden that evening. And now come Marcellina, Bartolo, Basilio, and the lawyer, Don Curzio, and the hilarious "trial scene" takes place.

The lawyer demands that Figaro repay his debt to Marcellina or else fulfill his contract and marry her. But Figaro has other things on his mind. He has suspected for some time that he is of noble birth. He was stolen from his parents as a small child and bears on his arm a mysterious birthmark. Marcellina becomes excited at this news, identifies the birthmark, and embraces Figaro as her long-lost son! Susanna enters just at this point and it takes quite a bit of persuasion to convince her that Marcellina is in Figaro's embrace because she is his rediscovered mother and not Susanna's successful rival.

That episode over, we have a charming duet between Barberina, the gardener's daughter, and Cherubino the page-boy. This is followed by the Countess's beautiful aria, *"Dove sono"* ("It is past"), in which she sings of her love for the Count, which she now thinks she has all but lost.

But the plotting is not over. In the delightful "Letter Duet"—*"Che soave zeffiretto"* ("What gentle zephyr"), the Countess dictates to Susanna a note confirming the rendezvous with the Count in the garden, the scheme now being to have the Countess herself, disguised as Susanna, keep that appointment.

Now Barberina and a group of her young girl friends come in to bring a gift of roses to the Countess. Cherubino, disguised as one of the girls, is with them, a fact that Antonio, the gardener, discloses by pulling off the page-boy's headdress. Poor Cherubino—he is always being discovered in suspicious circumstances! The Count's jealousy is aroused once more, but Barberina saves the situation this time by announcing that she and Cherubino are in love and wish to be married.

Curtains at the back of the stage are pulled aside revealing a large staircase down which troops a stage-full of people ready to celebrate the wedding of Figaro and Susanna. And so, with the dancing of a Fandango, the act comes to an end in an atmosphere of gaiety and frolic incidental to the wedding festivities.

ACT FOUR

SCENE: *Garden of Count Almaviva's home.*

The final act brings about a happy solution to all the plots and counterplots. It takes place at night in the garden and the comedy revolves around the idea of mistaken identity (you will remember how Susanna and the Countess had planned to change costumes in order to catch the Count in his attempted flirtation with Susanna).

Near the beginning of this scene Figaro sings an aria in which he asks the men in the audience if nothing will ever teach them that women are faithless, *"Aprite un po' que gl'occhi"* ("Open your eyes a little"). We also hear Susanna sing her expressive aria, *"Deh vieni non tardar"* ("Ah, why delay so long?"), in which she tells of her love for Figaro. But Figaro, listening on one side of the dark garden thinks she is singing about her love for the Count.

Now, wandering in the dark in search of his Barberina, Cherubino comes on the Countess disguised as Susanna and starts to make love to her. The Count discovers them and, thinking his wife is Susanna, chases Cherubino away and starts to make love to her himself. Figaro, who is gradually catching on to what is happening, finds Susanna (disguised as the Countess, you must remember) and starts to make love to her too. It is all quite complicated and is made still more complicated when the Count discovers Figaro and, thinking that his servant is making love to the Countess (whereas it is really Susanna), he seizes Figaro and calls in everyone else. Susanna keeps up her disguise and starts to apologize to the Count—a mock apology, of course—when the real Countess comes in and reveals herself.

The Count, realizing that he has been fairly caught, kneels before the Countess and asks for mercy. This is, of course, granted by the Countess and the opera closes with all the couples happily united—the Count with the Countess, Figaro with Susanna, Cherubino with Barberina and, for special good measure, Dr. Bartolo with Marcellina.

Don Giovanni

by WOLFGANG AMADEUS MOZART (1756–1791)

Two Acts. Libretto by da Ponte, based on the legend of Don Juan.
First produced in Prague, 1787.

Don Giovanni	*Baritone*
Don Pedro, Commandant of Seville	*Bass*
Donna Anna, his daughter	*Soprano*
Don Ottavio, Donna Anna's Fiancé	*Tenor*
Donna Elvira	*Soprano*
Leporello, servant to Don Giovanni	*Bass*
Zerlina, a peasant girl	*Soprano*
Masseto, a peasant, engaged to Zerlina	*Bass*

Peasants, dancers, musicians.

TIME: *Eighteenth Century*.
PLACE: *In and near Seville*.

ACT ONE

SCENE ONE: *The garden of the Commandant's palace.*

In heavy, bumptious tones, we hear the servant Leporello complain because his master, Don Giovanni, has left him outside (as is his custom) to wait while the master makes love to a lady inside. But this time the famous lover is not successful; for he comes running out pursued angrily by the lady, who is Donna Anna, daughter of the Commandant. She calls for help and runs off before she has even discovered who her would-be lover is. Then her father, the Commandant, comes out and challenges Don Giovanni to a duel, in which the old gentleman is killed. The Don and his servant escape before Donna Anna returns with her fiancé, Don Ottavio, and a group of servants with torches. There, in the dark square, lighted only by the torches, the grief-stricken lady and her fiancé, Don Ottavio, swear to avenge the Commandant's murder.

121

SCENE TWO: *A street*.

Don Giovanni and Leporello meet a lady who seems to be in distress but when the Don offers his assistance, he discovers that she is Donna Elvira, whom he had deserted some years before, and she has been voicing her desire for vengeance on the Don himself. Making feeble apologies, the Don slips away, leaving Leporello to console the lady. This is done in a very odd way: Leporello reads to her a list of the Don's conquests. It includes no fewer than two thousand sixty-five ladies—Italian, German, French, Spanish, tall ones, short ones, blondes, brunettes. As Leporello sings this famous *"Catalogue Song"* he brings out a huge notebook, which unfolds and stretches halfway across the stage.

SCENE THREE: *A village green*.

As the curtain rises, we are in the midst of festivities on a village green to celebrate the engagement of the charming and coquettish Zerlina to her village swain, Masetto. Don Giovanni soon arrives with Leporello, and the quick-eyed nobleman picks out Zerlina for his next conquest. On his instructions, Leporello gets rid of the peasants, including Masetto, by inviting them to the castle for refreshments.

In a charming duet, *"Là ci darem la mano"* ("Thy little hand, love"), the Don proposes marriage to Zerlina who virtually consents. Fortunately for her, Donna Elvira arrives to denounce him and rescue the innocent young girl. Donna Anna and her fiancé arrive a moment later still in search of the man who killed Donna Anna's father. They do not know yet that Don Giovanni is the murderer, but Donna Anna now begins to suspect the truth. This is one of the most dramatic moments in opera, when Donna Anna sings the magnificent aria, *"Or sai, chi l'onore"* ("The wretch now thou knowest").

The scene closes as Don Ottavio steps before the curtain and sings his beautiful aria, *"Dalla sua pace"* ("On her appeasing"), declaring that he will devote himself only to the peace of mind of his beloved Donna Anna.

SCENE FOUR: *A room in Don Giovanni's palace.*

Don Giovanni is putting the finishing touches to a gay costume he is to wear at his own party, and as he does so he sings a merry drinking song, *"Finch han dal vino"* ("For a carousal").

SCENE FIVE: *Don Giovanni's garden.*

Zerlina is pleading with Masetto for forgiveness for her little flirtation with the Don, and she does so in one of the most charming melodies in the whole opera, *"Batti, batti, o bel Masetto"* ("Scold me, dear Masetto"). Masetto is won over and, a moment later, the Don enters and, taking the young people by the arm, he leads them inside the palace.

Then the masked figures of Elvira, Anna, and Ottavio come into the garden as dusk descends. From the balcony the Don (with the music of the famous *"Minuet"* playing in the background) invites the three nobles in disguise to join the party, and they accept. The scene then ends with the very beautiful "Mask Trio," *"Protegga, il giusto cielo"* ("O guard, all bounteous heaven"), in which they invoke the aid of heaven in securing revenge on the Don.

SCENE SIX: *Ballroom of the palace.*

At the height of the festivities, the wicked Don persuades Zerlina to go off into another room with him. Presently, we hear her scream off-stage, and Masetto tries to follow. However, it is the servant Leporello who dashes out followed by the Don with drawn sword, making believe it is Leporello who has molested the young girl.

ACT TWO

SCENE ONE: *In front of Donna Elvira's house.*

The Don is about to serenade a new love of his—Donna Elvira's maid. He and Leporello exchange cloaks and hats and, standing behind his servant in the darkness, the Don serenades Donna Elvira in order to get her out of the way so that he may pay his attentions to the maid. His scheme works. She comes down, and Leporello (whom, of course, she mistakes in the darkness for Don Giovanni) starts to make love to her. Out jumps the Don from a hiding place, threatens them, and they run away.

Now, the Don takes out his mandolin and sings another serenade, *"Deh vieni alla finestra"* ("Come to the window"), to the servant girl. However, he is interrupted by Masetto and a group of his peasant friends who are armed and bent on destroying the wicked Don Giovanni.

Still disguised as Leporello, Giovanni manages to get them all off in various directions to look for him, but he keeps Masetto with him. By another trick, he gets Masetto's gun and pistol away from him, and then knocks him to the ground, beats him and moves off. Thus Zerlina, his pretty fiancée, finds Masetto and eases his wounds with one of the most touching melodies in the opera, *"Vedrai carino"* ("Dearest, shall I tell you").

SCENE TWO: *In front of Donna Anna's house.*

Leporello is still with Donna Elvira and she still mistakes him for Don Giovanni. He tries to get away from her, but Donna Anna arrives with Don Ottavio and, a few moments later, Masetto and Zerlina also put in an appearance.

In order to save his life, Leporello tells who he really is and insists that he, too, has suffered cruelly at the hands of the wicked Don Giovanni. Finally Leporello runs away.

Don Ottavio, convinced that Don Giovanni is the murderer of the Commandant, promises revenge, and then he sings his aria, *"Il mio tesoro intanto"* ("To my beloved"). While he desires to bring the Don to justice, his greatest concern is the comfort of his beloved Donna Anna.

SCENE THREE: *A cemetery.*

The Don and Leporello are joking about his many love affairs, but suddenly they are interrupted by a solemn voice which is coming from a nearby equestrian statue. "Your laughter will change to mourning with the dawn," the statue declares. The unfrightened Don commands Leporello to invite the statue to dinner. The servant is aghast by such impiety, and he barely manages to blurt out the invitation. The statue nods his head to indicate acceptance; but just to make sure, Giovanni himself repeats the invitation.

Again it is accepted by the statue, this time with one word, *"Si"* ("Yes"). Despite these supernatural manifestations, the Don retains his off-hand manner and, as the curtain falls, he instructs his servant to see that everything is made ready for their prospective guest.

SCENE FOUR: *A room in the house of Donna Anna.*

Don Ottavio urges Donna Anna to marry him, promising that Don Giovanni will soon be brought to justice. In a beautiful aria, full of dignity and nobility, Donna Anna tells Ottavio that she loves him but that until her father's murderer is brought to justice she cannot think of the joy to come. This is the aria, *"Non mi dir, bel idol mio"* ("Do not say, my own beloved").

SCENE FIVE: *Banquet hall in Don Giovanni's palace.*

Don Giovanni is having a fine time joking with Leporello, eating his dinner, and listening to his own private orchestra. The musicians are on the stage in a gallery of their own, and they play several light tunes for the master, including an aria from Mozart's own opera, *Marriage of Figaro,* to which Leporello comments "I've heard too much of that."

Suddenly Donna Elvira comes rushing in, throws herself on her knees before the Don, and begs him to repent before it is too late, to show just one single virtue. The Don, however, only makes fun of the poor distraught lady, and she rushes out of the door, and we hear her scream in horror.

The Don orders Leporello to see what this is all about. Leporello goes to the door, looks out, and returns almost speechless with fright. He has seen nothing less than the stone statue of the Commandant walking up to the door. In stalks the supernatural visitor and refuses his host's polite offer to dine, saying that spirits from Heaven eat only Heavenly manna—*"Ferma un pò"* ("No need of food"). However, he asks the Don whether he will not come to *his* dwelling to dine. Poor Leporello, who hides in fright under the table, urges his master to decline, but to no avail.

Don Giovanni accepts, and finds his hand sealing the bargain. It is so rigid a clasp of stone that he cannot escape.

The statue asks him to repent his sins, but he only cries, "No, no! I scorn repentance." Thereupon, the statue pronounces Don Giovanni doomed to Hell. He disappears as flames and smoke shoot up and envelop the room.

All the surviving characters step before the curtain. Now Don Ottavio can marry his Donna Anna, and Masetto can marry his Zerlina. Now too, Leporello can go in search of a less wicked, less exasperating master. But poor, deserted Donna Elvira, who tried to save Don Giovanni, even to the end, must remain alone. The opera ends like a fairy tale, with the singing of a joyful little septet about the justice of the doom the Don has met.

Cosi Fan Tutte

(All Women Are Like That)

by WOLFGANG AMADEUS MOZART (1756–1791)

Two Acts. Libretto by Lorenzo da Ponte.
First produced in Vienna, 1790.

Ferrando ⎱ Young officers		*Tenor*
Guglielmo ⎰		*Bass*
Fiordiligi ⎱ Sisters		*Soprano*
Dorabella ⎰		*Mezzo-soprano*
Despina, their maid		*Soprano*
Don Alfonso, an elderly bachelor		*Baritone*

Townspeople, soldiers, musicians, servants.

TIME: *Eighteenth Century.*
PLACE: *In and near Naples.*

ACT ONE

SCENE ONE: *A café.*

Three men, who have been indulging in idle conversation, suddenly find themselves involved in a heated argument. The oldest of them, Don Alfonso (who is a bachelor), has just made the statement that all women are fickle and that there is really no such thing as a faithful woman.

The two younger men, Ferrando and Guglielmo (who are officers in the army and very much in love with two young ladies), indignantly deny this. They are confident that their own fiancées (two young sisters named Fiordiligi and Dorabella), are models of constancy and could not under any circumstances be otherwise. Don Alfonso tells them that they are just young and inexperienced, and he finally offers to bet a hundred sequins that the young ladies would not remain faithful to their lovers when put to the test. The young men are only too willing to take up the bet, and they agree to carry out their part in any plan which Don Alfonso may devise. They are so sure of winning the bet that they start planning what they will do with the money.

SCENE TWO: *Garden of the villa of the two sisters near Naples.*

The two sisters gaze fondly at miniatures of their lovers and sing of their love and happiness. But a discordant note is brought into the scene when Don Alfonso enters the garden with the news that Ferrando and Guglielmo have received orders that their regiment is marching away on the following day and that they must go with it. Don Alfonso says that the two young men would like to say goodbye but, fearing that the parting may be too painful, they have sent Don Alfonso on ahead to break the sad news.

At that, the two officers appear and the two pairs of lovers sing a melodious farewell, expressing their mutual sorrow and promising eternal fidelity. Ferrando and Guglielmo call Don Alfonso's attention to the fact that the two young ladies are just as much distressed at the parting as they are, but the older man tells them that the test is not over yet.

There is the sound of martial music; a troop of soldiers marches in, followed by a small crowd of townspeople. The farewells and vows of fidelity are repeated, and the two officers join the troops and march away, followed by the crowd. The two sisters express their hopes for a safe and speedy return. They leave the garden. Don Alfonso feels quite satisfied with the beginning of the plot. Three things are as hopeless and futile, he says, as putting your trust in women: trying to sweep up the ocean, trying to grow crops in sand, and trying to catch the wind in a net.

SCENE THREE: *A room in the villa.*

The two sisters have a maid, Despina, who is a worldly-wise and rather cynical young woman with not much more faith in woman's constancy than Don Alfonso has. She thinks her two young mistresses are capricious and whimsical, and she has grown weary trying to satisfy their demands. One of the sisters, Dorabella, enters the room in a very depressed state of mind and gloomily orders Despina to draw the shades and darken the room so that she, Dorabella, may mourn in appropriate surroundings. In a few moments, Fiordiligi comes in. She also is feeling very sad, although apparently she does not take the separation quite as emotionally as Dorabella does. The maid, Despina, who is used to expressing herself quite frankly, reminds the sisters that, after all, there are plenty of men in the world and, if they lose these two, others just as good can speedily be found to take their places. Fiordiligi and Dorabella are greatly incensed at such an unsympathetic attitude toward their sorrow, and they indignantly leave the room.

When Despina is alone, Don Alfonso slips in quietly, and it does not take him long to find out that she is quite willing to accept a liberal bribe to act as an accomplice in his plot. She agrees with Don Alfonso's statement that the two young ladies require male companionship while their lovers are away, and when he calls in two young men who have been waiting in the next room, she gives no sign that she recognizes them as Ferrando and Guglielmo. They wear bushy beards, one blonde and the other brunette, and Don Alfonso introduces them as two Albanians.

Fiordiligi and Dorabella are heard approaching, and Don Alfonso hastily hides as they enter the room. They are shocked to find two strangers in their home and still further shocked when these two strangers fall on their knees before them and declare that they are madly in love with them. Don Alfonso reappears and assures the young ladies that the strangers are friends of his. The supposed Albanians renew their protestations of love, but the young ladies spurn them with scorn and indignation, both declaring that their undying love has been given to their fiancés and nothing can swerve them from their devotion.

The comedy is played out to the end when Dorabella and Fiordiligi leave the room haughtily. Ferrando and Guglielmo are delighted at the result of the experiment. They offer to remit half of the bet to Don Alfonso, but the old Don reminds them that he laughs best who laughs last, and the two young men agree to carry on the plot for another day. They leave joyfully, and Don Alfonso and Despina are left with the apparent failure of their plot. But Despina assures the Don that it is only a matter of time, and she tells him that she has a little plan of her own which will be developed if he will bring his two supposed Albanians into the garden.

SCENE FOUR: *In the garden.*

Despina's contribution to the plot proves to be quite melodramatic. The two bearded Albanians rush into the garden in a great state of excitement, followed by Don Alfonso, who endeavors to calm them. His efforts are in vain, and the two young men, declaring that life without love is unbearable, drink the contents of two small bottles they are carrying and sink to the ground. Don Alfonso cries that they have taken poison, but before they die, they reproach the two young ladies for their heartlessness. The indispensable Despina comes in; and she, with Don Alfonso, runs for a doctor.

During their absence, Dorabella and Fiordiligi kneel down and do what they can to comfort the sufferings of the dying men. In a few moments Don Alfonso returns with a doctor, who is none other than Despina in disguise. After a brief and perfunctory examination, the doctor produces a huge magnet which he holds over the two bodies while he utters an incantation. As if by magic, the two dying men revive. At first they pretend to regard Dorabella and Fiordiligi as angels, but when convinced that they are still on earth, they demand that their sufferings be rewarded with a kiss from the fair ladies for whom they had tried to die. The two girls indignantly refuse, and in the closing moments of the scene, Ferrando and Guglielmo forget their Albanian disguise long enough to call Don Alfonso's attention to the fact that their fiancées have again resisted temptation and are still faithful to their vows.

ACT TWO

SCENE ONE: *A room in the villa.*

Despina is giving her young mistresses a lecture on the art of love. After all, women are made to be loved and men are made to love them; and, in her opinion, Dorabella and Fiordiligi are depriving themselves of a lot of pleasure by rejecting the ardent Albanians for the sake of two absent young officers. Dorabella and Fiordiligi are a little doubtful as to how they should treat the Albanians, (if they decide to see them again) and Despina tells them that any girl of fifteen knows all the coy tricks and sly deceptions by which a man's love is caught and held. Don Alfonso enters and invites them to come with him to the seashore where he promises them a delightful experience.

SCENE TWO: *A spot on the seashore.*

Anchored a few feet off shore is a boat gaily festooned with flowers. In it are the two Albanians and a small band of musicians. When Dorabella and Fiordiligi appear on the shore, accompanied by Despina and Don Alfonso, the musicians strike up a merry tune and the two young men sing a serenade, after which they come ashore and greet the ladies. But the latter are rather self-conscious, and things are not going very well when Don Alfonso and Despina give them an object lesson in how two lovers should greet each other.

After Despina and the Don have left, Dorabella consents to talk to the Albanian who is really Guglielmo, while Fiordiligi strolls off with the disguised Ferrando. This is just the opposite of the situation in real life, for Dorabella is engaged to Ferrando and Fiordiligi to Guglielmo. The Albanian Guglielmo presents Dorabella with a heart-shaped pendant and takes from her a necklace from which hangs a miniature of Ferrando. They, too, stroll away and as they leave, Fiordiligi and the disguised Ferrando reappear. He, however, has not been as successful as his friend. Fiordiligi rewards his wooing by denouncing him as a villain who is trying to tempt an innocent maiden from the straight and narrow path. His protestations are in vain and she orders him to leave her. He goes off in one direction and she in the other, but in a few minutes both young men return to compare notes.

Ferrando reports to Guglielmo that his beloved Fiordiligi has resisted all blandishments and remains faithful to the absent Guglielmo. This, of course, delights Guglielmo, but he has to confess to his friend that *his* sweetheart Dorabella, has not been so steadfast. When Guglielmo brings out the miniature of Ferrando which he had taken from Dorabella, Ferrando flies into a rage and vows revenge. But Guglielmo persuades him that women are not worth the breaking-up of a life-long friendship, and intimates that perhaps Don Alfonso is right—all women *are* fickle. The Don himself comes in at this point and reminds them that the test is not yet over.

SCENE THREE: *A room in the villa.*

Dorabella regrets that she has been unable to resist the blandishments of the bearded young Albanian; but Fiordiligi, on the other hand, insists that she is firmly determined to remain true to her absent Guglielmo, although she confesses that she has fallen a *little* bit in love with her new suitor. Fiordiligi has an idea for settling the whole dilemma. In her wardrobe are uniforms, helmets, and swords. She and Dorabella will don these uniforms and join their faithful lovers at the front and share with them whatever fate may bring.

The faithful Despina brings the uniforms, and Fiordiligi immediately puts on one of them and declares herself impatient to begin the adventure at once. Dorabella has left the room, so that when Ferrando enters he finds Fiordiligi alone. In spite of the uniform he recognizes her and, as he is still angry with Guglielmo for having had too much success with his own fiancée, Dorabella, he sees an opportunity for revenge and starts making violent love to Fiordiligi. This time Fiordiligi finds it more difficult to resist the ardent Albanian, and she yields to his pleading. They embrace lovingly.

As they leave the room, Guglielmo bursts in, raging over his friend's treachery. Ferrando returns at once and the two irate young men, caught in their own trap, are

restrained from a violent quarrel by the intervention of
Don Alfonso. He advises them to marry the two young
ladies at once before they can change their minds again,
and he reminds them of his original contention,*"Cosi fan
tutte"* ("All women are like that").

SCENE FOUR: *A banquet room.*

The farce is now nearing its climax. A banquet to celebrate the marriage of the two "happy" couples is about
to begin. The two Albanians are not comfortable over the
deception they have practiced on their fiancées, and Guglielmo especially wishes that the guests at the banquet
would all drink poison instead of wine.

Don Alfonso brings in a notary who is to witness the
signing of the marriage contracts. This notary is the ver-
satile Despina in disguise. She (or he) reads the contracts
—Fiordiligi is to be married to "Sempronio" and Dorabella is to be married to "Tizio." No sooner are the contracts signed when martial music is heard outside and
Don Alfonso rushes out, only to return in a moment with
the disquieting news that Ferrando and Guglielmo have
returned from the wars.

Fiordiligi and Dorabella are panic-stricken and push
their new fiancés out of the room, while Don Alfonso
tries in vain to quiet them. In the next room, Ferrando and
Guglielmo doff their Albanian beards and cloaks and return as themselves. They greet the young ladies ardently
but their embraces are not received cordially. Guglielmo
asks why a notary is present, and the quick-witted Despina
explains that she has been wearing the costume at a fancy-
dress ball.

Ferrando picks up the marriage contracts and reads
them. He and Guglielmo accuse the ladies of having betrayed them, and Fiordiligi and Dorabella, stricken with
remorse, admit that they have been faithless. Don Alfonso
assures the two men that they will find further proof in
the next room. They follow him and do another quick
change, returning in a few moments with the beards and
cloaks of the alleged Albanians.

And now the masquerade is over. The two young men
reveal their identity, Guglielmo gives Dorabella the minia-

ture he took from her and she returns his heart-shaped
pendant. The two young ladies are happy to have their
true-loves back again, but blame Don Alfonso for all the
trouble. He defends himself by saying it was all a joke,
intended only to prove that all women are fickle.

The Magic Flute

(Die Zauberflöte)

by WOLFGANG AMADEUS MOZART (1756–1791)

Two Acts. Libretto by Schikaneder.
First produced in Vienna, 1791.

Tamino, a prince	*Tenor*
Pamina, daughter of the Queen of Night	*Soprano*
Sarastro, High Priest of the Temple of Isis	*Bass*
Papageno, a bird-catcher	*Baritone*
Old Woman, later Papagena	*Soprano*
The Queen of Night	*Soprano*
Monostatos, a dwarf slave	*Tenor*
Three ladies, attendants of the Queen of Night	*Soprano* *Soprano* *Mezzo-soprano*
Three Genii	*Soprano* *Mezzo-soprano* *Contralto*
Two Guards	*Tenor* *Baritone*

Priests, attendants, slaves.
TIME: *Ancient.*
PLACE: *Egypt.*

ACT ONE

SCENE ONE: *A wild mountain pass near the Temple of Isis.*

The young prince, Tamino, is being pursued by a fearsome serpent. He has shot all the arrows from his quiver
and, praying for help, falls unconscious to the ground.
Three lady attendants of the supernatural Queen of Night

rescue him from his fate by killing the monster, and then they stay to admire the handsome young hero.

And now, we hear the characteristic five ascending notes of the scale played on a Pan-pipe as Papageno comes in— *"Der Vogelfänger bin ich ja"* ("I am the bird catcher"). Papageno is a simple-minded fellow who earns his living by catching birds. He carries a large birdcage on his back and is outlandishly dressed in leaves and feathers.

When Tamino awakes, Papageno (first making sure the snake is dead) claims that he himself choked the mighty monster with his strong right arm and, a minute later, the three ladies-in-waiting place a lock on his lips for having told such a fib. They also bring with them a picture of Pamina, the beautiful daughter of the Queen of Night and Tamino immediately falls in love with the girl—*"Dies Bildnis ist bezaubernd schön"* ("This is wondrously beautiful"). And so the Queen herself, heralded by thunder and a darkening stage, appears against a background of stars and dramatically tells the young man that Pamina has been kidnapped by what she calls "an evil fiend"—*"Zum leiden bin ich auserkoren"* ("My days are spent in sorrow").

At once Tamino undertakes to rescue his unknown beloved. Now the three ladies-in-waiting present him with a magical flute to guide and protect him, and then they turn to Papageno, unlock his lips, and give him a set of magical bells for his protection when he accompanies Tamino on his quest.

SCENE TWO: *A richly furnished room.*

The Princess Pamina is being held a prisoner in the palace of Sarastro, guarded by three slaves and a horrible little dwarf named Monostatos. Papageno wanders into the room and Monostatos is quite as much afraid of him as he is of Monostatos.

Finally Monostatos, overcome by fright, rushes from the room, and Papageno arouses the Princess. He informs her that Prince Tamino, who already loves her, is going to set her free from bondage. Pamina, as is the fashion in fairy tales, immediately falls in love with her unknown would-be rescuer, the Prince. They sing a magnificent duet, *"Bei Männern, welche Liebe fühlen"* ("Manly heart").

SCENE THREE: *Sacred grove, with the Temples of Reason, Nature, and Wisdom.*

Prince Tamino, in quest of the Princess Pamina, is solemnly warned away by hidden voices from the Temples of Reason and Nature; but when he approaches the central temple, the Temple of Wisdom, a white-robed priest appears and tells him of the good Sarastro, whose country Tamino has now entered. The Queen of Night has told Tamino that Sarastro is the man who kidnapped Pamina, and the priest has a hard time dispelling Tamino's prejudices.

Now Tamino hears Papageno's characteristic notes on the Pan-pipe and hurries off in search of him while Papageno himself, from the other side of the stage, runs in with Pamina, frantically fleeing from Monostatos—"*Nur geschwinde*" ("Hasten, hasten!")—who chases after them with his slaves. Just as the two are about to be seized, Papageno remembers his magical bells; and by striking them musically, so charms his enemies that they dance harmlessly away.

Then Sarastro himself, the High Priest of Isis and Osiris, comes on with his entire entourage. He reveals that he has been holding Pamina in his palace as her mother, the Queen of Night, is plotting to overthrow the priests and the Temple, but he warns the loathsome Monostatos against any mistreatment of Pamina. He then orders that Tamino and Papageno be prepared and properly robed for the trials and ceremonies which are to come.

ACT TWO

SCENE ONE: *A sacred grove.*

Sarastro and his priests are assembled, all of them in white robes, with Sarastro in the center. Under a tree three priests question Sarastro concerning Tamino—his virtue, his ability to keep silence, his benevolence and courage. Sarastro assures the company that Tamino is worthy on every score to become a member of the holy order, and then he sings that deeply religious and dignified melody, "*O Isis und Osiris*".

SCENE TWO: *The court of the Temple*.

Amidst thunder and lightning Tamino and Papageno await their first trials. Two priests ask them questions about their desires, and all that Papageno wants is sleep, food, and drink, and, if you please—a nice little wife. And then both men are warned that they are to remain silent no matter what happens now, and to beware the wiles of women.

As soon as the priests leave, the test really begins; for now three ladies-in-waiting of the Queen of Night appear and try to tempt them away from adherence to the rules of Sarastro. Tamino maintains his silence steadfastly, while Papageno almost fails, but with the moral support of the Prince, manages to come through this test. Once more, we have thunder and lightning, frightening away the ladies-in-waiting. The priests reappear and commend Tamino for having come through his first trial successfully.

SCENE THREE: *Garden of Sarastro's palace*.

Pamina is sleeping under a great, exotic fern. Once again she is threatened by the dwarf, Monostatos, who creeps in to gloat over his prey—*"Alles fühlt der Liebe Freuden"* ("All confess the tender passion"). But suddenly, there is a clap of thunder and Pamina's mother, the Queen of Night, appears high up at the back of the stage. Monostatos retires to one side to watch, and the Queen of Night sings her great *"Revenge"* aria. She gives her daughter a dagger which she is to use to slay the Queen's enemy, Sarastro; and then, having completed her brilliant music (one of the most difficult coloratura arias ever written), the Queen disappears in another clap of thunder.

Immediately Monostatos jumps forward, takes the dagger from poor, frightened Pamina, and threatens her with death if she will not love him. But again Pamina is saved, this time by Sarastro, who consigns the villainous Monostatos to punishment. And then, in an aria full of comfort and nobility, *"In diesen heil'gen Hallen"* ("Within these sacred portals"), he assures her that revenge in his domain is unknown.

SCENE FOUR: *A great hall.*

Prince Tamino and the birdman, Papageno, are being tested once more for their ability to keep silence. A little old woman appears to tempt Papageno, and he promptly fails the test and chatters away gaily when she tells him that she has a sweetheart named Papageno.

Meantime, Prince Tamino has a much harder time of it. When his beloved Pamina comes in, he resolutely refuses to speak even when she completely misunderstands and goes off, broken-hearted, bemoaning the loss of his love, *"Ach ich fühl's"* ("Ah, I feel it"). Now three blasts on a trumpet summon the two men for further tests.

SCENE FIVE: *The inner shrine of the Temple.*

The priests, led by Sarastro, march in, chanting a solemn invocation to Isis and Osiris. Tamino is about to be led into the inner shrine to undergo his final test, and Sarastro instructs Pamina to bid him a last farewell.

When they have gone, Papageno enters, and a priest informs him (as we already know) that he has failed his first test. But Papageno doesn't care a bit; all he wants is a glass of wine. So quickly is his wish granted that he now asks for a sweetheart, *"Ein Mädchen oder Weibchen"* ("A maiden, fair and slender"), and in comes the little old woman he had met in the previous act. She says she is his sweetheart, and she demands that he be faithful to her. Papageno, goodnatured fellow that he is, agrees, and immediately she turns into a pretty little girl dressed just like Papageno, feathers and all.

Papageno is about to embrace her when one of the priests intervenes. Papageno is not worthy of her, and the priest takes the girl away from him.

SCENE SIX: *A garden near the Temple.*

Princess Pamina, who believes the Prince has left her forever, prepares to end her own life with the dagger her mother, the Queen of Night, gave her. But three benevolent Genii intervene just in time, telling her that Tamino is enduring his trials in the hope of being united to her, for he loves her still.

SCENE SEVEN: *Near the Temple.*

On either side of the stage is a rocky cavern with a grilled gate before it, and in the center is a large stairway leading up to a heavily studded doorway before which are two armed guards. The two men sing a brief duet from which we learn that the man who wishes to share the holy mysteries of Isis and Osiris must endure the tests of fire and water. Prince Tamino is led in and is about to enter one of the gates when Pamina calls out and demands to share these trials with him.

So with her arm about his shoulder, Prince Tamino playing his magic flute, they enter the gate on the left. Flames rise within the cavern, but Prince Tamino and Princess Pamina pass through them safely, untouched. They pass across the stage, singing, as great waterfalls tumble and rise in the cavern on the right, and through this ordeal the happy lovers pass, too. And now, Sarastro, the High Priest of Isis and Osiris, and all the other priests, greet them, congratulate them, and, as the scene ends, they are led through the great central gate, into the very Temple itself.

SCENE EIGHT: *A garden.*

Papageno enters with a rope fashioned into a noose; he is all ready, he says, to hang himself, for life without a Papagena is not worth living.

After some time, just as he is at the end of his ingenuity in devising ways to put off his act of self-destruction, the three Genii come in and rescue him, just as they rescued Pamina a little earlier. They advise him to try his magic bells which saved him once before.

Happily he takes their advice; he plays his bells, *"Klinget, Glöckchen"* ("Let my maiden hear"), and the great leaves of a giant artichoke slowly unfold to disclose pretty little Papagena sitting inside and waiting for him. Half-stuttering for joy, the two greet each other as "Papa-papa-papa-geno" and "Papa-papa-papa-gena."

SCENE NINE: *Near the Temple.*

The Queen of Night has assembled her forces outside the great, forbidding walls of the Temple in an effort to steal Princess Pamina back again. The Queen has promised the dwarf, Monostatos, that he shall marry Pamina. Accompanied by the ladies-in-waiting, they advance on the temple with flaming torches. But a great storm, with bolts of lightning, strikes them, and they sink into the ground with cries of despair, to be seen no more.

And now the scene is flooded with brilliant sunlight. In the background is the glittering golden Temple and before it are gathered Sarastro, his priests in their white robes, and a great multitude of worshipers. Sarastro tells them that the forces of evil have been vanquished, and all unite in singing the praise of Isis and Osiris.

Prince Tamino and Princess Pamina both have shown their devotion to each other and their fearlessness in facing death and danger. Now they are united and the opera ends with a joyous chorus—*"Heil sei euch Geweihten"* ("Hail, ye true and faithful").

The Tales of Hoffmann
(Les Contes d'Hoffmann)

by JACQUES OFFENBACH (1819–1880)

Prologue, Three Acts, and Epilogue. Libretto by Barbier and Carré.
First produced in Paris, 1881.

Hoffman, a young poet		*Tenor*
Nicklause, his friend		*Soprano*
Olympia		
Giulietta	the young ladies with whom	
Antonia	Hoffman falls in love	*Sopranos*
Stella		
Coppélius		
Dapertutto	various aspects of his	
Doctor Miracle	Evil Genius	*Baritones*
Lindorf		
Luther, an innkeeper		*Bass*
Schlémil, Giulietta's lover		*Bass*
Councillor Crespel, father of Antonia		*Baritone*
Spalanzani		*Tenor*

TIME: *Early Nineteenth Century.*
PLACE: *Nuremburg, Venice, Munich.*

PROLOGUE

SCENE: *Luther's Tavern in Nuremberg.*

Each act of this opera is a complete short story, but there is a certain similarity among the three stories which holds the entire opera together. In each story the young poet Hoffmann is in love, and in each story there is a rather mysterious evil influence working against him. This evil influence works through certain little tricks of magic and the whole atmosphere of the story is highly imaginative and fantastic.

In the Prologue, we meet the first of Hoffmann's Evil

Geniuses, known in this episode as Councillor Lindorf. Hoffmann is in love with a popular opera singer named Stella who is singing, that very evening, in a performance of Mozart's "Don Giovanni" in the opera house next to the tavern. Lindorf is his rival for the lady's affection.

The first thing this Evil Genius does is to bribe away from a servant a letter from Stella addressed to Hoffmann making a rendezvous with him and enclosing a key.

A crowd of students enters, singing a jolly drinking song. Soon they are joined by Hoffmann and his friend Nicklause.

It is intermission time at the opera house and they have all come to the tavern for a drink. Hoffmann does not like the beer and orders punch, which is brought in in a huge bowl and lighted. Hoffmann sings a weird song about a hideous dwarf named Kleinzach, *"Il était une fois à la cour d'Eisenach"* ("Once at the court of Eisenach"). The students tease Hoffmann about being in love and he holds his glass up and declares he will never fall in love again.

Lindorf reminds him that he is at that moment in love with the opera-singer Stella, and Hoffmann asks the company if they would like to hear about his three great loves and they enthusiastically encourage him.

"The name of the first," he begins, "was Olympia," and the curtain falls on the Prologue.

ACT ONE

SCENE: *A room in the home of Spalanzani.*

There are alcoves on each side of the stage partitioned off by heavy curtains. Spalanzani enters and draws aside the curtain of one of these alcoves and looks proudly at the latest of his inventions, a mechanical doll named Olympia. He is worried, however, about his friend, Coppélius, who claims to be part-inventor of the doll.

Spalanzani has invited a large party to his house to demonstrate his latest invention and the first to arrive is the young man, Hoffmann. Spalanzani offers to take him as a pupil and promises to make a great scientist out of him.

Spalanzani then goes off to make ready for the party and Hoffmann gazes rapturously on the beautiful Olympia—

"Allons! courage et confiance" ("Come! courage and confidence"). His friend Nicklause enters and is amused at Hoffmann's infatuation—*"Une poupée aux yeux d'émail"* ("A doll with china eyes"). Coppélius is the next to enter and he brings with him a big bag containing all kinds of scientific gadgets, including a pair of spectacles which will enable the owner to see into a woman's soul. The gullible Hoffmann is delighted to buy the magic spectacles.

Spalanzani returns and he and Coppélius have an argument about who is the true inventor of the mechanical doll. Spalanzani finally buys off Coppélius, who relinquishes his claim in return for a check for five hundred ducats.

The other guests now arrive and Spalanzani brings out Olympia who moves about the room in stiff mechanical motions. Hoffmann, having put on his magical spectacles, is of course more deeply infatuated than ever. Spalanzani proudly says that the doll will do anything the guests desire. A harp is brought in and Spalanzani plays an accompaniment while Olympia sings a charming aria, *"Les oiseaux dans la charmille"* ("The birds in the bower"), sometimes called "The Doll's Song". When her voice seems to falter, a servant steps up behind her, there is the sound of a spring being wound up, and the voice recovers itself and goes on.

Spalanzani guides the doll to the sofa and seats her on it, and then invites his guests into the next room for supper. Hoffmann remains behind with Olympia and immediately begins to make love to her. To all his protestations of affection she answers "Yes" and the poor deluded Hoffmann does not know that this is the only word she can utter. He seizes her hand and thereby touches part of the mechanism by which she operates and she rises from the sofa, circles the room and disappears through the curtains. Nicklause comes in and endeavors to bring Hoffmann to his senses, but the infatuated young man rushes after Olympia.

And now Coppélius enters in a great rage for he has found out that the check for five hundred ducats, for which he sold his rights to a share in the doll, is worthless. Just then, Spalanzani and his guests return and begin to dance to waltz music. Hoffmann and Olympia waltz into the room together and soon are the center of attention as the mechanical doll dances faster and faster. Finally Spalanzani comes to the rescue and touches a secret spring in the doll and she comes to a sudden stop. Hoffmann falls exhausted on the sofa, breaking his glasses.

Olympia has been led from the room and in a moment we hear a loud crash. Coppélius has revenged himself for the worthless check by smashing the doll. Hoffmann rushes into the alcove and returns with a piece of mechanism in his hand. As he realizes what a fool he has made of himself, the guests all laugh at him.

ACT TWO

SCENE: *Giulietta's house in Venice.*

This episode begins and ends with the lovely haunting melody of the famous *Barcarolle,* which we hear first as a prelude played by the orchestra. When the curtain rises, the *Barcarolle* is sung as a duet by Giulietta and Nicklause, *"Belle nuit"* ("Night of love").

The scene is a luxurious one. The room is strewn with bright colored fabrics and flowers, the chandeliers glitter with bright lights, through the lofty arches of the portico we catch glimpses of gondolas as they float by. Nicklause warns his impressionable friend, Hoffmann, not to fall in love with Giulietta, and Hoffmann assures him that there is not the slightest chance of that happening.

Among the guests is a mysterious character named Dapertutto, who turns out to be Hoffmann's Evil Genius. He has a magnificent diamond ring which he uses to bribe Giulietta to accomplish his evil designs. His strange request is that she secure Hoffmann's reflection in a mirror, *"Scintille, diamant, fascine, attire-la"* ("Sparkle, diamond, fascinate, attract her"). It seems that she has already accomplished one such task for Dapertutto by depriving one unfortunate young man named Schlémil of his shadow!

Card games have been going on in the next room and presently Hoffmann approaches Giulietta to tell her that he is leaving as he has lost all his money gambling. But she exerts her bewitching charm and in a few minutes he is hopelessly in love with her and declares that he will never leave her, *"O Dieu! de quelle ivresse"* ("Ye gods, with what bliss do you fire my heart?"). When she asks for his reflection in a mirror, he thinks it is a strange request, but readily grants it.

As Hoffmann and Giulietta are embracing, the young man Schlémil enters and flies into a jealous rage. Giulietta manages to let Hoffmann know that Schlémil has the key to her private apartment and intimates that if Hoffmann can get the key, he may come to see her later in the evening. She and most of the guests then leave and Hoffmann confronts Schlémil and demands the key.

Schlémil refuses and the two prepare to fight a duel—a strange duel between two men, one of whom casts no shadow, and the other who makes no reflection in a mirror! Hoffmann has no sword, but Dapertutto offers him one. The duel is a short one. Hoffmann kills his opponent, snatches the key from the dead body and runs off. But it is too late. Giulietta is already entering her gondola with another lover. Once more the Evil Genius has triumphed and once more Hoffmann is in despair.

ACT THREE

Scene: *Crespel's House in Munich.*

The girl with whom Hoffmann is in love in this story is named Antonia. When the curtain rises, we find her sitting at her clavichord, singing, *"Elle a fui, la toutterelle"* ("She has fled, the pretty dove"). Her father, Crespel, enters and begs her not to sing again as it was while singing that her mother had died. Antonia promises not to sing again and leaves the room. Crespel instructs the servant not to admit anyone to the house, but only a few minutes after he has gone, the servant disobeys him and admits Hoffmann.

When Antonia returns the two young lovers sing a charming duet together, Antonia in her happiness forgetting her promise to her father. But the effort is too much for her, and she almost faints. She goes to her room as her father enters and Hoffmann hides behind a screen to discover, if he can, the mystery behind Antonia's strange behavior.

And now enters the Evil Genius, in this act known as Dr. Miracle. He is a weird character. After announcing that he will cure Antonia, he draws up an empty chair, addresses it as if it contained Antonia, and soon we hear Antonia in the next room singing at his command. In horror, the father forces the evil doctor to leave with him. Antonia returns to the room and Hoffmann begs her to give up singing. Sadly, she agrees and Hoffmann leaves.

But now the evil doctor appears by magic and works his wicked spell on the poor girl. He urges her to sing and he causes a portrait of her mother to come to life and also urge Antonia to sing, *"Chère enfant que j'appelle"* ("Dear child, whom I call"). Antonia succumbs and sings wildly as Dr. Miracle seizes a violin and plays fiendishly with sparks of fire flying from the strings. Dying, Antonia falls on the sofa.

Her father returns just in time to take her dying form in his arms. Hoffmann enters and, frantic with grief, Crespel attacks him with a knife, but Nicklause is on hand again to save his friend. Dr. Miracle has disappeared with the death of Antonia, but now he makes one last magical appearance and pronounces his patient dead. "Antonia!" cries Hoffmann despairingly as the curtain falls.

EPILOGUE

Scene: *Luther's Tavern.*

So Hoffmann's tales are told and in the epilogue we find him in the tavern as in the prologue. The students sing again their jolly drinking song, but by this time Hoffmann has had too much to drink and is half asleep. While Hoffmann has been telling his tales, the opera performance next door has been finished and we hear the applause of the audience, with cries of "Stella, Stella!"

Nicklause remarks that all Hoffmann's three loves are really one—Stella, who is three women in one. The dreaming Hoffmann sees a vision in which the Muse of Poetry offers him the serenity of art in place of the torments of passion. Now Stella comes in looking for Hoffmann, but by this time his drunken stupor is too deep to be shaken off.

The Evil Genius conquers again, and Stella goes off with Lindoro.

La Gioconda

by AMILCARE PONCHIELLI (1834–1886)

Four Acts. Libretto by Boïto. Based on Hugo's tragedy, *Angelo*. First produced in Milan, 1876.

La Gioconda, a street singer	*Soprano*
La Cieca, her blind mother	*Contralto*
Enzo Grimaldo, a Genoese nobleman	*Tenor*
Barnaba, a spy of the Inquisition	*Baritone*
Alvise Badoero, Chief of the Inquisition	*Bass*
Laura, his wife	*Mezzo-soprano*
Zuane, a gondolier	*Bass*
Isepo, a public letter-writer	*Tenor*
A monk	*Baritone*

Townspeople, sailors, monks, ladies and gentlemen, children, dancers.

TIME: *Seventeenth Century.*
PLACE: *Venice.*

ACT ONE

SCENE: *Courtyard of the Ducal palace.*

It is a festival day and the crowd is singing gaily, *"Feste e pane"* ("Sports and feasting"). On one side, however, stands Barnaba, chief inquisitorial spy for the ruling Council of Ten watching grimly and taking no part in the festivities. After the people have left to watch a boat race, Barnaba notes the entrance of the beautiful street-singer known as La Gioconda, accompanied by her blind mother, La Cieca. When Gioconda leaves her mother to go in search of her lover, Enzo Grimaldo, Barnaba tries to force his attentions on her, only to have her elude him and run off.

And now the people return, carrying in triumph the winner of the boat race. Barnaba sees his chance to carry out his evil designs, and by suggesting to the loser of the race that La Cieca, the blind woman, is really a witch who has caused him to lose the race through her magic, he works up the whole crowd into a furore against her. They drag her from the church steps, crying, "Kill her, burn her!" Just then Gioconda returns with Enzo, who tries single-handed to save La Cieca. The rescue comes, however, from another source, Alvise Badoero, the chief of the Council of Ten that rules Venice, appears at the top of the staircase with his beautiful wife, Laura (who is wearing a mask), and it is through the warm-hearted intercession of Laura that La Cieca is finally saved.

In gratitude, La Cieca gives the younger woman the rosary with which she has been saying her prayers. There is a very lovely aria at this point sung by La Cieca—"*Voce di donna o d'angelo*" ("Voice of woman or angel").

Meantime, however, Enzo (Gioconda's lover) and Laura (the wife of Alvise Badoero) have recognized each other and the significance of their glances is revealed in a conversation between Enzo and the evil Barnaba. Barnaba addresses Enzo as the Prince of Santa Fior, for this spy knows the other's whole history. Enzo is not a merchant sailor from Dalmatia (which is the disguise he wears) but a nobleman who, in Genoa, has been in love with Laura and has lost her to Alvise. Barnaba thinks he can gain Gioconda's affection if he proves her lover, Enzo, to be unfaithful. Accordingly, he tells Enzo that he can arrange that Laura will visit Enzo's ship that very evening for he suspects that, in spite of his affair with Gioconda, Enzo still loves Laura.

When Enzo has left, Barnaba dictates (to a public letter-writer)—"*Regia e bolgia dogale!*" ("O mighty monument!")—a letter to Alvise betraying the plans of his wife and her former lover. The people once more come in joyfully singing. Gioconda, who has overheard the plot concerning her beloved Enzo, bewails her misfortune. The church bells sound the evening prayer and the curtain falls as the populace joins in the vesper service and Gioconda and her blind mother sorrowfully leave the scene.

ACT TWO

SCENE: *Enzo's ship.*

This is one of the most spectacular scenes in all opera. It represents Enzo's ship, the "Hecate", anchored by the side of an island near Venice. A large portion of the ship can be seen with the ocean shimmering in the moonlight in the background.

The deck of the ship is filled with sailors and there are more sailors on the island itself. The moon is rising above a cloud in the night sky, and the sailors sing a gay song, the *"Marinaresca"* chorus. Barnaba, the Inquisition spy, comes on disguised as a fisherman and joins the sailors in their song. After they have left, Enzo comes on deck and leaning pensively on the rail, gazes at sky and sea, and sings one of the most famous of all tenor arias, *"Cielo e mar"* ("Sky and sea").

Soon Laura comes, brought in a small boat by Barnaba, and a thrilling love duet follows as she and Enzo plan to elope. When Enzo goes below to complete preparations for the elopement, Laura comes down from the ship and kneels in prayer at a crude altar on the island. Now Gioconda arrives, for, as we know, she has overheard the plot for elopement. Laura, of course, knows nothing of the relationship between Enzo and Gioconda and besides, Gioconda, dressed in black, wears a mask over her face. Her anger, her threats, frighten Laura. As each declares her own love for Enzo to be the stronger, the street-singer is about to kill the aristocrat with her dagger when Laura lifts up her rosary and begins to pray. Suddenly Gioconda recognizes the rosary—it is the gift that La Cieca gave Laura. Now Gioconda knows that Laura is the lady who saved her mother's life, and her jealous rage leaves her.

She sees a boat approaching and knows that it brings Laura's husband, Alvise. She resolves to save her rival's life and forces her into a small boat and orders the rowers to take her to safety. And so when Enzo returns to the deck of his ship to meet Laura, he finds only Gioconda.

"Your Laura has fled," she cries. "She has returned to her Alvise." "Be silent," he answers. "I will follow her!" But Gioconda points out the Venetian galleys approaching, bringing the vengeful Alvise. Enzo realizes that he has been trapped by the treachery of Barnaba. He is surrounded by enemies. His sailors are ready to fight, but Enzo knows that the followers of Barnaba and Alvise outnumber them and the odds are hopeless. Rather than yield to the vengeful husband, he sets fire to his own ship.

As the flames rise, Enzo leaps over the side of the boat into the water.

ACT THREE

SCENE ONE: *A room in Alvise's palace.*

Alvise wanders nervously up and down, planning to avenge his honor by poisoning his wife. Last night, he says in his soliloquy, Laura escaped from the island where she had met Enzo, but now she must die, dramatically, while a gay party is going on in the next room.

When Laura enters, magnificently attired for the party, he at first treats her with ironic politeness, but soon reveals the fate he has in store for her. Flinging her violently to the ground, he disregards her pleas for mercy and, even as we hear a gay chorus singing a boating song off-stage, he gives her the poison and tells her she must drink it before the song is ended.

He leaves her then, but at that moment, Gioconda appears in the room, seizes the poison, and gives Laura another phial in its place. "Drink this instead," she says. "It will save you." Laura at first suspects her rival, but it is her only hope. She drinks the potion and rushes into the alcove behind a curtain where there is a bier ready to receive her supposedly dead body. Alvise now returns, sees his wife lying on the bier and solemnly declares that she is dead.

But, before the scene ends, Gioconda appears once more, declaring that she is giving up her lover to Laura in gratitude for saving her mother's life.

SCENE TWO: *Ballroom of Alvise's palace.*

Into Alvise's magnificent, brilliantly lighted ballroom come his guests and he receives them graciously, even though he knows that in the adjoining chamber lies the body of his wife, Laura, whom he thinks he has sent to her death. For the entertainment of his guests, Alvise has provided an elaborate ballet. The lights in the hall are lowered, and we hear the familiar strains of the ballet, *"The Dance of the Hours"*—the Hours of Daybreak, the Hours of Day, the Hours of Evening, and the Hours of Night— each of the four divisions of the day illuminated by changing and appropriate lights.

Scarcely has the applause died down after the ballet when Barnaba drags in La Cieca, whom he has discovered in the room where Laura lies.

"I meant no harm," she cries. "I was praying for the soul of my benefactress. She is dead!" The guests listen in amazement and slowly the ringing of the death knell sounds through the palace.

The guests are horrified, but Alvise attempts at first to make them keep up their gay spirits. And now Enzo steps forward, reveals himself as the Prince of Santa Fior, and the enemy of Alvise. He has taken this step so that, in death, he may be reunited with his beloved Laura. In a magnificent concerted number, Alvise charges Barnaba, on pain of death, not to permit Enzo to escape and Enzo sings of his despair over the loss of Laura and his hope of again meeting her in Heaven.

Dramatically, Alvise draws aside the curtain to show the body of his wife lying on her deathbed, clad all in white. Shamelessly, even with pride, he announces that he himself has slain her to avenge his honor. Enzo attacks him with his dagger but is arrested by the guards. Just as the curtain descends, Barnaba seizes La Cieca and drags her off through a secret door.

ACT FOUR

SCENE: *A ruined palace on an island near Venice.*

Gioconda is at first alone in the room but presently two men bring in the body of Laura who is still unconscious from the effects of the sleeping potion she drank in place of poison.

The two men, street-singers like Gioconda, refuse her offer of money, and agree to go in search of her mother, La

Cieca, who was abducted by Barnaba at the close of the previous act.

When she is alone once more, Gioconda sings her great suicide aria, *"Suicidio,"* in which she tells of her intention to take her own life. But Enzo appears and, in the ensuing dialogue, we learn that Gioconda has contrived to free him from his prison. He seeks only to die at Laura's tomb and Laura (who has been placed in the darkness of an adjoining chamber) at this moment wakens and appears before them.

She and Enzo embrace each other joyfully and they acknowledge Gioconda as their savior, kneeling before her. And now there is a fine trio, in which Gioconda renounces her claim to Enzo, and directs the lovers to the safety of the boat. When the two have left, Gioconda once more considers death, only to be interrupted by Barnaba. Gioconda promised to give herself to him if he would contrive Enzo's escape and now he has come to claim his reward.

"I shall keep my promise," she tells him as she adorns herself with jewels, but at the last moment she seizes the dagger and strikes herself dead. Bending over her body, Barnaba calls to her, "Last night I killed your mother!" But now Gioconda is past hearing these horrible tidings, and with a cry of baffled rage, the villain rushes away and the curtain falls.

The Love for Three Oranges

by SERGE PROKOFIEFF (1891–1953)

Two Acts. Original libretto by Serge Prokofieff after the comedy by Carlo Gozzi. English version by Victor Seroff.
First produced in Chicago, 1925.

Sylvio, King of an imaginary kingdom	*Bass*
Prince Tartaglia, his son	*Tenor*
Princess Clarissa	*Mezzo-soprano*
Leandro, Prime Minister	*Baritone*
Pantalone, a Councilor	*Baritone*
Truffaldino, Cook and Jester	*Tenor*
The Magician, Celio	*Bass*
The Sorceress, Fata Morgana	*Soprano*
The Princess Linetta	*Contralto*
The Princess Nicoletta	*Mezzo-soprano*
The Princess Ninetta	*Soprano*
The Cook	*Bass*
Farferella, a devil	*Dancer*
Smeraldina, black servant of Fata Morgana	*Mezzo-soprano*

Fans of tragic plays, fans of romantic plays, fans of comedies, Empty Heads, doctors, courtiers, court servants, soldiers, circus performers, four heralds.

SCENE: *An imaginary kingdom.*
TIME: *Long ago.*

ACT ONE

SCENE ONE: *Prologue.*

The advocates of different types of theatrical entertainment quarrel among themselves until the heralds announce that the evening will be devoted to a comedy. At this the bickering fans leave the stage and sit down in boxes closely overlooking it. Their comments form a part of the vocal score, and occasionally one or more of them will actually participate in the fantastic proceedings.

SCENE TWO: *The bedchamber of Prince Tartaglia.*

The old King is in despair. His only son and heir is ailing with so many complaints that the doctors can hardly catalogue them. He has pains in his liver, and elsewhere; everything makes his heart beat faster; his thoughts are depressing. In fact, the doctors believe, his ills are mental, and unless he plays and laughs he has no chance to survive. If he dies, the King must leave his kingdom to his wicked niece, Clarissa. This he cannot bear to contemplate.

Pantalone begs to introduce Truffaldino, who can make the Prince laugh if anyone can. Truffaldino, a merry fellow who has no respect even for kings, immediately suggests a celebration. Pantalone takes up the idea, but the King insists that Leandro, his Chief of State, be sent for. This does not suit Pantalone, for there is a deep rivalry between the two men. Leandro wishes death to the young Prince, Pantalone is sure.

The champions of gaiety, including many of the spectators, eventually win out over the more gloomy element, and the King orders festivals and bacchanalias. Leandro is left alone to brood.

Clarissa joins him, promising that if the Prince dies, she will share the kingdom with Leandro.

"Why, this is simply thrilling!" the chorus breathes. "She is the villain!"

Clarissa demands to know what Leandro has accomplished towards the desirable end of bringing about the Prince's demise. She is impatient at his half-way measures. It is not enough, she insists, to feed him on prose that cannot be digested, doses of silly notions, and poetry mixed in his porridge.

"Why not poison?" she demands. "Or just shoot him."

Leandro warns her that Truffaldino is dangerous—as he is a very funny man. Their conspiracy is overheard by Smeraldina, whom Leandro drags out from behind a table. She is not an ordinary eavesdropper, however, but a messenger from the witch, Fata Morgana. This all-powerful character is on their side. But ranged against them and with Truffaldino is another all-powerful character, the Magician Celio. The battle of the sorcerers is about to be joined.

Truffaldino tries to amuse the Prince by little antics and caperings, but this is not effective medicine. The Prince complains bitterly at being dragged off to the circus; but Truffaldino insists, and finally carries the Prince, wailing loudly, off on his back.

SCENE THREE: *The Circus.*

Horses prance, clowns tumble, processions form and re-group, monsters battle, drunkards and gluttons fight for food and drink, and a dazzling array of entertainers present themselves before the dismal Prince—all to no avail. The celebrated *"March"* introduces these antics.

In the midst of the festivities, a sinister figure appears. It is Fata Morgana. When Truffaldino discovers her, he gives her a push that sends her flat on her back, feet in the air.

The Prince, who has regarded all the merry-making with a jaundiced eye, sees something funny at last. A small giggle escapes him. The court cannot believe its ears. But another giggle follows, and then a rapidly growing torrent of mirth. The Prince's laughter at last threatens to inundate the theatre. Its tessitura is of the highest and lowest; in scope it resembles a grand concert aria. It seems inexhaustible. But at last it subsides.

The jubilation of the court is immediately silenced by the venomous witch, who cannot stand ridicule. She curses the Prince with a dreadful curse. He must fall in love. With three oranges! And these three oranges thousands and thousands of miles away!

The Prince is instantaneously enamored. Nothing will do but that he must set out at once, in spite of the King's pleading. Truffaldino is nominated to go along as chaperone, and the two depart on a breeze summoned up by the devil, Farferello, with his small but effective bellows. This is the *"Scherzo,"* almost as famous as the *"March"* to which it is often joined in concert performances.

ACT TWO

SCENE ONE: *The Desert.*

The two wayfarers have come near their goal, the distant kingdom of the giant Creonta, who has placed a formidable Cook as guard over the oranges. The Prince is all for pressing on, but the sudden appearance of their good genie, Celio, stays them momentarily. Celio gives them some good advice, which the Prince hardly heeds in his impetuosity—to cut open the oranges only if water is handy. Celio also gives Truffaldino a talisman to distract the Cook, a gaudy bow of red ribbon. The pilgrims depart.

SCENE TWO: *Outside Creonta's kitchen.*

This dreaded place, innocuous as it may seem to an outsider, strikes fear into the hearts of the Prince and Truffaldino. They withdraw slightly as a menacing voice comes from within.

"Who is whining?" demands this voice, a rugged bass-baritone. Out comes its owner, a fat cook, dressed in stiffly starched skirts, a fetching wig, and the brightest rouge imaginable. Truffaldino does not hide fast enough; the Cook pounces on him. Poor Truffaldino, shaking in his shoes, presents a pitiable sight. Yet the Cook finds something fascinating about him—it is the magic ribbon.

"But it is adorable," she simpers, in that unbelievable voice. "Oh, what a lovely ribbon. I love it so!" And she is lost to the world in a dainty dance, displaying the ribbon to best advantage.

This is the opportunity the Prince has waited for. Quickly he pops into the kitchen and out again, holding fast his prize, the three oranges. He and Truffaldino make their escape to the *"Scherzo"* music while the cook is still bemused by the ribbon.

SCENE THREE: *Another part of the desert.*

The travelers are footsore and weary; furthermore, they are thirsty. The Prince settles for a nap, but Truffaldino is tempted beyond his strength at the thought of refreshing orange juice. By now, the oranges have grown to considerable size, and appear to be plump and juicy. Truffaldino yields to temptation.

What is this? A comely young maiden! Truffaldino is disappointed. Nothing to drink. But the lady, the Princess Linetta, is in even more dire straits—without a drink she will die immediately. There is no drink, so she droops and dies. Truffaldino in dismay opens another orange with the same result: a dead Princess. At last the Prince wakes and is much disturbed at the sight of the pair of beautiful corpses. He summons help to take them out of his sight. Two harlequins obligingly appear out of nowhere and cart them away.

Now the third orange remains. The Prince gently opens it and there is his love, the Princess Ninetta. His joy soon turns to anguish when the inexorable fate descends upon her—for lack of water she must die.

At this point, the spectators take a hand. Moved by the suffering of the young couple, they consult among themselves and come up with a bucket of water, which one of them solemnly conveys across the stage. The Princess is saved!

The Prince urges her to return with him to his kingdom. But she, all too feminine, protests that she has nothing to wear. He must go fetch her some regal robes befitting her station.

His departure is the signal for the wicked forces in the person of Smeraldina, backed by Fata Morgana. With a magic pin, Smeraldina pricks the Princess and turns her into a pigeon, whereupon the Chorus comments that this is a very old trick indeed. Can't the author do better?

The trick works, however, for Smeraldina takes the place of the Princess, and in spite of the Prince's protests, is accepted by the King and his retinue. They march off.

SCENE FOUR: *The royal kitchen.*

Celio and Fata Morgana engage in a duel of words, whereupon the Chorus intervenes once again. Summoning Fata Morgana to hear a secret, they close in on her and send her packing off to the nether regions—via a trap-door, of course.

This leaves the field clear for Celio, who immediately brags about his strength.

"*His* strength!" the Chorus jeers.

Truffaldino has burned the roast. This seems to be the excuse to draw the Court into the kitchen, where the pigeon appears. Celio, now unhampered by his adversary, lifts the spell and the Princess Ninetta appears, to the joy of the Prince, to the confounding of Smeraldina, Fata Morgana, and Leandro, and to the pretended astonishment of the Chorus. What punishment will the King impose on the wicked ones? He ponders, then delivers judgment: the three traitors shall sweep the kitchen forever. But Fata Morgana has the last word. Summoning Leandro and Smeraldina to her side, she gives the sign and whoosh! Down they go, by the convenient trap-door, never to be seen again.

"A lovely, lovely show!" the Chorus sums it all up.

La Bohème

by GIACOMO PUCCINI (1858–1924)

Four Acts. Libretto by Giacosa and Illica, based on Murger's *Vie de Bohème*.
First produced in Turin, 1896.

Mimi, a seamstress	*Soprano*
Rodolpho, a poet	*Tenor*
Musetta, a girl of the Latin Quarter	*Soprano*
Marcello, a painter	*Baritone*
Colline, a philosopher	*Bass*
Schaunard, a musician	*Baritone*
Benoit, a landlord	*Bass*
Parpignol, a vendor of toys	*Tenor*
Alcindoro, an admirer of Musetta	*Bass*
Customs guard	*Bass*

People of the Latin Quarter, shop-girls, students, artists, soldiers, waiters.

TIME: *About 1830.*
PLACE: *Paris.*

ACT ONE

SCENE: *An attic studio.*

It is Christmas Eve. The low-ceilinged room is poorly furnished with a table, a few chairs, and a bed. The fireplace is empty and Rodolfo, the poet, and his friend, Marcello, the painter, complain of the cold. Through the wide window, we can see the snow-covered roofs of Paris. Marcello picks up a chair and proposes that they break it up and make a fire. Rodolfo says he will contribute the manuscript of his five-act tragedy for kindling.

Their friend Colline, the philosopher, comes in, tosses a few books on the table and complains disgustedly that the pawnshops are not open on Christmas Eve. In spite of the cold and hunger, their spirits are high and they make joking remarks about the warm qualities of Rodolfo's play which is now going up in smoke. In a few minutes Schaunard, the fourth of the Bohemian friends, enters the room with great news. Their luck has turned. He has suddenly acquired an unexpected music student and, with the resulting money, has purchased food, wine, and firewood.

All four are having a grand time when a knock is heard. It is Benoit, the landlord, who comes for the rent. The four Bohemians ply him with wine and wit, and are so successful in keeping him off the subject of his visit that in the end he leaves without any money at all. Three of them then leave to continue their merry-making below at the Cafe Momus, and Rodolfo stays home to continue writing.

He has barely begun when another knock is heard at the door—a timid knock this time. It is Mimi, a pretty little neighbor whose candle has blown out on the drafty stairway. Rodolfo invites her in, and, when she is attacked by a fit of coughing, offers her a glass of wine.

Feeling better, she starts to leave, but on the stairs her candle goes out again and she returns. This time, Rodolfo, who has been very much attracted by the girl, sees to it that *his* candle goes out too. At the same moment (on purpose, perhaps—we are never told) Mimi drops her key and there in the darkness they search for it on the floor. Rodolfo finds it and surreptitiously puts it in his pocket.

Then, "accidentally-on-purpose," their hands touch. "How cold your little hand is!" he exclaims, singing the aria, *"Che gelida manina."* In it he tells her about himself, his poverty, his poetry, his delight in pretty girls like Mimi, and then she replies in an aria, *"Mi chiamano Mimi"* ("They call me Mimi"), telling how she lives alone and earns a meager living by embroidering.

Rejoicing in their new-found love, Rodolfo and Mimi

sing a charming duet, *"O soave fanciulla"* ("O lovely maiden").

The voices of his friends are heard from the street below calling Rodolfo. He opens the window and moonlight floods the attic. "We'll be with you in a few minutes," he tells them. "Keep two places for us at the cafe." Mimi accepts Rodolfo's invitation to join the party and they depart arm in arm—slowly, tenderly. They go down the stairs, out of sight, and we still hear them singing as the curtain falls.

ACT TWO

SCENE: *The square in front of the Cafe Momus.*

A gay holiday crowd is strolling about in the square with street vendors, students and shop-girls, parents and children all mingled together in a motley throng. Parpignol, a vendor of toys, passes through the square, his pushcart decorated with lanterns, followed by a noisy group of children, laughing and singing.

Our bohemian friends have brought a table out of the cafe and are seated at it, ordering a bigger supper than they can afford. Mimi and Rodolfo have eyes and ears for no one but themselves. Marcello is in a gloomy mood and sarcastically asks the waiter to bring him an order of poison. The reason for his bitter mood is soon made clear.

A pair of late arrivals make their appearance and have to take a table on the other side of the stage. These two are much more richly dressed than any of the others, for they are Musetta and her wealthy admirer, Alcindoro. Now, Musetta and Marcello, the painter, were once lovers but quarreled and parted; and Musetta, seeing her old friend once more, finds the rich but elderly Alcindoro most unattractive. She tries to get Marcello's eye, but he resolutely turns his back.

And so Musetta makes a great fuss ordering Alcindoro around, and finally she breaks into the famous Waltz Song, *"Quando me'n vo soletta"* ("As through the streets I wander"), telling quite frankly and with complete conviction what a great charmer she herself really is. The situation is quite clear (to everyone, that is, but Alcindoro), and with Marcello leading the voices, the Waltz Song becomes a great concerted number.

Now, Musetta utters a piercing shriek. Her shoes are pinching her, she complains—and Alcindoro is sent to look for another pair. This is, of course, nothing but an excuse to get rid of him. Musetta, one shoe off, hops across the stage and flings her arms around the welcoming Marcello's neck. The disagreeable matter of the bill comes up, and merry, irresponsible Musetta solves it. Just add the whole party's bill to Alcindoro's, she says.

Off-stage, we hear the sound of a military band approaching. The patrol marches by; the whole crowd joins in behind it. As Musetta has only one shoe, she cannot walk very well and Marcello and Colline hoist her to their shoulders and carry her. When the last of the merry crowd has left the square, old Alcindoro comes rushing in breathlessly with a new pair of shoes for Musetta. But there is no Musetta and no supper party, only the outrageous bill. Alcindoro looks at it, groans and drops into a chair in a state of collapse.

ACT THREE

SCENE: *An open space near an entrance to the city.*

It is now an icy February morning, and the scene is a small square on the outskirts of Paris. In the background, we see the toll-gate at the entrance of the Orleans road into Paris. At one side of the stage is a small hotel where Musetta and Marcello are living, but perpetually quarreling—mostly because Musetta just can't help flirting with every man who comes within her view.

Mimi and Rodolfo have also been quarreling, and when the act begins Rodolfo is inside the hotel with Marcello ready to tell him of his troubles. Snow is falling softly. Presently, Mimi comes in, looking very ill and unhappy and asks for Marcello. When he comes out of the tavern, she tells him that she must at last leave Rodolfo, and asks Marcello's help in telling him so, for she just does not have the courage to do so. She tells of their frequent quarrels and of Rodolfo's intensely jealous nature. Then Rodolfo comes out of the hotel and Mimi hides behind a large tree. At first Rodolfo tells Marcello that he is leaving Mimi because she is a heartless coquette. Marcello does not believe this, and tells his friend that he is unreasonably jealous and stubborn. Rodolfo then admits that he still loves Mimi, but that she is terribly ill with a racking cough. Unfortunately, he has no money, and thinks she should have medical care. Poor Mimi has not realized before how bad her illness is, and she is deeply moved by Rodolfo's reiterated protestations of his love for her. Suddenly, she begins to cough and Rodolfo, discovering her, takes her into his arms.

Marcello tactfully leaves the lovers together and, in a very moving duet, they recall the days of their happiness, but agree that they must now part. Mimi sings, *"Addio, senza rancor"* ("Farewell, I wish you well"). But even while this lovely duet is going on, we hear the smashing of dishes inside the house. Marcello and Musetta are at it, quarreling again, and they carry their violent bickering outside. In a quartet, Mimi and Rodolfo sing, *"Addio, dolce svegliare"* ("Farewell, sweet love"), while the other pair of lovers hurl insults at each other.

Mimi and Rodolfo find their love has been rekindled and they agree that they will remain together until Spring has come—"Our time for parting is when the roses bloom." Musetta rushes down the street wildly. Marcello goes back sadly into the tavern while Mimi and Rodolfo, their arms around each other, stroll off together and their duet fades away softly in the distance as the curtain falls.

ACT FOUR

SCENE: *Same as Act One.*

Once more we are in the garret studio of Rodolfo and Marcello. The poet writes, the painter paints, but neither can concentrate for they are thinking of their lost loves. "Girls are fickle creatures," they agree in the famous duet, *"Ah, Mimi, tu più non torni"* ("Ah, Mimi, false and ficklehearted").

But their spirits are revived, as they were in the first act, by the arrival of refreshments which Colline and Schaunard bring with them, and the mood of these youthful artists is so much lightened that they engage in such pranks as an impromptu Spanish dance and even a mock duel fought with poker and fire-tongs as weapons and a couple of chairs as horses.

But a sudden end is put to this gaiety when Musetta enters, white and agitated. Poor Mimi has become desperately ill and Musetta has brought her back, perhaps to die in the arms of her lover. A cot is drawn forth hastily to accommodate the sad little seamstress, and happiness returns to her momentarily as she once again embraces her beloved Rodolfo.

But what she needs, and needs desperately, is medical attention, and none of them has any money. Musetta gives her precious earrings to Marcello and tells him to pawn them and bring a doctor. And Colline removes his overcoat and sings a sad and simple farewell to his old friend, *"Vecchia zimara"* ("Farewell, garment antique and rusty"), and leaves to pawn it.

For a brief while Rodolfo and Mimi are left alone to relive their romantic past—their meeting, their first party together, the little bonnet Rodolfo bought her.

Softly, sadly, we hear the music that accompanied their first love in this very garret. Then Mimi goes quietly to sleep as the others return from their mission of mercy.

Musetta shields the light of a candle so that it will not shine in Mimi's eyes; Rodolfo busies himself trying to cover the garret window with a blanket. Suddenly Schaunard, who has been hovering over the cot, notices that Mimi has stopped breathing. "She is dead," he whispers to Marcello—and Rodolfo, turning from the window, reads the dread news in the eyes of his friends. Crying "Mimi! Mimi!" distractedly, he rushes across the stage and takes the body of his beloved in his arms and the curtain falls.

Tosca

by GIACOMO PUCCINI (1858–1924)

Three Acts. Libretto by Giacosa and Illica, based on Sardou's play.
First produced in Rome, 1900.

Floria Tosca, a famous singer	*Soprano*
Mario Cavaradossi, a painter	*Tenor*
Baron Scarpia, Chief of Police in Rome	*Baritone*
Cesare Angelotti, an escaped political prisoner	*Bass*
Sacristan	*Baritone*
Spoletta, an agent of the police	*Tenor*
Sciarrone, a police officer	*Bass*
A shepherd boy	*Contralto*
A jailer	*Bass*

A cardinal, an executioner, soldiers, police, townspeople.

TIME: *June, 1800.*
PLACE: *Rome.*

ACT ONE

SCENE: *Interior of the Church of Sant' Andrea Della Valle.*

On one side of the stage a grilled iron gateway marks the entrance to a small private chapel; on the other side of the stage stands an artist's easel with a painting on it which is partially covered by a cloth. A man in ragged prison garb enters furtively. He is Angelotti, a revolutionary republican who has escaped from prison. When he hears someone coming, he hides in the small chapel.

A moment later, the Sacristan enters carrying a handful of paint brushes. Then the artist Mario Cavaradossi comes in, removes the cloth covering the picture, and goes to work on it. It is a portrait of the Madonna, and Cavaradossi has used for his model a beautiful woman whom he has seen praying in the church—*"Recondita armonia"* ("Strange harmony"). As he works, the Sacristan busies himself cleaning the brushes and gossiping.

After a few minutes he leaves and Angelotti emerges cautiously from the chapel. Cavaradossi recognizes him and, realizing the situation, he locks the door of the church, then gives the half-starved man the basket of lunch which has been sent into the church for his own use. Then Tosca's voice is heard outside and Angelotti once more hides in the chapel.

Cavaradossi now unlocks the church door and Tosca enters. She is a very beautiful woman and a famous singer. The artist and the singer are very much in love with each other, but it is very evident that the course of their love does not run smoothly. Tosca has a very jealous nature and is suspicious because Cavaradossi has kept her waiting before admitting her to the church. Her suspicions are increased when she observes that the Madonna Cavaradossi is painting is a blonde, while she is a brunette. But her love for Cavaradossi is stronger than her suspicions and before she leaves she invites him to meet her that evening—*"Non la sospiri la nostra casetta"* ("In our cottage").

When Tosca has left, Angelotti comes out of his hiding place and tells Cavaradossi that the beautiful woman he has used as his model for the Madonna is the Marchioness Attavanti, Angelotti's sister, and that she has taken part in the plot which effected his escape from prison and has hidden clothing under the altar to aid him in his escape. Cavaradossi gives him a key to his villa on the outskirts of the city and tells him to hide himself there. They both leave hurriedly and there is a short merry scene in which the Sacristan tries, not very successfully, to discipline a group of unruly choir boys.

The scene is cut short when the elegant and evil Baron Scarpia, Chief of the Roman police, enters with his evil-looking assistant, Spoletta, and questions the trembling Sacristan. He is looking for the escaped prisoner, Angelotti. A search is made of the church and Spoletta finds a fan belonging to Angelotti's sister, who is the model for the Madonna that Cavaradossi is painting. The empty lunch basket is found also and this confirms Scarpia's suspicions that Cavaradossi is implicated in the escape. Soon Tosca reappears and Scarpia shows her the fan and suggests that possibly some lady dropped it hastily when a rendezvous in the church was interrupted. Tosca remembers how she was kept waiting at the locked door of the church and her jealousy is kindled anew. Scarpia hopes to trap both Cavaradossi and Angelotti, and also to win the beautiful Tosca for himself through a villainous plan which is maturing in his mind. Now the church is filling up. We hear the solemn sound of organ music. The Cardinal enters and a religious procession files through the church, with priests, choristers, and a Cardinal in magnificent scarlet vestments, and the service begins while Scarpia stands at one side meditating his evil schemes in a counterpoint to the Chorus which sings a *"Te Deum."*

ACT TWO

SCENE: *The luxurious apartments in the Farnese Palace.*

It is evening and Baron Scarpia is sitting alone at the supper table. Through the window at the left, we hear occasionally the sounds of a cantata that is being sung in celebration of a victory over Napoleon. Floria Tosca is the soprano soloist in this cantata and Scarpia sends her a message which will bring her to him after the performance. Now the police agent, Spoletta, enters and reports to his chief that they have searched Cavaradossi's villa thoroughly but can find no trace of Angelotti. Instead they have arrested Cavaradossi and he is brought in. He is in a defiant mood and to all of Scarpia's cross-questioning, he replies scornfully that he knows nothing of Angelotti.

The cantata is over and Tosca comes in and she embraces Cavaradossi. But Scarpia has Cavaradossi taken to the next room to "give testimony", as he euphemistically puts it, and in the meantime, he questions Tosca about the whereabouts of Angelotti. Of course, she says that she knows nothing. Then Scarpia tells her that Cavaradossi is being tortured in the next room. In the grim scene that follows, Scarpia suavely works on Tosca's nerves and her love for Cavaradossi by giving orders to be "more insistent"—that is to tighten the band of steel around Cavaradossi's head till it spurts blood and he cries out in anguish. The door to the torture chamber is opened so that Tosca can see what is taking place. She begs Cavaradossi to tell the secret but he refuses and implores her not to do so. But

she cannot bear the sight of her lover's agony and she tells
Scarpia, "You will find Angelotti in a well in the garden."

The limp body of Cavaradossi is brought in and laid on a
sofa. Tosca embraces him tenderly and he slowly regains
consciousness. He is horrified when he learns what Tosca
has done.

Just then news is brought in that the battle which was
celebrated as a victory over Napoleon was in reality a defeat for the Italians and a victory for Napoleon. Cavaradossi's misery turns to joy and he hurls defiance at Scarpia
and says that tyranny will eventually be overcome by freedom, *L'alba vindice appar*" ("O may vengeance awake").
Contemptuously Scarpia orders Cavaradossi to be led away
to be executed the next morning. Then he turns to Tosca
and tells her that the price of Cavaradossi's life is—herself.
She draws back in horror from his embraces. "I have done
evil to no one," she cries. "I have lived only for music and
love!"—this is the famous aria, *"Vissi d'arte"*.

Finally, loathing the very thought of him, she agrees to
his terms. With an irony that escapes Tosca, he now gives
an order to Spoletta that in order to comply with formalities
Cavaradossi must undergo a mock execution, as has been
done before in a similar case. Spoletta indicates that he
understands and leaves the room. Tosca demands that
Scarpia write out a safe-conduct for herself and Cavaradossi to leave the country. While he is at his desk writing
out the passport, Tosca picks up a knife which is lying on
the supper table and conceals it behind her. Scarpia rises
from his desk and approaches her holding out the passport.
Suddenly, Tosca drives the knife deep into his breast and
he falls dead at her feet. She wrenches the passport from
his lifeless hand, then places a crucifix on his breast. Then
she picks up her cloak and steals out of the room as the
curtain descends on one of the most tensely dramatic
scenes in all opera.

ACT THREE

SCENE: *The roof of the prison-castle of Sant' Angelo.*

It is just before dawn. From the roof-top, we look out
over the city of Rome with the dome of St. Peter's showing
clearly against the sky. The sound of sheep bells echoes

from the distance and we hear the far-off sound of a shepherd singing a simple little song that dies away as the church bells ring for matins. A jailer emerges from a trap-door, lights the lanterns, and seats himself at a small table on which are writing materials. Cavaradossi is led in and the formalities are quickly finished. Cavaradossi begs the guard to bear one last message to Tosca and when this is granted, he seats himself at the table and picks up the pen. As he writes he recalls—in the deeply moving aria, *"E lucevan le stelle"* ("The stars were brightly shining")—the many happy hours he spent with Tosca. He is overwhelmed by despair and buries his face in his hands and, just at that moment, Tosca appears at the trap-door accompanied by Spoletta and a soldier. Both men soon withdraw and the two lovers are alone.

Excitedly Tosca tells Cavaradossi that she has secured his release and shows him the passport. Now they are free to go away and love each other always—*"O dolci mani"* ("O gentle hands").

But there is still the mock execution to be undergone, and Tosca tells Cavaradossi how to act. It is daylight now and the firing squad files in, and the officer in charge places Cavaradossi in front of the wall. Knowing that the rifles are loaded with blanks and that the execution is not a real one, Cavaradossi smilingly refuses the blindfold which is offered him. With Tosca watching excitedly at one side, the officer lifts his sword, lowers it, and the shots ring out. Cavaradossi falls to the ground just as Tosca has told him to do. "How well he acts!" she exclaims. The soldiers file out and Tosca, whispering "Do not move yet", waits until they have disappeared down the stairway, then tells him to rise. But he does not move. Horror-stricken, she throws herself on his body and discovers that this has been no mock execution. Cavaradossi is dead.

Just at that moment, Spoletta and the others rush in. Scarpia's dead body has been found. Spoletta tries to seize Tosca but, pushing him violently aside, she screams, *"Scarpia, avanti a Dio!"* ("Scarpia, we meet before God!") and climbs the low parapet and leaps to her death. Paralyzed with horror, Spoletta stands motionless. The others look over the edge of the parapet where Tosca has disappeared and the curtain falls.

Madame Butterfly

by GIACOMO PUCCINI (1858–1924)

Three Acts. Libretto by Giacosa and Illica, based on John Luther Long's story.
First produced in Milan, 1904.

Cio-Cio-San (Madame Butterfly)	*Soprano*
Lieutenant Pinkerton, U. S. Navy	*Tenor*
Sharpless, American Consul	*Baritone*
Suzuki, Cio-Cio-San's maid	*Mezzo-soprano*
Goro, a marriage broker	*Tenor*
The Bonze, Cio-Cio-San's uncle	*Bass*
Prince Yamadori	*Baritone*
Kate Pinkerton	*Mezzo-soprano*
Trouble, Cio-Cio-San's child	

TIME: *About 1900.*
PLACE: *Nagasaki, Japan.*

ACT ONE

SCENE: *Garden of a Japanese house overlooking Nagasaki.*

There is a brief orchestral introduction which suggests in its exotic rhythms the Oriental setting of the opera. When the curtains part, we see the garden outside Pinkerton's rented house, a flimsy little Japanese dwelling with matchbox walls and sliding panels, situated at the top of a hill. There is a flowering terrace on the right from which we catch a glimpse of the distant town and harbor. Pine branches overhead and flowering cherry trees add to the Japanese atmosphere.

Goro, the fussy, self-important Japanese marriage broker, who has arranged the international match, is showing Lieutenant Pinkerton the garden, the view, and the cute little sliding panels in the paper-walled house. The name of the bride-to-be is Cio-Cio-San, but she is known in English as Madame Butterfly. The three servants come out and bow low as they are introduced. "Call them Scarecrow One and

Scarecrow Two," says Goro, and then there is Suzuki, Madame Butterfly's personal maid. Goro dismisses the servants and tells Pinkerton that Cio-Cio-San has twenty-four relatives, all of whom will attend the ceremony.

Then Pinkerton's friend, the American Consul, Sharpless, arrives, a little out of breath after the climb up the hill. As Sharpless talks with Pinkerton, he becomes concerned as he realizes that the young lieutenant is taking the marriage contract as a joke. He is only going to be in Japan a short while and wants to make his stay as enjoyable as possible. *"Dovunque al mondo"* ("The whole world over"), he sings, the American sailor goes where he pleases and does what he pleases. "I leased the house and the wife for nine hundred and ninety-nine years," Pinkerton says, "with the option to cancel both at a moment's notice."

Sharpless warns him that the little Japanese girl may not have the same idea, but Pinkerton flippantly proposes a toast to America. As the two men drink the toast the orchestra plays the opening strains of "The Star-Spangled Banner."

Goro returns to announce the coming of the bride and her family and friends. As they slowly climb the hill, the girls sing a happy bridal chorus and at last Cio-Cio-San appears at the little wicket opening into the garden—*"Spira sul mare e sulla terra"* ("Across the earth and sea")—her arms filled with flowers, a lovely vision of youth and happiness. Sharpless is still more concerned when he sees how rapturously happy she is, but Pinkerton won't listen to his warnings.

Then the many relatives of Cio-Cio-San troop in and the quaint ceremony of signing the marriage contract is performed and toasts are drunk to the happiness of the young couple.

While the guests are enjoying the food and drink, Cio-Cio-San and Pinkerton draw aside. She tells him that her family was formerly wealthy, but her father is dead now and she and her mother are dreadfully poor and she has to earn her living as a geisha. "But now," she says, "I am the happiest girl in all the world." She asks Pinkerton to guess her age and laughingly tells him she is fifteen. Cio-Cio-San asks Pinkerton if she may bring a few of her keepsakes, and she takes from the wide sleeves of her kimono a handkerchief, a mirror, a fan, and, last of all, she draws out a dagger in a ceremonial sheath. Goro whispers that it was sent to her father by the Emperor and indicates by gesture that it was used for hara-kiri.

Suddenly, the festivities are interrupted by the appearance of Butterfly's uncle, who is a Japanese priest. He has learned that Butterfly visited the Christian mission and renounced the gods of Japan. He furiously denounces her for deserting the faith of her ancestors to marry a foreigner. Her relatives, who have been enjoying the wedding feast, now turn against her and add their curses to those of the priest as they all hastily depart, leaving Pinkerton to comfort the weeping Cio-Cio-San.

It is growing dark now and Suzuki brings out Butterfly's snowy white kimono which she puts on in place of the elaborate ceremonial dress she has been wearing. Fireflies flash their twinkling lights through the garden as the two lovers sing of their happiness, *"Viene la sera"* ("Evening is falling").

Butterfly tells of her fears and hesitations at the idea of marrying a foreigner, but that she is blissfully happy and knows that all will be well. Clasped in each other's arms, they sing, *"Notte serena!"* ("Peaceful night!").

ACT TWO

SCENE: *Living room of Butterfly's house.*

Three years have gone by since Pinkerton and Cio-Cio-San sang of love beneath the stars. His ship has sailed away long ago, but Butterfly is still living in the house he bought for her and with her is her faithful servant Suzuki and her little child. Her money is almost gone, but she is still unwavering in her belief that her husband is faithful to her and will return.

When the curtains part, Suzuki is praying before an image of Buddha, but Butterfly refuses to pray to a Japanese god, and assures Suzuki that Pinkerton will return—he promised to come when the robins nest. Then she sings the thrilling aria which sums up her deep faith, *"Un bel dì"* ("One fine day"). "One day," she says, "we shall see a thread of smoke rising from the ocean." And she describes how Pinkerton's ship will come into the harbor and how he'll rush up to the little house on the hilltop to greet her.

And now, the kindly American consul, Sharpless, arrives, and with him is the marriage broker, Goro. Sharpless tells Butterfly he has received a letter from Lieutenant Pinkerton. Without waiting to hear what is in the letter, Butterfly expresses her joy at this justification of her faith.

But Goro urges her to remarry and says that he has brought with him a wealthy suitor named Yamadori. The wealthy suitor is brought in, but he is pompous and affected and Butterfly laughs at him. "How can I marry?" she says, "I am already married." Goro tells her that the desertion of her husband constitutes divorce. "Not in my country, America," answers Butterfly, proudly.

After Goro and Yamadori have left, Sharpless tries to persuade Butterfly to accept her wealthy suitor. She runs out of the room and in a moment comes back carrying a yellow-haired baby. "Is this his child?" cries Sharpless in surprise. "Who ever heard of a Japanese baby with yellow hair and blue eyes?" answers Butterfly scornfully. "His name today is 'Trouble'," she adds, "but soon he will be called 'Joy'."

And now Sharpless tries to read to her the letter he received from Pinkerton. It tells of Pinkerton's marriage to an American wife, but Butterfly keeps interrupting and finally he gives up and leaves without having broken the news to Butterfly. After he has gone, there is a commotion outside in the garden, and Suzuki drags in the cringing Goro. He has been hanging around the house, hoping to get Butterfly to change her mind and marry Yamadori and he has told Suzuki that in America, Butterfly's baby would be considered an outcast. On hearing this, Butterfly seizes the sacred dagger of her father and threatens the thoroughly frightened Goro, but she lets him escape as the sound of a cannon-shot is heard from the harbor.

It is Pinkerton's ship. Cio-Cio-San is overjoyed at the apparent fulfillment of her faith. She orders Suzuki to fill the house with flowers from the garden and the two sing their beautiful "Duet of the flowers"—*"Gettiamo a mani"* ("In handfuls, let us scatter petals")—as they strew the floor with blossoms. "Put some rouge on my cheeks and bring out my wedding garment," says Butterfly to her faithful servant.

Then, as twilight steals over the room, Butterfly, Suzuki, and the baby wait silently by the window for Pinkerton to come, watching through small peep holes made in the paper window panes. There is a haunting melody of yearning tenderness from the orchestra and an unseen chorus of humming voices.

ACT THREE

SCENE: *Same as Act Two.*

When the curtain rises, we are again in the living room of Butterfly's house. Three motionless figures are still in the same position where we left them at the end of the second act—watching by the window for the return of Lieutenant Pinkerton. But whereas the last act ended in the darkness of early evening, this one begins in the gray dawn. Suzuki and the child are asleep, but Butterfly has watched the long night through. Then as morning brightens, she tenderly carries the sleeping baby to an inner room with the song, *"Dormi, amor mio"* ("Sleep, my love").

Hardly has she gone when Pinkerton arrives and with him the Consul, Sharpless. Suzuki at first is overjoyed, but they caution her to be silent. She notices an American woman out in the garden and she asks hesitatingly who she is. Sharpless breaks the news. It is Pinkerton's American wife. She and Pinkerton have come to adopt the child. At this, Suzuki wrings her hands in despair. Pinkerton leaves, and a few moments later, Butterfly comes into the room. She sees Sharpless, a strange American woman in the garden, and her own Suzuki in tears. The cruel truth begins to dawn upon her—*"Tutto è finito"* ("All is dead for me, all is finished").

Butterfly agrees to give up her son and asks only that Pinkerton come for him in half an hour. She is left alone. Quietly, she takes the dagger from its sheath and reads the inscription, "Die with honor when it is impossible to live with honor."

Then, pushed through the sliding door by the trembling Suzuki, her little child comes in. Butterfly bids him a heart-breaking farewell, *"O me, sceso dal trono"* ("My son, sent to me from heaven"), blindfolds him and gives him a doll and an American flag to play with. Then taking the dagger, she goes behind a screen. Pinkerton's voice from outside calls, "Butterfly, Butterfly!" But he is too late. We hear the sound of the dagger falling to the floor. Butterfly staggers out, groping for her child and falls beside him. Pinkerton rushes in and kneels beside her lifeless body, sobbing with grief and shame, and the curtain slowly falls.

Le Coq d'Or

(The Golden Cockerel)

by NIKOLAI RIMSKY-KORSAKOV (1844–1908)

Three Acts. Based on a fairy tale by Pushkin.
First produced in Moscow, 1909.

The Astrologer	*Tenor*
King Dodon	*Bass*
The Queen of Shamakhan	*Soprano*
Prince Guidon	*Tenor*
Prince Aphron	*Baritone*
General Polkan	*Bass*
Amelfa, the royal housekeeper	*Soprano*

TIME: *Mythical.*
PLACE: *Imaginary.*

ACT ONE

SCENE: *Court of King Dodon.*

Before the curtain rises, an odd little old man in the costume of an ancient astrologer, with signs of the Zodiac on his robe and tall hat, comes out in front of the curtain and, in a cracked, high-pitched voice, informs you that he is about to present an ancient story, which is not entirely true, but which still has a message.

Then the curtain rises on the gorgeous and utterly fantastic court of fat old King Dodon. His council of noblemen are seated on benches and the ancient king himself is seated on a magnificent high throne in the center of the room. Dodon tells his court that he is not as vigorous as he once was and that he does not know what to do about the enemies who keep threatening his kingdom from all sides. If they would only let him alone to eat and sleep and enjoy a quiet life, but they will not!

The king has two sons and the older one, Guidon, now speaks up. He says it is all quite simple. The trouble is that the armies are too close to each other and hence they are always fighting. Let King Dodon withdraw his army from the frontier and then they can have a little peace and quiet. To be sure the enemy will undoubtedly burn and pillage the outlying villages, but they will tire themselves out doing that and when they are exhausted, Dodon's army can attack them and defeat them easily.

The councilmen are all delighted with this plan, all except old General Polkan, who says what will happen if the enemy does not tire himself out burning villages, but advances at once and attacks the capital?

Then the king's younger son, Aphron, speaks up and says that his brother is wrong, as he always is. Aphron's plan is to disband the army entirely. Send them all home and this will lull the enemy into a false sense of security. Then in exactly one month, call the army together again and annihilate the enemy in a surprise attack.

This plan meets with even greater applause than the first one and King Dodon embraces his younger son and compliments him on his brilliant military genius. But old Polkan again says that the enemy might fool them and not wait a month to attack the capital.

And now the noblemen start a silly quarrel about whether it would be better to foretell the future by consulting the dregs of beer or by counting beans. When the argument reaches its height, our old friend the astrologer comes in and solves everything.

He has brought a present for the king, a golden rooster which he carries in a bag. "This rooster," he says, "should be placed on a spire where he will be always on the lookout for danger. When an enemy approaches, he will warn you by crowing."

So grateful is the king for this magical bird (which is immediately placed high on a pole), that he offers the astrologer any gift he may desire. The astrologer demands nothing at the moment, but asks the king to put the promise in writing. But the king is loathe to do this, and the astrologer is content with his verbal promise.

Now the court disbands. A large bed is brought on for the sleepy old king, the housekeeper Amelfa prepares his bed for him, sees that he has something to eat, and Dodon falls asleep. In his dreams he sees beautiful maidens dancing, but soon the rooster cries "Cock-a-doodle-doo" and warns everyone of approaching danger.

The people rush in and the king orders his sons to lead the armies off to battle. Then Dodon once more lies down to sleep. Again he dreams of beautiful maidens, and again the cock awakens him with cries of danger. This time, he realizes he must do something himself. He calls for his armor (which is old and rusty) and for his sword (which is too heavy for him) and for his horse, which he says must be a gentle one. When they finally get his armor buckled on him, it is impossible for him to get into the saddle by himself and this is accomplished only by much pulling and pushing and lifting. The housekeeper, Amelfa, is distressed that he is going off without eating, but King Dodon says he will get something to eat on the way.

And so, King Dodon rides off to battle, while the populace cheer him wildly and hail him as their glorious leader and beg him to stay in the rear, out of all possible danger.

ACT TWO

SCENE: *A battlefield.*

It is just before dawn. Dimly through the darkness can be seen many bodies lying around, among them the corpses of King Dodon's two sons, Guidon and Aphron, in awkward postures on the ground, their swords thrust through each other, their horses mournfully standing by. In the confusion of battle, they have slain each other!

The king and his army come upon this dismal scene, and Dodon sings of his bitter loss. But dawn is beginning to break and in the dim light they descry a tent. It must be the enemy, they decide. They draw up their ridiculous little cannon, load, aim, fire—and out of the tent comes a beautiful maiden with oriental attendants.

It is the Queen of Shamakhan, and everyone is enchanted

as she sings the famous *"Hymn to the Sun"*, a song of the love she has to offer in her distant, oriental land.

Dodon, completely forgetting his lost sons (whose bodies have been considerately carried off) at once approaches her, backed by his General Polkan. She entertains them with wine and invites them to sit beside her on soft cushions. She tells Dodon that she has come to conquer his country, but when he asks her where her army is, she replies that anyone as beautiful as she is does not need an army. But Polkan asks such silly questions and makes such silly remarks that she asks that he be sent away. Polkan thereupon retires behind a rock to watch what happens. And what happens is very odd, indeed.

For the beautiful, languorous young Queen of Shamakhan proceeds to win the heart of the foolish old King Dodon, singing for him, dancing for him. And she even gets him to sing too, and finally to dance, although he is dreadfully embarrassed over having to do this in front of his whole army. However, he goes through with the dance (very awkwardly) and the queen both flatters and teases him in such a bewildering fashion that the poor old fellow offers her his hand and his kingdom both—and even the head of General Polkan if she wants it. She very promptly accepts and has herself gorgeously bedecked by her attendants, and the whole troupe marches off victoriously to a strange and wonderful combination of military and wedding march.

ACT THREE

Scene: *Before the palace of King Dodon.*

A large crowd has collected in the square in front of the palace. They are worried about the war and also badly frightened on account of the heavy storm-clouds in the sky. The golden rooster stands motionless and voiceless on his spire. Messengers come running in and finally Amelfa, the royal housekeeper, comes out on the steps of the palace and informs the crowd that King Dodon has conquered no less than four kings, named Hearts, Diamonds, Clubs, and Spades.

She also tells them that the king has had his two sons executed because they had been quarreling and warns the populace that they had better be good or their heads will be lopped off next. But most important is the news that King Dodon has rescued a beautiful princess and is bringing her home as his bride.

A moment later the triumphant procession of the homecoming king and his bride begins to appear. Soldiers, dwarfs, giants, all sorts of queer people appear and the crowd cheers wildly.

Finally Dodon and the Queen of Shamakhan appear in a golden chariot. Amid wild shouts of joy, they descend from the chariot and take their seats on two thrones on one side of the square. And the victory celebration begins with an elaborate ballet.

When the ballet is over, the astrologer appears once more and reminds the monarch of his promise to reward him with anything he wants in return for having brought the golden cockerel. And what the astrologer wants is nothing less than the Queen of Shamakhan herself!

Dodon at first thinks the astrologer must be joking; but when the queer old fellow insists, he takes his sceptre and strikes him on the head. A clap of thunder is heard, everything suddenly grows dark and the astrologer falls to the ground. Dodon is surprised and shaken and turns to the queen, but she only laughs and pushes him away and calls him a doddering old fool.

Suddenly the golden cockerel flies down from his perch, pecks Dodon on the head, and *he* falls dead.

Again everything goes dark and through the darkness we hear a mocking laugh from the queen. When the lights go up again both the queen and the golden rooster have disappeared. Now the populace bewail the loss of the king. What a good old soul he was, how wisely, mercifully, and yet justly he had ruled without ever doing anything! How will they ever get along without a king!

But the opera is not quite over. For the astrologer once more wanders across the stage before the curtain and in his cracked high voice tells us not to worry about the sad ending to the story. No one, he says, was real—excepting only himself and the queen.

The Barber of Seville

(Il Barbiere di Siviglia)

by GIOACCHINO ROSSINI (1792–1868)

Two Acts. Libretto by Sterbini, based on the comedy by Beaumarchais.
First produced in Rome, 1816.

Count Almaviva	*Tenor*
Dr. Bartolo	*Bass*
Rosina, his ward	*Soprano*
Figaro, the barber	*Baritone*
Don Basilio, a music teacher	*Bass*
Fiorello, Count Almaviva's servant	*Bass*
Berta, Dr. Bartolo's housemaid	*Soprano*
Ambrosius, Dr. Bartolo's servant	*Bass*

A magistrate, a notary, an officer, musicians, soldiers.

TIME: *Seventeenth Century.*
PLACE: *Seville.*

ACT ONE

SCENE: *A street in Seville.*

The handsome and wealthy young Count Almaviva has fallen in love with a beautiful young girl whom he has seen on a number of occasions, but has never met. When the curtain rises on the first scene, we discover the Count, very early in the morning, on a street in Seville before the house of his beloved where he is about to serenade her.

He has brought along with him his servant, Fiorello, and a whole band of musicians. He sings his lovely and very florid serenade, *"Ecco ridente in cielo"* ("Lo, the skies are smiling"), and pays off the musicians so liberally that he has considerable difficulty getting them to stop saying "Thank you."

His unknown lady-love fails to appear, but the Count

178

lingers on beneath her balcony. After he has finally dismissed his musicians, he hears someone else coming down the street and he hides in a doorway.

The newcomer is Figaro, the barber, whom Count Almaviva has known in another town. Figaro, accompanying himself on the guitar, describes his own irrepressible, high-spirited and ubiquitous self in the most famous patter song in all opera, *"Largo al factotum"* ("Make way for the factotum"). He is a barber, but he is much more than a barber. He is a master-intriguer, "the town's most useful citizen". His profession gains him admission into all the houses in town and he is an expert at plotting secret meetings, carrying notes, planning elopements, and goodness knows what else. No rest day and night, Figaro here, Figaro there, the busiest and apparently the happiest of men.

Now Almaviva comes out from his hiding place. They recognize each other and Almaviva tells Figaro he does not want his identity or his presence in town to be known. He learns from Figaro that his Rosina is the ward (not the daughter, as he had thought) of the fat old physician, Dr. Bartolo, with whom she lives and before whose house they stand.

Just at that moment Rosina steps out on the balcony, followed by Dr. Bartolo. She has a piece of paper in her hand and Bartolo asks her what it is. She replies that she has written down the words from a popular opera called *The Vain Precaution*. But alas, she (quite accidentally, of course) drops the note and it falls in front of Almaviva who is hiding beneath the balcony. Dr. Bartolo angrily orders his ward into the house and Almaviva picks up the note, which informs him that Bartolo will soon be leaving the house and suggesting that this might be an opportunity for her unknown admirer and serenader to identify himself.

In a moment, Dr. Bartolo appears calling orders to his servants that no one but Don Basilio, the music teacher, is to be admitted. Then he hurries off to get a notary so that he and Rosina can be married immediately.

Almaviva now accepts Rosina's invitation by singing another serenade, *"Se il mio nome"* ("If my name you would know"), in which he tells her that his name is Lindoro and that while he cannot offer her wealth or fame, he can give her boundless devotion. He does not tell her his real name or rank because he wants her to love him for himself alone, and not for his wealth and title. Rosina attempts to reply from within the house, but is rudely cut short.

Figaro and Almaviva plot together as to how Almaviva may, with Figaro's assistance, get a chance to win Rosina before Dr. Bartolo can carry out his designs to get the girl, and her fortune, for himself.

The Count is frantic and begs Figaro to figure out some way for him to get into the house. The fertile imagination of Figaro is not lacking in this emergency. "I have it," he cries. "A new regiment is coming to town. You dress up as a soldier—the old man will believe everything you say." And the act ends as the two conspirators sing a rollicking duet, *"Ah che d'amore"* ("Love's own enchantment").

SCENE TWO: *A room in Dr. Bartolo's house.*

Rosina is declaring her undying love for Lindoro—the name Count Almaviva has assumed in his incognito visit to Seville, and by which he has been carrying on his long-distance courtship. This is the famous aria, *"Una voce poco fa"* ("There's a voice within my heart"), and through its fascinating brilliant pyrotechnics she also tells us what an amiable, yet determined, creature she is.

When Rosina has left the room, in comes her guardian, the elderly and rather ridiculous Dr. Bartolo, accompanied by Don Basilio, the music-master. Dr. Bartolo tells Basilio, who is really a matrimonial agent, that he wishes to marry Rosina himself. But Basilio tells him that the fair Rosina has another suitor, one Count Almaviva. Of course, neither he nor Dr. Bartolo realize that Count Almaviva is really the anonymous serenader.

The problem now is how to get rid of the Count. Basilio suggests that they start some disgraceful rumor about him which will make him impossible as a husband for Rosina. It is here that Don Basilio sings his extraordinary aria, *"La calunnia"* ("Slander's whisper"), describing graphically how a faint breath of detraction can develop into a whirlwind of slander. This description of the devastating effect of gossip is set to music that grows, in an amazing crescendo, to a climax of fury.

When the two old cronies leave to get a marriage contract drawn up for Bartolo, Figaro returns and persuades Rosina to write a letter to Lindoro (who, he says, is a cousin of his but who is really, of course, Count Almaviva), but the letter has already been written by the eager little minx. Bartolo once more interrupts proceedings by inquiring about all this letter writing. Rosina manages to put him off with clever little lies.

Then, in comes the Count disguised now as a drunken soldier, in accordance with the plot he has hatched in Scene One with Figaro. He claims to be billeted in Bartolo's house, and nothing can persuade him he is not.

A lively scene follows (in which the Count manages to get another letter into Rosina's hands), and it is all brought to a climax by the entrance of a group of soldiers who have been sent for by Bartolo. He claims he has a paper which exempts him from billeting and, after some rummaging, he finds it. He tries to get his supposedly drunken intruder arrested; but Almaviva takes aside the officer in charge and proves to him that he really is a nobleman. That's enough for the officer, who does not make the arrest, and in this complex muddle of cross purposes and, with a brilliant ensemble depicting it, the curtain falls.

ACT TWO

Scene: *The same room in Dr. Bartolo's house.*

Bartolo has succeeded in getting rid of the drunken soldier but he is suspicious of the strange incident and is inclined to think it has something to do with Rosina, but just what, he is not sure. There is a knock at the door and a young man comes in who says that he is a music-master and that he has come to give Rosina her music lesson in place of Don Basilio, who is ill. The young man is Count Almaviva, and this is another scheme thought up in the fertile brain of Figaro. The Count is so well disguised that Dr. Bartolo does not recognize him as the drunken soldier. But he is a suspicious old man and, in order to get in his good graces, Almaviva tells him he has just come from the apartment of Count Almaviva where he has picked up a letter from a lady which indicates that the Count is not sincere in his desire to marry Rosina. The letter is really the one which Rosina herself had written, but Bartolo does not know this and is glad to have what he considers evidence to be used against Rosina's suitor.

And so the music lesson takes place. The music which Rossini wrote for this scene has been lost, and it is customary for the soprano who takes the part of Rosina to sing anything she chooses. Almaviva, posing as the music teacher, praises Rosina's voice and artistry. Bartolo starts to sing a song which was popular in his younger days, but is interrupted by the entrance of Figaro, who insists he must shave the Doctor at once as he will have no time later on. Bartolo reluctantly gives him a bunch of keys to get the shaving things from their cupboard. Figaro goes out of the room and we hear the sounds of breaking crockery. This is just a little foolishness on Figaro's part. His real purpose (which he accomplishes) is to get the key to the balcony door for his patron, Count Almaviva.

There now follows a comic scene in which Figaro puts the Doctor out of commission by covering his face with lather and getting some of it in his eyes, while the young couple carry on their love-making on the other side of the room. In the midst of all this, Don Basilio, the real music teacher comes in. Of course, he is astonished and mystified but after Almaviva slips a well-filled purse into his hand, he is willing to admit that he really is sick and must return home and go to bed.

The shaving is resumed while Rosina and the Count at the harpsichord plan their elopement that night. But Bartolo overhears enough of this to realize that something is going wrong, and he springs up from the chair, lather and all, and denounces Figaro and the young people as conspirators. They laugh at him and leave the room. In a towering rage, Bartolo sends for his man-servant and orders him to bring Basilio back at once. Then he tells his housekeeper, Berta, to make sure that no one enters the house. Left alone, Berta has a few caustic remarks to make about this silly business of love and marriage.

Basilio comes in, and he and Bartolo have an argument as to the identity of the false music-master, and Bartolo insists that his marriage to Rosina must take place that evening. Basilio goes off to get the notary and the marriage papers, and Bartolo calls for Rosina and shows her the letter picked up in Almaviva's apartment. Of course, she does not know that Count Almaviva is none other than her lover Lindoro, and she thinks she is being tricked by Lindoro and impulsively agrees to marry Bartolo.

There is a brief interlude, enlivened by a thunderstorm, during which two figures come in from the balcony. They are Figaro and Almaviva. Rosina accuses the supposed Lindoro of treachery, but all is well when he reveals that he is not Lindoro but Count Almaviva.

Figaro urges the young lovers to hurry, but when they go to the balcony they discover that their ladder is gone. Now, the notary appears to draw up the marriage papers for Rosina and Bartolo, but is easily persuaded to put in the name of Count Almaviva instead of Bartolo. Basilio is bribed again and signs the papers as witness. And so it happens that by the time Dr. Bartolo returns, his ward is already married and, when he hears that the bridegroom is a wealthy nobleman and is ready to give him Rosina's original dowry, Dr. Bartolo is reconciled and joins in the happy finale.

La Cenerentola

(Cinderella)

by GIOACCHINO ROSSINI (1792–1868)

Two Acts. Libretto by Jacopo Ferretti.
First produced in Rome, 1817.

Prince Ramiro	*Tenor*
Dandini, his servant	*Bass*
Don Magnifico, a nobleman	*Baritone*
Clorinda ⎱ Don Magnifico's daughters	*Soprano*
Tisbe ⎰	*Mezzo-soprano*
Angelina, Don Magnifico's step-daughter, known as Cinderella	*Mezzo-soprano*
Alidoro, a philosopher	*Baritone*

TIME: *Whenever you wish.*
PLACE: *A true Prince's kingdom.*

ACT ONE

SCENE ONE: *The decrepit old mansion of Don Magnifico.*

In a large room that seems to be kitchen, dining room, dressing room and hall in one, Cinderella's two step-sisters are primping at a dressing-table, each fighting to take the mirror from the other in order to evaluate her charms, even to brag about them a little. Their preoccupation with their own fussily-dressed selves is broken into by a sad song from near the fireplace. Cinderella, tending a coffee pot, amuses herself in the only way she can. She sings *"Una volta c'era un re"*, a ballad telling of a king who picked a simple, innocent maid for a wife, a piece of wishful thinking the two sisters do not relish. They stop her before she can complete a second verse.

An incipient quarrel is forestalled by a knock on the door. It is a friend of Prince Ramiro, the philosopher Alidoro, who has disguised himself as a beggar in order to see the true inwardness of the people he visits. The sisters chase him off, but Cinderella gives him a little food and coffee surreptitiously, and is beaten for her generosity. The viragos stop their persecution only at the entrance of a pompous chorus of courtiers. They have come to announce a ball at the near-by summer palace of Prince Ramiro, and they tell the twittering sisters that the most beautiful woman at the ball will be chosen by the Prince as a bride.

In the tizzy to which this announcement reduces them, the sisters pull Cinderella about like a dummy, a fact she bemoans in a little passage similar to that of another Rossini character, Figaro in *The Barber of Seville,* who also had to *"va la, va su, va giu",* at the beck and call of patrons. The chorus comments on the excitement, and Alidoro remarks that the stupid sisters' downfall is already in sight. He hints mysteriously that by tomorrow, Cinderella's troubles may be over.

Don Magnifico, wakened by the clatter, scolds his daughters, and relates a magnificent dream they interrupted, *"Mi sognai fra il fosco e il chiaro".* He interprets it to mean a rise in his station, and is amazed at the coincidence of the news about the Prince's search for a wife, which the impatient sisters finally manage to tell him. In his excitement, he orders Cinderella to take coffee to his room, and bustles out, giving his daughters sage advice about behavior and toilettes. They hurry to their rooms to dress. The hall is deserted.

Quietly a figure appears in the doorway. It is Ramiro, disguised as his valet, playing the same game as his philosopher friend. He muses on the fate which condemns him to a loveless marriage—that is, unless he finds the girl Alidoro has told him is in this very household.

Cinderella, coming back with the coffee cup, does not see the visitor. She begins to sing her little song, and suddenly finds herself face to face with the Prince. In her astonishment she drops the dishes and they break. Her dismay is soon replaced by another emotion, but when the Prince tells her he has come to inquire about Magnifico's daughters, she believes there is no hope for her. But Ramiro has seen magic in her face and presses her for details about herself. She answers in confusion and departs. Ramiro sings longingly after her as Magnifico bustles in.

The Prince is coming? The girls aren't ready. "They need a century!"

"What a clown!" says Ramiro. Then preceded by a wave of expensive perfume, and attended by courtiers, Dandini makes an entrance, more princely than the Prince, though in reality he is only Ramiro's valet. The chorus warns him to select a mate, and he sings *"Come un' ape ne' giorni d'aprile"*. Like a bee in April, he cannot make up his mind which flower to choose. The stage is wholly Dandini's from now on: the girls fawn and simper; Magnifico gloats. The courtiers escort the sisters to the ball. Cinderella piteously begs to be allowed to go; Magnifico brutally refuses in spite of Alidoro's hints that there is a third daughter. Magnifico disclaims her, saying that she has died. The five now on stage express themselves in short phrases of varying emotions until at the climax they all scatter. Alidoro comes back shortly, dressed as a pilgrim. He summons Cinderella, waves his wand, and—presto, he is the traditional fairy godmother. Cinderella shall go to the ball.

SCENE TWO: *In Ramiro's palace.*

Don Magnifico, having sampled the contents of the Prince's notable wine cellar and therefore knowing whereof he speaks, has given a noble discourse on the subject, when Dandini sends him off with the promise to make him Royal Wine Steward. In a vain attempt to learn their fate, Clorinda and Tisbe buzz around Dandini like gnats until he brushes them off.

SCENE THREE: *The park of the palace.*

Don Magnifico wins the title! He has sampled thirty casks and hasn't yet staggered. The courtiers announce his appointment as Wine Steward and a number of other high-sounding positions—he wants it in writing, and the courtiers oblige. As they go off to celebrate, Ramiro and Dandini tiptoe in and compare notes about the girls. They must be very quiet about it all, so they sing, *"Zitto, zitto: piano, piano. . . . Sotto voce a mezzo tuono"*. Dandini reports the sisters "a mixture of insolence, capriciousness and vanity." Speak of the devil: there they are! *"Princi-*

pino, dove siete?" "Where are you?" Dandini cannot escape. He announces that a man cannot marry two girls; therefore he will take one sister and the other shall be given to his groom. Their horror at the very idea is cut short by a commotion outside.

"An unknown lady, veiled, is arriving," says Alidoro. All wonder who it can be. When the fair stranger at last lifts her veil, the startling resemblance to the cindery maid confuses and perplexes Magnifico and his daughters. The entire assemblage wonders audibly who this stranger can be? if the Prince already loves her? are we dreaming?—all but Dandini, who vows to eat enough for four while he is still playing prince. They finally join in a brilliant crescendo of rolling "r's", predicting all sorts of dire happenings. On this note of mock disaster, the curtain falls.

ACT TWO

SCENE ONE: *A room in the palace.*

Magnifico's mind turns over and over the disturbing resemblance between the fair stranger and his shamefully wronged stepdaughter. We learn that he has defrauded her of her inheritance. As his only escape from his troubles, he looks to one of his daughters to save him by marrying the Prince. But the Prince has other ideas. He comes on the scene singing of *"questa bella incognita"*, who resembles the one who has stirred his heart. The lady of his dreams appears at the moment, pursued by Dandini, who hastily proposes. "I cannot," says the lady, "for I love another— your groom!" Hearing this, the Prince comes forward joyfully, but Cinderella is still shy. However, she gives him a bracelet from her arm; when he finds her and she is wearing its twin, she will be his. The bracelet is as near as may be to the more familiar glass slipper. *"Sì, ritrovaria io giura!"* he promises ardently. "I will find her, I swear it." The chorus comments on the evident tumult in his breast. "But he has love to guide him," they sing sagely.

Now it is time for Magnifico to hear the news: which daughter? In a hilarious scene with Dandini, the old rogue, already on pins and needles, is led on farther and farther, until finally the great secret is revealed: Dandini is the valet! This insult is not to be borne. Magnifico rushes out in rage and despair. Alidoro who has carefully planned that the Prince's carriage shall break down near Magnifico's castle, prepares to leave. A storm is coming up—it will further his project.

SCENE TWO: *Don Magnifico's mansion.*

Cinderella is alone before the fire. The ball is over for her. She has only the bracelet to remind her of those happy hours—and of him whom she loves with all her heart. A few moments of reverie remain to her—then her stepfather and his daughters burst in, hardly disguising their disdain and suspicion of her. That distressing resemblance to a certain witch!

While Cinderella is fetching some supper, Dandini ventures in. The Prince's coach has overturned, and the Prince and he seek shelter, not realizing whose home they have come to. Don Magnifico is enraged at the sight of the man who has so humbled him, and the revelation of the real Prince's identity does nothing to calm him. He vents his anger on Cinderella, who comes running back when she hears his shouts.

Now is the time for all tangled skeins to be smoothed out, for the lovers to be known to each other, for the wicked to be punished. It requires, however, considerable ensemble singing, explaining just how complicated the situation is, with individual comments spicing the concoction. The tumult dies down and Clorinda is left alone to voice her despair and chagrin and eventual hope for better things in *"Sventurata! mi credea comandar seduta in trono."* Rossini gives this brilliant aria to Clorinda who is a coloratura, rather than to her sister, a mezzo whose voice would be in competition with that of Cinderella, herself a dark-voiced heroine.

SCENE THREE: *Throne Room in the palace.*

With great pomp Cinderella is escorted to the throne that she will share with her beloved Prince. The chorus salutes her, the instrument of goodness triumphant. She, modestly, remembers that not so long ago she was among the ashes, and asks pity for her step-father and the two shrews who have done her nothing but ill. She sets this plea to one of the most exacting and effective arias in existence, *"Nacqui all'affano"*, and melts everyone's heart with her generous sentiments as well as her vocal fireworks. The sisters repent; Don Magnifico is humbled; the Prince forgives; the Chorus sings its blessing on the entire company. The happy couple will, no doubt, live that way ever after.

Samson and Delilah

by CAMILLE SAINT-SAËNS (1835–1921)

Three Acts. Libretto by Lemaire.
First produced in Weimar, 1877.

Samson, leader of the Israelites	*Tenor*
Delilah, priestess in the Temple of Dagon	*Mezzo-soprano*
Abimelech, Satrap of Gaza	*Bass*
High Priest of Dagon	*Baritone*

Hebrews, Philistines, dancers.

TIME: *1150 B. C.*
PLACE: *The city of Gaza in Palestine.*

ACT ONE

SCENE: *A public square in Gaza.*

A group of Hebrews has gathered together in the open space before the temple of the Philistine god, Dagon, and are lamenting their unhappy lot under the tyranny of their hereditary enemies, the Philistines. "Why has our God forsaken us?" they cry, but one among them, Samson, rebukes them and tells them the hour of deliverance is at hand and that soon they will be raising their voices in praise and not in protest.

The Philistine military leader and governor of the city, Abimelech, strides into the square with a company of Philistine soldiers and orders the Hebrews to be quiet. He taunts them with their defeat and disgrace. Their God,

Jehovah, is of no avail against the Philistine god, Dagon. Samson defies Abimelech and denounces him for his tyranny and cruelty. The hour of deliverance for the Hebrews is at hand—*"Israël! romps ta chaîne"* ("Israel, break your chains"). Their God, Jehovah, will come to their aid as He has in the past. The Hebrews take courage from Samson and repeat his defiance. In a rage, Abimelech draws his sword against Samson, but before he can strike him, Samson wrests the sword from his grasp and slays him with a mighty blow.

The Philistine soldiers fall back in dismay at this sudden reversal of fortune and Samson and the Jews leave the square, Samson flourishing aloft the sword of Abimelech. The great doors of the Temple of Dagon swing open and the High Priest comes out and angrily demands from the Philistine soldiers why they have allowed the murderer of Abimelech to escape. They cower before his wrath, and two of them attempt to explain to the High Priest that some mysterious power seemed to hold them back. But the High Priest pours contempt and scorn upon them for their cowardice and declares that the Jews must be destroyed in punishment for this terrible crime.

A messenger rushes in with the news that a growing Hebrew army, led by Samson, has put the Philistines to rout. The High Priest calls down a terrible curse on Samson and the Hebrews, but the Philistines are thoroughly frightened and insist that nothing remains for them but flight. They take up the body of Abimelech and hurry away.

And now the square fills up again with Hebrews, no longer lamenting their sad fate but rejoicing in victory. They hail Samson as their leader. The doors of the temple swing open once more but this time it is not the High Priest who appears, but the beautiful priestess, Delilah, accompanied by a group of maidens, carrying wreathes and garlands of flowers. They descend the steps and move among the Hebrew warriors in a sensuous pagan dance. Delilah approaches Samson seductively, but he is warned by one of the older men not to yield to her charm or she will surely lead him to destruction. Samson is fascinated by Delilah's beauty, but prays that he may be delivered from her power. In a lovely melody, *"Printemps qui commence"* ("Spring voices are singing"), she tells him how she will await his coming in her flower-scented home in the valley of Sorek. The ancient Hebrew repeats his warning as Delilah and the dancing girls slowly retire into the temple.

ACT TWO

SCENE: *Delilah's dwelling in the valley of Sorek.*

It is an evening in early spring and Delilah, gorgeously attired and bedecked with jewels, awaits Samson in the luxuriant tropical garden surrounding her home in the valley of Sorek. She invokes the power of the god of love to aid her in destroying the enemy of her people, *"Amour! viens aider ma faiblesse!"* ("O love, come aid my weakness").

Distant flashes of lightning indicate a coming storm. The High Priest enters the garden to make sure of Delilah's assistance and to strengthen her resolve. He tells her that the Hebrews are masters of the city and that Samson seems to have supernatural strength. Delilah must learn his secret so that he can be vanquished. "All the wealth of the shrine of Dagon is yours if you succeed," he tells her. But Delilah reassures him that she hates Samson as much as he does and that the destiny of her people is safe in her hands.

The High Priest leaves and it grows dark in the garden and the sound of thunder in the distance is heard at intervals. Samson gropes his way through the darkness, hesitating and doubtful, torn between his infatuation and his sense of duty. Delilah greets him rapturously but he turns away from her caresses and tells her that he is the instrument of the holy will of God and that he has been chosen to liberate his people and lead them to victory. But she assures him that the god of love is even stronger than the God of the Israelites. He can resist her no longer as she sings the famous aria, *"Mon coeur s'ouvre a ta voix"* ("My heart at thy sweet voice"). Samson cries out that it is his destiny to love her and that his love is so great that it defies even his God.

And now Delilah demands that, as an assurance of his great love for her, he confide to her the secret of his supernatural strength. Samson tries to tear himself away from her as the sounds of the approaching storm grow louder. Suddenly, she pushes him away and rushes into the house.

There is a vivid flash of lightning and a loud roll of thunder as Samson stands hesitating for a moment and then follows her into the house. Delilah has won.

Shadowy figures of Philistine soldiers creep silently through the dark garden and surround the house. Presently Delilah appears at a window, calling for help and the soldiers rush in to seize their victim. From within we hear the despairing voice of Samson crying out that he has been betrayed. In the weakness of his surrender to passion he had told Delilah that the secret of his great strength lay in his hair and she has cut it off leaving him powerless to resist his enemies.

ACT THREE

SCENE ONE: *The prison at Gaza.*

Samson has been blinded by his captors and is chained to a huge millstone in the prison of Gaza and spends his days in despair and remorse walking round and round as he grinds corn for the Philistines. From other cells in the prison and from outside the walls voices come to him, voices of the Hebrews taunting him with his failure to lead them to victory as he had promised. Samson is overcome by shame and falls on his knees praying to Jehovah to take his life in atonement for his sin and to save his people. As he is praying, a prison guard comes in, unchains Samson from the millstone and leads him away.

SCENE TWO: *Interior of the Temple of Dagon.*

A crowd has assembled in the great Temple of Dagon. In an impressive procession the High Priest enters with princes of the Philistines. Following them comes Delilah and a group of dancing girls, garlanded with flowers and bearing golden cups of wine. They sing in praise of the dawn which puts the darkness to flight and they dance the "*Bacchanale*", at first softly and voluptuously, increasing gradually in intensity. and climaxing in a dance of wild abandon.

And now the blind Samson is led in by a little boy, his drab prison garment contrasting with the gorgeous dress of the victorious Philistines. They gloat over him and mock him. Delilah, goblet in hand exults in her triumph and mockingly offers him her hand to guide him. Samson raises his sightless eyes and prays for a rebuke from heaven. "Grant me my old power that Thy glory may be avenged!" The High Priest and Delilah now begin the sacrificial rites. They pour libations on the flaming altar and at length Samson is ordered to offer his oblation to the pagan god. "Guide my steps toward the two pillars supporting the roof," he says to the boy who is his guide, and when the child has done so, Samson orders him to flee from the temple at once. Then, as the exulting chant of the Philistines reaches its climax, Samson repeats his prayer for a return for only a moment of his old supernatural strength. Standing between the massive columns, he heaves their massive weight apart. There is a shriek of horror from the crowd as the pillars give way and the stone roof of the temple crashes down upon Samson and his enemies.

Fledermaus

(The Bat)

by JOHANN STRAUSS (1825–1899)

Three Acts. Original German libretto by Haffner and Genée.
Many English adaptations exist. This account is based on the
Metropolitan Opera version, with text by Garson Kanin,
lyrics by Howard Dietz.
First produced in Vienna, 1874.

Gabriel Von Eisenstein, a "well-to-do"	*Tenor*
(*Alias* Marquis de Renard in Act II)	
Rosalinda, his wife	*Soprano*
(*Alias* the Countess in Act II)	
Adele, their maid	*Soprano*
(*Alias* Olga in Act II)	
Alfred, a "wild oat"	*Tenor*
Dr. Blind, Eisenstein's lawyer	*Tenor*
Dr. Falke, noted Ballmaster	*Baritone*
(The "Bat")	
Frank, a warden	*Baritone*
(*Alias* the Duke de Bastille in Act II)	
Prince Orlofsky	*Mezzo-soprano* (or *soprano*)
Ida, Adele's sister	*Speaking part* (*Ballerina*)
Frosch, a jailer	*Speaking part*

Servants, guests, dancers, singers, prisoners.

TIME: *1874.*
PLACE: *Bad Ischl, Austria.*

ACT ONE

(In the Metropolitan Opera version, as the overture ends,
Dr. Falke appears before the curtain in a spoken prologue.
He is dressed for evening, wearing a flowing opera cape.
Explaining how he came to be called the "Bat", he reveals
that his friend Eisenstein played a trick on him, leaving
him, dressed as a bat, to "sleep it off" in a public square

after a fancy dress party. He has been called "Dr. Fledermaus" ever since. Now he thirsts for revenge. And it will be forthcoming that very night.)

SCENE: *The morning room of Eisenstein's house, overlooking a garden.*

From the garden, Alfred appears, looking in the window and finally daring to enter the room. He is dressed like the conventional poet, for that is what he is—a poetic singer. At sometime in the not too distant past, he has courted the lady of the house—before she became Mrs. von Eisenstein —and he proceeds to recall those days in song. *"Do you still belong to me?"* he carols melodiously. But Rosalinda is not there to hear, so Alfred retreats to the garden, just as Adele, the pert and pretty maid, comes into the room. She does not notice him, for her thoughts are with a letter she has received, purporting to be from her sister, who has become quite well known as a dancer. *"I've a sister rarely writes,"* she tells us. Ida has invited Adele to a grand ball. When Rosalinda enters, agitated at the sound of the voice she has just heard, Adele begs for the night off. Rosalinda refuses absent-mindedly, and Adele leaves in tears. This is the signal for Alfred's re-entry. His singing voice, which he uses at every opportunity, almost melts Rosalinda's heart, but she is saved by the voice of her husband outside. Eisenstein is angry, which spoils his debonair good looks. He enters arguing furiously with his lawyer, Blind; and in a fast exchange of insults the two reveal to Rosalinda, who joins them in a lively trio, that her husband must go to jail for two weeks. He has kicked a tax collector. The sentence was for one week, but an irate judge has doubled it. "You've made your bed and you must lie in it," Rosalinda scolds.

The trio grows faster and more furious until Blind rushes out. Adele comes in, and receives an order from her master for a fancy dinner and some very plain clothes—not to embarrass his jailmates. Dr. Falke is announced, and congratulates Rosalinda on getting rid of her tiresome spouse. When she goes to fetch some wine, Falke conspiratorially invites Eisenstein to drop off at Prince Orlofsky's glamorous ball on his way to jail. Eisenstein is very easily persuaded. The two men sing a duet, dwelling joyfully on the anticipated pleasures of the evening, and can hardly conceal their glee when Rosalinda returns. She looks thoughtful. An idea is beginning to simmer behind her beautiful brow.

"Is your aunt still sick? Well, take the evening off," she commands the astonished Adele, who has already forgotten the excuse she gave for absence. Both women turn to gape in astonishment at Eisenstein's entrance. He has arrayed himself in his finest evening clothes, and now is on pins and needles to go to the place of his "incarceration". Rosalinda and he engage in a tender farewell duet, soon joined by Adele, in which each of the partners seems a bit absentminded. *"The graying sea, the leaden sky,"* are Rosalinda's prospects. "When you're away, we'll try to carry on," all three promise. The husband goes off with a flourish, followed by Adele.

Alfred loses no time. At once he is in the room, putting on Eisenstein's dressing gown, eating his supper, drinking his wine, and making himself very much at home. Of course, he has to sing and of course it is a love song, *"What a lovely rendezvous!"* in which Rosalinda eventually joins, "Here we are—we two alone." But the "two alone" are rudely interrupted by Frank, the warden, who has come to escort Eisenstein personally to jail. Mistaking Alfred for the head of the house, he drags the now besotted tenor off, after some sly (and extremely musical) comments on the domestic scene. Rosalinda protests a little too much that the man is her husband—"A lady is only as good as her name"; Frank begs her pardon over and over; Alfred takes advantage of the situation to exact a kiss that Frank thinks is "longer than a kiss should be".

"Oh come with me and you'll agree it's great to be in jail," he urges Alfred. Off they go, after a sprightly trio, and Rosalinda is left alone.

ACT TWO

SCENE: *Prince Orlofsky's party.*

The gay company is enjoying the party more than the host, who confesses himself bored. Falke guarantees to make him laugh, and explains the plot which will bring master, mistress, and maid together, each disguised from the other. Orlofsky agrees it may be faintly amusing, and gives orders for everyone to have a good time. It's his motto, he says in a jaunty song, *"Chacun à son goût"*.

Eisenstein, suddenly confronted by Adele, tries to unmask her, but she responds so devastatingly that he is silenced. *"Look me over once, look me over twice,"* she invites him. And in a number of flattering self-estimations, she points out that she could not possibly be a chambermaid. She laughs so merrily at the idea that the company wholeheartedly joins in.

Now the real complications begin. Frank, the jailer, is introduced as the Duc de Bastille, and he and the phony Marquis (Eisenstein) become bosom, and boozy, friends. The glamorous Countess appears, and behind her mask bewails the faithlessness of her own spouse, who makes bold love to the supposed stranger. By a ruse she gets away from him his prized chiming watch. He is further bemused by her singing of a haunting Czardas, *"Some days you're lonely"*.

Orlofsky, by now a trifle more animated, proposes a toast to the king of wines, champagne, and the company joins in zestfully: "Up with the wine and drink her down!" Then a gentle mood dedicated to love falls on the crowd, and they sing, first one and then the other, two of the most beloved songs in the opera, *"Happy Days"* and *"You and I"*. The lights come on with brilliance, and the corps de ballet dances an enchanting waltz, led by Adele's sister, Ida. The guests join in singing the famous waltz, *"Oh the delight of a night with you"*. Suddenly, the clock chimes six. It is morning; the revelry must end. Eisenstein and Frank, soon to meet in other surroundings, part affectionately. The ball is over.

ACT THREE

SCENE: *The Bad Ischl Municipal Jail.*

The jailer, Frosch, is a handy man with a tramp, a bail bond, or a bottle. His red nose and shambling gait testify to his long and comfortable association with the last of those three. His humor also is of vintage mold. When

Frank staggers in, groggy with memories of the charming girl who has made a deep impression on his susceptibilities, and almost stuporous with other, more alcoholic afterthoughts, Frosch attempts some light banter, but finds his boss unresponsive.

Frank comes to life only when Adele and Ida enter, the former determined to follow up the advantage she had gained at the ball. With rapid changes of character in three brilliant songs—from a simple farm lass to a dramatic queen to a gay Paris Apache—she proves beyond doubt that she has talent as an actress, and as a singer. Her dismay at discovering that her prospective benefactor is a jail warden is cut short by a knock at the door. Eisenstein wants to come in. Frosch escorts the girls out.

Frank having deposited the pseudo Eisenstein in a cell himself, refuses to believe that his erstwhile drinking companion is that wanted gentleman, and goes to fetch *his* Eisenstein. Blind now bustles in, having been sent for by Frosch at Alfred's behest. Eisenstein quickly changes coats with his lawyer, puts on the latter's fuzzy wig and concealing spectacles, and prepares to confront his wife's lover— and his wife. Rosalinda has not been able to stay away. Perhaps she can straighten it all out before Eisenstein suspects anything. But she is too late.

Assembled in a furious little group, Frank, Frosch, Eisenstein, Alfred, and Rosalinda try to sort things out, once and for all. Alfred sings his story while the fake Blind fumes; Rosalinda and Alfred bemoan "The legal mind" that makes tangles where none were before; the scene works up to a pitch where Rosalinda feels she must defend herself. This she does in a plaintive aria centering around pots and kettles calling each other black, "You call me an improper noun". Both men join in. Eisenstein is at last moved to reveal his identity and the three principals engage in a lively trio, which Rosalinda resolves by producing her trump card—the chiming watch. Her husband is aghast. He makes a feeble attempt to deny his identity in order to escape imprisonment and placate his wife, but there are too many witnesses that he is Eisenstein. Suddenly the stage is crowded with Orlofsky's entire party, who salute Fledermaus, and resolve to leave everything unsettled— up in the air. They take up favorite strains once again.

Then to the melody of *Chacun à son goût,* the merry Viennese assemblage bids the audience farewell, counseling it at the last curtain to take up glasses, "Then up with the wine and drink her down until the sun appears."

Salome

by RICHARD STRAUSS (1864–1949)

One Act. Based on Oscar Wilde's play.
First produced in Dresden, 1905.

Salome	*Soprano*
Herod, Tetrarch of Judea	*Tenor*
Herodias, his wife	*Mezzo-soprano*
Jokanaan (John the Baptist)	*Baritone*
Narraboth, Captain of the Guard	*Tenor*

Soldiers, Jews, slaves, a page, and an executioner.

TIME: *30 A. D.*
PLACE: *Judea.*

SCENE: *A terrace in the palace of Herod.*

In pale moonlight a group of soldiers is standing guard outside the banqueting hall of Herod, the King of Judea. Narraboth, the young Syrian captain of the guard, gazes intently into the hall and cannot take his eyes off the beautiful Princess Salome, daughter of Herodias and stepdaughter of Herod. "How beautiful she is!" he exclaims, but is warned by a young page that it is dangerous for him to show so plainly his infatuation for the daughter of Herodias.

In the center of the terrace is an iron grating in the floor. It is the opening to a large well which is in reality a dungeon. Suddenly, we hear from the depths a voice intoning the mysterious words, "After me will come One who is greater than I!" One of the group on the terrace asks who the prisoner is and is told that it is a "holy man from the desert".

"The princess is leaving the table!" cries Narraboth in excitement. "She is coming this way!" And the beautiful Salome comes out into the cool night air to seek relief from the revelry in the banquet hall and from the intense gaze of her stepfather, Herod, who has been staring at her all evening with all too evident significance.

As she comes out on the terrace the voice is heard again. She is told by the soldiers that it is the voice of Jokanaan, a prophet, and she inquires if he is young or old, and she is told he is young. A message is brought to her that Herod wishes her to return to the banquet table, but she declares that she will not go back and demands to have the prisoner brought forth. The soldiers will not obey her and tell her that Herod has ordered that no one, not even the High Priest, shall even so much as speak to Jokanaan.

Then Salome exerts all her charm on the infatuated Narraboth and promises him that if he will grant her request, she will smile upon him. The unhappy young man is helpless under her spell and orders the prophet to be brought forth. The grating in the floor of the terrace is thrown back and in a moment Jokanaan emerges slowly, an impressive figure clad in a rough garment, with long hair and unkempt beard.

Salome is fascinated. "I am the daughter of Herodias," she says and Jokanaan bursts forth in a terrible denunciation of Herodias as the very incarnation of evil and depravity. Instead of being repelled by this, Salome tells him that his voice is music to her ears. He urges her to leave the court of Herod and to go into the wilderness to seek salvation, and she only speaks more amorously of the beauty of his body. "Enough!" he cries, "I will not listen to you!" "Jokanaan," she murmurs, *"Ich will deinen Mund küssen"* ("I must kiss your lips"). But he calls her a daughter of sin and urges her to the lake of Galilee to seek forgiveness from the Saviour.

Overcome with remorse and horror, the young captain, Narraboth, steps between Salome and Jokanaan and with a swift movement stabs himself and falls dead at their feet. But his death has no effect upon Salome who continues to gaze at the prophet with hypnotic fascination and repeat, "Your lips, Jokanaan, I must kiss your lips!" "You are accursed" are his last words as he turns his back on her and descends again into his prison cell. The iron grating is replaced and Salome crouches above it looking down into the well with a strange look of wild joy on her face.

The wine-besotted Herod and his drunken courtiers come out from the banquet hall and Herod asks at once for Salome. Herodias turns on him savagely and berates him for his obvious infatuation with his stepdaughter. Herod stumbles on the body of Narraboth and, recalling that the young Syrian captain also gazed with ardent longing on Salome, he orders the body to be carried away and the blood stains to be removed. The superstitious ruler is frightened by the suicide of Narraboth and fears it may be an evil omen. He fancies he hears the beating of unseen wings and cowers in fear.

Herodias mocks him but he recovers himself when he discovers Salome still crouching over the grating in the terrace floor. He invites her to drink wine with him and as she refuses, the voice of the prophet is heard again denouncing Herodias and the evil court. Herodias demands that he be silenced and accuses Herod of being afraid of him. The Jews have asked that Jokanaan be turned over to them and Herod has not done so. Five Jews now appear before the Tetrarch and renew their request. But Herod refuses, saying that the prophet is a holy man who has seen God. But the Jews reply indignantly that no man has seen God since the prophet Elijah and they denounce Jokanaan as a blasphemer. Among the Jews are two Nazarenes, disciples of Jesus, and they speak of the miracles which He has wrought in Galilee, even to the raising of the dead. Herod's superstitious fear is aroused again by this, and he exclaims, "I forbid it!"

The voice of Jokanaan is heard again and Herodias again demands that he be silenced. But now Herod's wandering thoughts have turned again to Salome. Ignoring his wife, he asks the princess to dance for him. Herodias indignantly forbids her to do so and she herself is reluctant. But Herod insists and promises to give her anything her heart may wish. Again he hears the mysterious beating of unseen wings. He tears the wreath of flowers from his head, crying that they are burning like a crown of fire.

In the meantime, slaves have prepared Salome for the dance and she moves with wild abandon over the terrace in *"The Dance of the Seven Veils."* Herod watches her intently as she discards her veils one by one, and when the last veil has been cast aside, she flings herself at his feet. When he asks her to name her wish, she replies that she wants the head of Jokanaan brought to her on a silver platter.

Herod cries out in horror at this terrible request, but Herodias praises Salome as a worthy daughter. Herod offers anything else, but Salome insists and he sinks back in his chair almost fainting with fear and dismay. With an evil smile, Herodias draws a ring from his finger and hands it to the executioner as a token of what he is to do. The executioner, with a scimitar poised on his shoulder, descends into the well. Salome crouches again at the entrance to the dungeon and there are a few moments of awful suspense, and then, silently the arm of the executioner comes up through the opening, bearing aloft the platter with the severed head.

Salome places the platter on the floor and grovels beside it as she sings of her passion and her hate, of her wild and unsatisfied longing and her revenge, *"Du wolltest mich nicht deinen Mund küssen lassen!"* ("You would not let me kiss your lips, Jokanaan, but now I will fulfill my desire.")

Herod can bear no more, and orders the slaves to extinguish the torches as he prepares to go back into the palace. Through the darkness comes the voice of Salome, "I have kissed your lips, Jokanaan, I have kissed your lips."

The moonlight has been obscured by clouds, but now a bright ray of moonlight floods the scene revealing Salome in her ghastly passion.

"Kill that woman!" screams Herod and the soldiers surround her and crush her to death beneath their shields.

Elektra

by RICHARD STRAUSS (1864–1949)

One Act. Libretto by von Hoffmannsthal.
First produced in Dresden, 1909.

Elektra, daughter of Agamemnon	*Soprano*
Chrysothemis, her sister	*Soprano*
Clytemnestra, their mother	*Mezzo-soprano*
Orestes, their brother	*Baritone*
Aegisthus, lover of Clytemnestra	*Tenor*

An overseer, trainbearer, and other servants.

TIME: *Remote antiquity.*
PLACE: *Mycenae (Greece).*

SCENE: *A courtyard in the palace of Agamemnon.*

On one side of the courtyard is the servants' quarters, on the other side, the rear of the royal palace. As the curtain rises, five serving maids, with a woman overseer, are drawing water from a well and gossiping among themselves. One of them speaks scornfully of Elektra, daughter of the dead king, Agamemnon, saying that this is the hour when they must expect to hear the screams and imprecations of this strange woman. At that moment, Elektra appears briefly in the shadows of a doorway. She is dressed in rags, her hair disheveled and her whole manner wild and distraught. As she sees the servants, she suddenly throws her arm before her face and springs back through the doorway.

The serving maids continue to express their hatred for this daughter of a king who has forsaken the royal apartments and taken up her abode in the stable yard, where she broods constantly over the murder of her father and dreams of vengeance. Only one of the young girls speaks up in defense of Elektra, declaring that if she could, she would gladly kneel before her and anoint her feet with oil and pay her the homage due a princess. The others ridicule the young girl for her sentimentality, and the overseer lashes her with a whip and drives her into the dingy servants' quarters. The other maids pick up their water-jugs and follow her and for a few moments the courtyard is silent and empty.

Evening is deepening into night as Elektra once more creeps out from her hiding-place. Completely absorbed in her dreams of vengeance, she calls upon the spirit of her dead father, Agamemnon—(*"Elektra's Monologue"*). "It is the hour when they murdered you," she cries, "your wife Clytemnestra and her lover, Aegisthus." She prays that the day of retribution may come speedily and that she and her sister and brother—the three children of Agamemnon—may soon dance in triumph beside his tomb and over the dead bodies of his murderers.

Absorbed in her dream of revenge, she is startled when the palace door opens and her sister, Chrysothemis, appears. Elektra turns away from her, but Chrysothemis approaches her quietly and whispers to her that Clytemnestra and Aegisthus are plotting to imprison Elektra in a dungeon. Chrysothemis begs Elektra to give up her plans of revenge and to go away with her from this gloomy palace. "I am young," she cries. "I want to live. I want to have a husband and children as other women do!" She reminds her sister that neither prayers nor imprecations can bring back to life their dead father, and as for their brother, Orestes, they have not heard from him for a long time and do not know whether he is alive or dead. But Elektra scornfully commands her to be silent.

Their conversation is interrupted by strange noises from a gallery which runs along one side of the courtyard—the cracking of whips and the sounds of hoofs and the groaning of beasts. Chrysothemis flees in terror but Elektra watches as a weird procession passes by illuminated by the flickering light of torches. Animals are being driven to the sacrificial altar, for Queen Clytemnestra has had a terrible nightmare and has ordered a sacrifice to the gods to bring her peace of mind. She appears at a window of the palace, and gazes into the courtyard where Elektra stands defiantly.

Clytemnestra, clad in purple and covered with jewels, is a ghastly figure as she is revealed by the light of the torches.

Her face is bloated and sallow and her expression is almost that of a sleep-walker. At first, Clytemnestra is enraged at the sight of her daughter and reproaches the gods for giving her such an unnatural child. But her anger soon subsides. She is lonely and full of foreboding, her sleep is troubled with hideous nightmares. Though she hates and fears Elektra, yet she feels that perhaps this strange creature may have some unearthly wisdom which will bring relief from her torment. Elektra declares she will not speak to her mother in the presence of the two ladies-in-waiting who attend her. Clytemnestra turns on her companions and denounces them as depraved creatures, slaves of the wicked Aegisthus. Then, alone and unattended, and supporting herself with a long ivory cane set with gems, she comes slowly down the palace steps and confronts Elektra.

An under-current of horror runs through the conversation of mother and daughter. Clytemnestra tells of her terrible dreams and asks if there is no sacrifice which may be made to dispel the evil influence—(*"Where art thou, O truth"*). Elektra replies that when the right blood flows, the evil will be wiped out and when Clytemnestra asks, "Whose blood?" Elektra replies, "A woman's." When Clytemnestra anxiously asks for further details, Elektra tells her that a man will officiate at the sacrifice. Then she asks her mother if she will permit her brother, Orestes, to return to the palace. Startled by this question, Clytemnestra declares that the people to whom her son had been entrusted have treated him so badly that he has lost his reason and adds angrily that she has forbidden his name to be mentioned in her presence.

"You lie!" cries Elektra. "You have sent money to have him murdered and your dreams are the visions of a guilty conscience!" Clytemnestra haughtily replies that she is queen in the palace and is well guarded against treachery, and she threatens Elektra with imprisonment unless she will reveal the sacrifice which will ease her tormented soul and bring her restful sleep.

"You are the sacrifice," bursts out Elektra savagely, "and your son Orestes will wield the ax of retribution. You will fly from him in vain and in the final moment you will behold the eye of your murdered husband gazing at you."

Overcome with horror at this terrible prophecy, Clytemnestra sinks to the ground but as she crouches at Elektra's feet, an attendant rushes out from the palace and whispers something in her ear. Suddenly transformed from despair into triumph, Clytemnestra rises to her feet and shakes her fist at Elektra menacingly. "Torches, torches!" she cries. Almost at once the courtyard is filled with attendants, many of them carrying torches, and they escort Clytemnestra into the palace.

While Elektra stands amazed at this sudden transformation, Chrysothemis rushes up to her with the terrible news that Orestes is dead. Elektra refuses to believe it, but Chrysothemis says that two messengers, an old man and a young man, arrived at the palace gates only a few minutes before with the story. As the two sisters huddle on the palace steps, overcome with grief, a young servant enters and orders that a horse be saddled at once, as he must hurry to the absent Aegisthus with an important message. As other servants go to do his bidding, Elektra rouses herself and rises slowly to her feet. She turns to Chrysothemis with the light of madness in her eyes. "Now, we must act alone," she murmurs and confides to her sister that she has hidden the ax with which their father was killed and that she has saved it for the day of vengeance. But Chrysothemis cannot bring herself to take part in this ghastly deed which Elektra is planning and she escapes into the palace.

In the dark courtyard Elektra now creeps stealthily along the wall until she comes to a spot near the doorway. Here she kneels down and begins digging in the ground with her hands, now and then looking apprehensively over her shoulder to see that she is not observed.

Suddenly she is startled as a young man comes into the courtyard and stands looking down at her. Elektra springs to her feet and angrily demands to know what he is doing there. He replies that he is the messenger who has brought the news of Orestes' death and he is now waiting to be summoned before Queen Clytemnestra. In reality the young man is Orestes himself, but he and Elektra do not at first recognize each other. She reproaches him with being alive while the young Orestes is dead, and the bitterness of her grief is so great that he asks her if she is perhaps related to the dead man. She proudly declares that she is Elektra, daughter of King Agamemnon and sister of Orestes. At first he cannot believe that this dirty and unkempt creature, clad in rags, is his sister, but as he looks at her more intently he recognizes that it is indeed Elektra. He whispers to her that Orestes is not dead, but still she does not recognize him and does not understand.

An old servant of the palace now approaches and, kneeling before Orestes, kisses the hem of his robe. Other servants enter and do likewise and Elektra realizes who he is and greets him with a shout of joy, that begins the aria of passion, *"Orestes, Orestes,"* which commences the *Recognition Scene*. But when he tries to embrace her, she draws away from him and looks down at her filthy and ragged dress with loathing. Once she was a proud and beautiful princess, but her whole life has been transformed by her vow of vengeance. Orestes assures her that her long vigil is over and that he will take upon himself the fulfillment of the vow—(*"Happy he who comes to end the work"*). He and his old teacher brought the false news of Orestes' death as a ruse to gain entrance into the palace. And just at that moment the older man appears and tells him that Clytemnestra is waiting to receive them. Before they go into the palace, they warn Elektra that she must remain silent and make no move which may undo all their plans.

Accompanied by servants bearing torches, Orestes and his companion enter the palace, while Elektra, in a torment of suspense, paces up and down like a wild animal. Suddenly she stops and exclaims, "The ax! I have forgotten to give them the ax!" Just at that moment a wild shriek comes from within the palace. It is Clytemnestra, and Elektra shouts exultantly, "Strike again!"

Chrysothemis and the servant maids, aroused by the clamor, rush out of the servants' quarters and Elektra greets them with insane laughter. One of the maids cries out in terror that Aegisthus is returning to the palace and they all run back into their quarters and Elektra is left alone to greet the queen's lover. As he strides through the gate, Elektra seizes a torch and bows before him with mock deference. He recognizes her as the woman he has always regarded as mad and looks at her suspiciously as she moves about him in a strange kind of slow, sinister dance. At the doorway of the palace, he hesitates, and asks in a shaking voice who are the shadowy figures he sees in the darkness. "They are those who wait to welcome you," replies Elektra.

He enters the palace and a moment later appears at a window, screaming for help. "Does no one hear me?" he shrieks. "Agamemnon hears you," shouts Elektra.

Chrysothemis rushes up to Elektra with the news that Clytemnestra and Aegisthus are dead and that the attendants and loyal followers of Orestes have conquered the palace. In a wild climax of madness, Elektra begins a weird, exotic dance. The courtyard fills with people and is ablaze with the light of torches, but Elektra is oblivious to them all. Her dance grows more wild and abandoned and suddenly she collapses in a lifeless heap. Her vow has been fulfilled—her life is over. Chrysothemis bends over her for a moment and then runs toward the palace doorway, shrieking, "Orestes, Orestes!" as the curtain falls.

Der Rosenkavalier

(The Cavalier of the Rose)

by RICHARD STRAUSS (1864-1949)

Three Acts. Libretto by von Hofmannsthal.
First produced in Dresden, 1911.

The Marschallin, Princess of Werdenberg	*Soprano*
Count Octavian, a young Viennese nobleman	*Mezzo-soprano*
Baron Ochs von Lerchenau	*Bass*
Von Faninal, a wealthy merchant	*Baritone*
Sophie, his daughter	*Soprano*
Marianne, Sophie's chaperone	*Soprano*
Valzacchi ⎫ blackmailers	*Tenor*
Annina ⎭	*Alto*
Major-domo to Faninal	*Tenor*

A young Negro servant, an attorney, a milliner, a vendor of animals, a widow with three daughters, a singer, a flutist, a head cook, a hairdresser, an innkeeper, a police commissioner, musicians, servants, coachmen, children, a doctor.

TIME: *Early Eighteenth Century.*
PLACE: *Vienna.*

ACT ONE

SCENE: *Boudoir of the Marschallin, Princess of Werden-berg.*

It is morning and sunlight streams through the window. In an alcove at the back of the room may be seen a large four-poster bed. The Marschallin is seated in a chair and her seventeen-year-old lover, Octavian, is kneeling at her feet, telling her how wonderful she is. A bell tinkles outside the door and Octavian hides behind a screen as the Marschallin's little Negro servant comes in with the Princess's morning chocolate. While he is arranging the breakfast tray on a table, Octavian dashes out, picks up his sword from a chair, and retires without being seen.

The servant departs and the Marschallin reproves Octavian for being so careless as to leave his sword in a lady's bedroom. They both speak of her absent husband, who is away on a prolonged hunting trip. When he returns, their little love affair will be over. The Marschallin, too, is conscious of the disparity in their ages and she hints that some day they will have to part, husband or no husband.

Soon there is a commotion in the next room and in a moment Baron Ochs forces himself in. He is a big pompous fellow and the Marschallin's cousin. Perhaps he can best be described as a country bumpkin aristocrat. Octavian, when he heard the Baron coming, slipped hastily into the dressing-room, where as a joke, he dresses up in the clothes of the Marschallin's maid-servant which he finds there. Baron Ochs has an eye for a pretty young girl and immediately starts flirting with Octavian when he emerges from the dressing-room and, playing the role of a servant, begins to serve the morning chocolate. The Marschallin is much amused at this and addresses the supposed maid as "Mariandel". Before the scene is over, the Baron has succeeded in making a date with "Mariandel".

Baron Ochs has come to ask the advice of his city cousin, the Marschallin, concerning his recent engagement to Sophie, daughter of the wealthy, middle-class Faninal, who has recently been made a baron for services rendered the state.

Baron Ochs needs some young nobleman to act as Rose

Cavalier, to convey a silver rose as a gift to the bride, a pretty custom observed by the nobility in Vienna at that time. The Marschallin assures him that she will help him out and secretly determines to make Octavian the baron's Rose Cavalier.

And now the Marschallin has to receive the crowd of people who have been waiting in the outer room. They all want something from her and it is her duty as wife of the Prince of Werdenberg to receive them and hear their requests. It is indeed a motley crowd which enters, including such varied characters as an animal dealer, a scholar, a milliner, an impoverished widow and her three daughters, a tenor, a flute player, and a couple of intriguing Italians. The Marschallin has seated herself before a dressing-table and her hairdresser goes to work on her as the various petitioners present their requests. The animal dealer wishes to sell her a dog or perhaps a pet monkey; the scholar wishes to dedicate a book to her; the milliner wants to sell her some hats; the widow, along with her three daughters, begs for some financial assistance in the name of her dear departed husband; the tenor and the flute player perform a showy aria, *"Di rigori armato il seno"* ("From harshness the armed soul"), hoping to secure the Marschallin as patroness. Most important, the two blackmailers, Valzacchi and Annina, bring her a copy of a local scandal sheet and intimate that their services are available for any kind of intrigue or spying.

The Marschallin is indifferent to their wiles, but not so Baron Ochs. He is quite willing to employ them and the first commission he gives them is to spy on the supposed maid, Mariandel.

Soon everyone is dismissed and the Marschallin, left alone, looks into her mirror which tells her that she is getting older, *"Kann ich mich auch"* ("I can remember in my youth").

So when the young Octavian returns once more (and once more dressed in proper masculine attire) she bids him a fond but firm farewell. There is a tone of melancholy throughout this closing scene, giving a sense of seriousness and sadness to follow the boisterous comedy which has preceded.

ACT TWO

SCENE: *A large room in the house of Faninal.*

This is the day when Faninal's daughter, Sophie, is to receive the silver rose from her fiancé, whom she has never seen, Baron Ochs. Coming at last into such close touch with the nobility, the wealthy and snobbish Faninal is in great excitement, but his major-domo instructs him that the father is never allowed to be present at the ceremony of the presentation of the rose. Accordingly, he retires, leaving his daughter and her chaperone, Marianne, to greet the messenger who is to bring the rose. This Cavalier of the Rose is, of course, young Count Octavian and he enters with great ceremony. Taking the silver rose from a jewel case held by a footman, he presents it to Sophie. She exclaims at its beauty and says that it is like a flower from Heaven. The footman hands the jewel case to Sophie's duenna, Marianne, who takes the rose from Sophie and replaces it in the case. The formalities having been complied with, the servants withdraw.

It is obvious that the two young people have fallen in love at first sight, *"Wo war ich schon einmal"* ("Where did I taste of old"). Their first interview is full of the charming embarrassment of youth but the charm quickly disappears when Sophie's father, Faninal, brings in Baron Ochs. This loutish nobleman behaves so badly and is so fat and ugly as compared with the slim and youthful Octavian that Sophie can barely stand the sight of him and she shrinks from his advances. Baron Ochs is rather more pleased than otherwise with this behavior and he leaves the two young people alone while he goes off to discuss business with his future father-in-law. Sophie now says she will never marry the Baron, and she and Octavian declare their love for each other and fall into each other's arms, *"Für uns zwei"* ("One together").

Their embrace is suddenly interrupted by a man and woman who come out from an alcove. They are Valzacchi and Annina, the two adventurers, and they have been in the alcove spying on the young lovers. They seize Sophie and Octavian and start screaming for the Baron. When Ochs enters, he takes in the scene at a glance and seems quite complacent about it. He compliments Octavian on his youthful spirit, which he says, reminds him of his own early days. Even when Octavian tells him that Sophie will not marry him, he regards this as a bit of youthful bravado. But when he tries to lead Sophie into the next room to sign the marriage contract, Octavian draws his sword and blocks his way.

The astonished Baron puts his fingers to his mouth and whistles for his servants. When they come trooping in, the Baron regains his courage and draws his own sword. But before he can do more than make an awkward motion, Octavian rushes at him and wounds him slightly in the arm. Ochs bellows that he has been murdered and collapses on a sofa. In addition to the Baron's servants, the servants of Faninal also rush in and add to the commotion. The climax comes when Faninal himself comes in. When he learns that Sophie and Octavian were surprised in an embrace, he is in despair for he has had his heart set on his daughter's marrying into the aristocracy.

Sophie declares that not under any circumstances will she marry Baron Ochs. Faninal retorts that he will force her to marry him—either that or back to the convent.

And now a doctor has arrived and announces that the Baron's wound is a mere pin-prick. The excited servants are herded out of the room, Octavian whispers a fond farewell to Sophie and bids her be of good courage, Marianne leads Sophie from the room as Octavian leaves, and Faninal is left alone with the Baron. The fawning Faninal tries to embrace the Baron which only causes that nobleman to howl with pain. He demands wine and Faninal departs more frustrated than ever. A footman enters and serves the Baron with wine and then at last the Baron is alone and the room is quiet after all the noisy hubbub.

The Baron sips his wine and begins to feel better. After a few minutes, the spy Annina slips quietly into the room and hands the Baron a note from "Mariandel." The note informs Ochs that his loving Mariandel is dying to meet him again. Completely revived by this bit of news, and now in excellent spirits, the Baron jumps up from his bed of pain and waltzes gaily around the room as the curtain falls.

ACT THREE

SCENE: *A dingy private room in a questionable inn.*

Here the Baron expects to keep his rendezvous with the
pretty little serving maid he was flirting with in the first
act. Little does he suspect that the maid is really young
Count Octavian in disguise and that he himself is being
made the victim of a plot. The whole affair is being en-
gineered by the unscrupulous pair, Valzacchi and Annina,
now in the employ of Octavian, who is determined to get
rid of the objectionable Baron so that he himself can marry
Sophie. When the curtain rises, Valzacchi, using trap doors,
false windows, candles, and all sorts of tricks, is instructing
his assistants in what they are to do. Soon Baron Ochs
enters, with Octavian on his arm, only Octavian is dressed
again as the little maid-servant.

A supper table is ready and a servant enters bringing
food and wine. Ochs urges Mariandel to have a glass of
wine but she answers shyly that she does not drink wine.
She is very coy and flutters about the room to the great annoyance of the amorous Baron. His little supper party is
not going well at all. There are too many candles and he
puts some of them out. And then there is the sound of a
small orchestra playing and he orders them to stop as he
declares he will not pay the bill. He thinks the room is too
warm and takes off his wig and urges Mariandel to loosen
her bodice.

The Baron tries to make some progress with his flirtation
but heads keep popping out of trap doors and false windows and the poor Baron grows more and more nervous.
The climax of his misery seems to be reached when Annina
enters and announces that she is the Baron's deserted wife.
To prove her claim, she brings along four children who
insist on calling the Baron "Papa." A police officer is called
in and, among other things, wants to know who Mariandel
is. Ochs says in desperation that she is his fiancée, the
daughter of Faninal, and, just at that unhappy moment, in
walk Faninal and Sophie.

To make matters worse, Mariandel goes into the bedroom which adjoins the supper room and apparently starts

taking her clothes off as various articles of feminine apparel come flying through the door.

It is time to end the comedy. The Marschallin comes in and sets all to rights by appeasing the police officer and then advising Baron Ochs that he can best serve himself by leaving town and forgetting all about Sophie.

And so we come to what is really the musical and emotional climax of the opera, a trio in which Sophie, Octavian (now properly dressed in male attire), and the Marschallin sing of their own individual feelings, *"Hab' mir's gelobt ihn lieb zu haben"* ("I made a vow to love him rightly"). The Marschallin renounces all her interest in the young Octavian in favor of the girl she knows he loves; Octavian is head over heels in love with Sophie, but still is conscious of the pain he is causing the Marschallin, and Sophie, who does not quite understand all this, sings simply of her love for Octavian. The Marschallin and Faninal give the two young people their blessing and all leave the inn.

The stage is dark and still for a moment, after all the excitement, and then the little black servant of the Marschallin returns, picks up Sophie's handkerchief from the floor where she dropped it and slips out once more as the curtain falls.

Mignon

by AMBROISE THOMAS (1811–1896)

Three Acts. Libretto by Barbier and Carré, based on Goethe's *Wilhelm Meister*.
First produced in Paris, 1866.

Mignon, a young gypsy girl	*Mezzo-soprano*
Lothario, an aged wandering minstrel	*Bass*
Wilhelm Meister, a young student	*Tenor*
Frédéric, another student	*Contralto*
Philine, an actress	*Soprano*
Laërte, an actor	*Tenor*
Jarno, a gypsy	*Bass*
Antonio, a servant	*Bass*

TIME: *Eighteenth Century.*
PLACE: *Germany and Italy.*

ACT ONE

SCENE: *Courtyard of an inn.*

On the left of the stage, the inn itself with its balcony and a flight of steps leading up to it. A crowd of jolly citizens is seated at tables in the yard singing and drinking. They stop while the aged Lothario, a tattered, white-haired, half-crazed old man, who carries a small harp, sings of his lonely life wandering about and searching for his long-lost daughter, *"Fugitif et tremblant"* ("Fugitive and trembling"). A group of gypsies, headed by a rough, bearded man named Jarno, comes into the courtyard to entertain the crowd, and while they dance to the accompaniment of fiddle and tambourines, two members of a traveling group of actors watch and make comments from the inn's balcony. These are Philine, the leading lady of the troupe, and Laërte, the leading man.

Now Jarno, the gruff leader of the gypsies, promises to make a young girl-gypsy dance her egg-dance for the crowd, and he drags a little waif, named Mignon, from the gypsy cart. Mignon refuses to perform, and is only saved from a beating at the hands of Jarno by Philine's tossing him some money and by the sudden appearance of the handsome and wealthy student, Wilhelm Meister, who threatens Jarno with a pistol.

The excitement over and the crowd having departed, Laërte introduces himself to Wilhelm and, a short while later, also introduces his companion, Philine, who it is clear, has taken quite a fancy to Wilhelm. After a bit of coquettish flirting, Philine departs on the arm of Laërte, and little Mignon comes forward to thank Wilhelm for having saved her.

In answer to his questions as to who she is, she answers vaguely but very beautifully in the celebrated aria, *"Connais-tu le pays"* ("Do you know the land?"), telling him all she recalls of her childhood is a beautiful country with orange trees and blue skies and a beautiful house. Very much touched, Wilhelm goes off with Jarno to arrange to purchase the freedom of the little gypsy, and the aged Lothario comes in to say he must again leave on his wanderings. Mignon plays Lothario's harp as the two join in a duet, for there seems to be a mysterious affinity between the girl and the old man that neither of them quite understands, *"Légères hirondelles"* ("Oh! swallows, gay and blithe").

Now Philine comes back, this time with another beau, the young dandy, Frédéric. She reads an invitation for the troupe of actors to perform at a neighboring castle belonging to Frédéric's uncle, and inflames the jealousy of Frédéric by inviting Wilhelm to join them. Mignon asks to accompany Wilhelm as a servant wherever he may go and, after first refusing, he finally agrees. The stage fills again with villagers, gypsies, and the actor troupe; and the curtain goes down on a general chorus of jollification as the actors depart.

ACT TWO

SCENE ONE: *A boudoir in the castle.*

Before the curtain goes up on the second act, the orchestra plays the popular and tuneful *"Gavotte"* as a prelude. On its closing strains, the rising curtain discloses the actress Philine in the elegant dressing room provided by the owner of the castle, and immediately her fellow-trouper, Laërte, enters and comments on the luxury. And, when Wilhelm Meister comes in, Laërte informs him that the play tonight will be *A Midsummer Night's Dream* by—as Laërte puts it—"someone called Shakespeare, really a pretty good poet."

Now Wilhelm calls in Mignon, who is dressed as a page, and who watches jealously as Philine makes herself up and carries on a flirtation with Wilhelm. Left alone, Mignon goes to the dressing table and starts to experiment with the make-up as she sings the charming *"Styrienne"*—*"Je connais un pauvre enfant"* ("I know a poor child"), finally going off into the next room to dress herself in one of Philine's pretty costumes. Then Frédéric, Philine's painfully youthful admirer, enters through the window and, finding no one there, sings a song to the absent actress—the charming little *"Gavotte"*—*"Me voici dans son boudoir"* ("Here I am in her bedroom"), which was heard as the prelude to the act. And when Wilhelm returns to the dressing room, the rash young Frédéric draws his sword and insists on a duel with his much taller rival.

But Mignon, now in a pretty white dress with rosettes, rushes in to save (as she thinks) Wilhelm. Enormously amused, Frédéric puts up his sword and leaves the room. Wilhelm, seeing Mignon for the first time as a grown woman tells her that she no longer can travel with him as his servant. He bids her farewell in the tender melody, *"Adieu, Mignon"* ("Farewell, Mignon"). She, for her part, refuses his offer of money and says that she will go back to being a gypsy once more.

But Philine returns at this moment (together with Frédéric) and sarcastically compliments Mignon on her new-found finery. In a burst of angry tears, Mignon tears the rosettes from the dress and rushes off again into the other room. "My word!" comments Philine, "it looks as if the child is jealous of me!" "Jealous," repeats Wilhelm. It is the first time it has occurred to the young man that Mignon may be in love with him. And as they all leave the scene, Mignon once more comes in from the other room dressed in her first-act gypsy clothes. "That Philine!" she cries. "I hate her!"

SCENE TWO: *The park of the castle.*

On the right-hand side of the stage is the conservatory where our company of actors is giving its performance for the local aristocracy. At frequent intervals we hear sounds of music and applause. To the left, is a lake. In the darkness, Mignon comes in, desperate now with jealousy, for she believes that Wilhelm and Philine love each other. In dramatic fashion, she sings of her own misfortunes and is about to fling herself into the water when she hears the harp of the old wandering minstrel, Lothario. The young girl and the old man have a duet, *"Pauvre enfant! Pauvre créature"* ("Poor child, poor creature"), in which they recount their sorrows—and once more we hear applause from inside the conservatory. "Ah," cries Mignon, "may God burn that palace down." The poor, half-crazed Lothario believes Mignon means this literally and wanders off to accomplish the deed.

And now, the park fills with the guests who have applauded Philine's performance as Titania in *A Midsummer*

Night's Dream. Last of all comes Philine herself, still costumed as Titania, the fairy queen, and she sings the brilliant coloratura polonaise, *"Je suis Titania"* ("I am Titania").

At its conclusion, the aged Lothario slips in and whispers to Mignon that she has been avenged—"The palace is on fire!" Then Philine, wishing to humiliate Mignon, tells her to go into the conservatory and get a bouquet of flowers she has left there. Philine, of course, does not know of the danger but Mignon does. Nevertheless, she obeys.

But no sooner has the girl gone on this errand, than Laërte rushes in to announce that the whole place is in flames. There is great excitement. Flames appear in the conservatory and Wilhelm rushes in to save Mignon. There is a huge crash, but Wilhelm comes running out in time, Mignon unconscious but safe in his arms. Lotharia, who has caused the fire, is quite unaware of what he has done and continues singing of his long-lost child—and Mignon lies unconscious, clutching the bouquet she had gone to fetch for her rival.

ACT THREE

SCENE: *A hall in an Italian palace.*

All the characters in the story are now in Italy. Off-stage, a chorus sings sweetly about the lovely countryside. Mignon (still not recovered from her adventure in the burning conservatory in the Second Act) lies in another room asleep and Lothario, the aged wanderer, sings her a lullaby.

Wilhelm Meister now comes in to tell Lothario that her new surroundings seem to have helped poor Mignon. He intends to buy this palace for her, once the palace of the Cipriani. At the word "Cipriani", the light of understanding comes to the old man's eyes, and he goes off to inspect the palace.

Left alone, Wilhelm sings of his love for the little waif, Mignon, *"Elle ne croyait pas"* ("Ah! little thought poor Mignon"). Soon after this, Mignon comes in, and learns that Wilhelm does not love Philine (as she had thought) but herself. But at that moment the voice of Philine is heard off-stage singing phrases from the aria *"Je suis Titania"*. Shocked by the presence of the woman she has learned to hate, Mignon declares that she cannot accept Wilhelm's love, that she can love only old Lothario.

But now, Lothario comes in once more, a completely changed man. He has been brought to a realization of his own identity by finding himself in his old surroundings, for this palace, the palace of the Cipriani, is his home. And now he is clothed in rich black velvet, like the aristocrat he is, and he brings a casket for Mignon to open, which contains a scarf and a bracelet that once belonged to his long-lost child, named Sperata. And, when he utters that name—"Sperata"—Mignon also begins to recollect her past, for it was her own name once upon a time. She takes a prayer book from the casket, starts to read a prayer to the Virgin that she finds in it and then, dropping the book, continues the prayer from memory. Moved by a sudden impulse, Mignon rushes from the room and returns in a moment crying "I have seen it—the portrait of my mother!"

Now, Lothario knows that she is indeed his long-lost daughter, and Mignon, Wilhelm, and the newly recovered Marquis Cipriani join in a beautiful trio, *"Mignon! Wilhelm! Salut à vous"* ("Mignon, Wilhelm, I greet you"), Mignon (or Sperata, as we should now call her) and Wilhelm embracing each other fondly and Lothario (Marquis Cipriani) giving them his paternal blessing.

Rigoletto

by GIUSEPPE VERDI (1813–1901)

Four Acts. Libretto by Piave, based on Hugo's *The King Amuses Himself*.
First produced in Venice, 1851.

The Duke of Mantua	*Tenor*
Rigoletto, his court jester	*Baritone*
Gilda, Rigoletto's daughter	*Soprano*
Sparafucile, a professional assassin	*Bass*
Maddalena, his sister	*Contralto*

Borsa		*Tenor*
Count Monterone	Members of the	*Baritone*
Count Ceprano	Ducal court	*Bass*
Countess Ceprano		*Mezzo-soprano*
Giovanna, Gilda's nurse		*Mezzo-soprano*

Ladies and gentlemen of the court, servants.

TIME: *Sixteenth Century.*
PLACE: *Mantua, Italy.*

ACT ONE

SCENE: *Ballroom in the Ducal Palace.*

A gay party is in progress, with everyone dancing and the Duke looking on. In a spirited aria, the Duke tells one of the courtiers—Borsa—that he finds *every* woman attractive. This is the famous *"Questa o quella"* ("Mid the gay throng"), which at once sets the character of the Duke as a gay trifler and deceiver.

The Duke joins the dancing with the Countess Ceprano with whom he is carrying on a flirtation, even though the jealous Count Ceprano is watching helplessly, furiously. Now the Duke has a hunchbacked court jester, named Rigoletto, and Rigoletto takes this occasion to taunt Ceprano, thinking to ingratiate himself still further with the Duke. It is not the first time Rigoletto has acted this way and, in a brief choral number, *"Che festa"* ("What sport"), the courtiers threaten vengeance on him. But Rigoletto only laughs at them, thinking himself quite safe in the all-powerful protection of the Duke.

The dancing begins again, but suddenly a white-haired gentleman of great dignity—the Count Monterone—appears on the scene. He denounces the Duke for that nobleman's behavior to his daughter, and Rigoletto, again in a rudely taunting manner answers for his master. Monterone, however, is not like the other courtiers. He turns upon his tormentor and utters a great curse upon the Duke and upon his jester. The Duke calmly orders the old man to be arrested, but the superstitious Rigoletto begs him to take back his curse. Instead, just as he is led off, Monterone repeats the curse, making it still stronger, and as the curtain goes down, Rigoletto quakes and cowers in fear.

ACT TWO

SCENE: *Outside Rigoletto's home.*

The stage is divided into two parts by the wall of Rigoletto's garden, with the street leading to his doorway on one side and the garden itself, including a stairway leading into an upper story of the house, on the other.

Rigoletto is in a black mood after the curse has been laid on him in the first act. He is on his way home when he is accosted by a tall and sinister figure in a long cloak. This is Sparafucile, an innkeeper by trade, who conducts a business as a professional assassin on the side. In this latter capacity he offers his services to the court jester, who notes his name and decides to use those services should occasion demand. When Sparafucile has gone on his way, Rigoletto sings his aria, *"Pari siamo"* ("We are equals, the assassin and I"), in which he rails bitterly against the Duke and the courtiers for his own low moral estate.

There is only one sacred thing in Rigoletto's life—his love for his daughter Gilda. When Gilda greets him as he enters his garden, there follows a long and lovely duet, *"Figlia!" "Mio padre!"* ("My daughter!" "My father!"). He expresses his love for his daughter and his adoration of the memory of her mother, who had died shortly after Gilda was born—*"Deh non parlare"* ("Speak not of one").

Rigoletto has to leave again, but before he goes he instructs Giovanna, Gilda's nurse, to let no one on any account enter the house. Giovanna, unfortunately, is not a very strong character. Even while Rigoletto is speaking, the Duke of Mantua, disguised as a student, slips into the garden behind the hunchback and with a bribe to the nurse, manages to stay hidden until Rigoletto finally leaves.

And now follows another duet, *"E il sol dell'anima"* ("Love is the sun"), this time between the Duke and Gilda, a duet in which he completely wins her heart. He tells her he is a humble student named Gaultier Maldé.

When he leaves her at last, promising to return, Gilda murmurs his name ecstatically—"Gaultier Maldé!"—and sings the renowned coloratura aria, *"Caro nome"* ("Dearest name"). She slowly mounts the steps into the house and the last notes are sung as she passes through the doorway.

The plot of the courtiers against Rigoletto now begins to take shape. It is twilight and a group of them slip quietly into the street outside the garden wall. They have heard of the lovely Gilda and, thinking her to be Rigoletto's sweetheart, they are planning to kidnap her to teach the old man a lesson.

Before they can take any action, Rigoletto himself appears, returning home. It happens that the palace of the Ceprano family is next door to Rigoletto's modest dwelling and a fiendish scheme occurs to the conspirators—they will make Rigoletto assist in the kidnapping!

So they tell him that they are planning to kidnap the Countess Ceprano for the Duke, and Rigoletto promises to join them. They are all masked, so he has no objection to putting on a mask, and hardly notices that after they have done so, they swiftly tie a blindfold over the mask. "How dark it is!" he says, innocently.

They guide Rigoletto to the wall, and place a ladder against it. Rigoletto thinks the wall is part of the Ceprano palace and does not suspect it is his own house. He holds the ladder while the conspirators climb up, and then in a moment return with their victim. After a moment he hears the voice of Gilda from a distance, calling for help. He tears the blindfold and mask from his face and realizes with horror what has happened. He searches the house and garden for Gilda, in vain, and then cries out, *"Ah, la maledizione!"* ("The curse!").

ACT THREE

SCENE: *A room in the Ducal palace.*

It is the same evening. The Duke returned to Rigoletto's home but found it deserted. Now he is back at the palace. He expresses his love and compassion for the girl in the aria, *"Parmi veder"* ("Each tear that falls").

Now his courtiers come in and, in a jolly, but somehow sinister, chorus relate their escapade, saying how, with Rigoletto's help, they kidnapped Gilda and brought her to the Duke's palace—*"Scorrendo uniti"* ("As we with glee").

The Duke rushes off to see her—*"Possente amor"* ("To her I love")—and Rigoletto enters: He who has so often laughed at the misery of others is now himself a pathetic object.

At first he tries to act his role of court-jester, but there is a tone in his voice which is anything but jesting, for he is really trying to find out from the courtiers what has happened to his beloved daughter. From the remarks of a page, who enters inquiring after the Duke, Rigoletto begins to suspect the truth. Desperately, he tries to get into the Duke's room, but is held back forcefully by the courtiers, who only now learn that it is his daughter, not his sweetheart, whom they have kidnapped. Finally Rigoletto turns on them and sings his great accusing aria, *"Cortigiani, vil razza dannata"* ("Vile race of courtiers").

Now Gilda rushes into the room and her father embraces her joyously. The courtiers leave them alone and Gilda sadly tells her father of her shame and humiliation, *"Tutte le festa al tempio"* ("Whenever I went to church"). Rigoletto consoles her tenderly and promises to take her away from Mantua to some place where they can begin life anew.

But an ominous procession interrupts them. Count Monterone, who cursed the Duke and Rigoletto, is being led through the hall to his execution. His curse, he says, has been in vain, for the Duke is still happy. Eagerly Rigoletto promises the Count vengeance, for both of them. But Gilda, who loves the Duke, begs her father to relent. It is in vain. Rigoletto is bound to gain his vengeance, and as the curtain falls, he repeats his oath.

ACT FOUR

SCENE: *An inn on the outskirts of the city.*

This is the spot where Sparafucile, the assassin, dispatches his victims. A wall divides the stage in two. On the right hand side of the stage is a road, and on the left hand side (within the wall), is the inn—thus the audience sees what is going on inside the inn as well as what happens on the road outside.

Rigoletto has hired Sparafucile to murder the Duke, who has been lured to the inn in quest of another lovely woman—in this case Maddalena, the sister of Sparafucile. Rigoletto has come to the outside of the inn, accompanied by Gilda, and he feels that his hour of vengeance is near. A storm is brewing and the night is dark. The Duke comes to the inn, enters and immediately orders wine. Then he sings the most famous melody in the opera, *"La donna è mobile"* ("Woman is fickle").

Outside, Sparafucile and Rigoletto meet briefly and now Maddalena, Sparafucile's sister, appears at the inn. The Duke begins at once to make love to her—as he does to all women—and very soon we hear the familiar quartet, *"Bella figlia dell' amore"* ("Fairest daughter of the graces"), in which the Duke sings his smooth, flattering melody, Maddalena answers coquettishly, Rigoletto bids his daughter sternly to forget about her lover, and Gilda sings despairingly of that lover's falseness. The quartet is sung by the Duke and Maddalena inside the tavern, and Rigoletto and his daughter on the road outside.

Having proved to his daughter that her lover is faithless and fickle, Rigoletto orders her to don boy's clothing and ride to Verona, where he will meet her. She leaves, and Rigoletto and Sparafucile confer once more about the coming murder. Now that his victim is safely within the inn, Rigoletto pays Sparafucile half the fee and tells him he will return at midnight to claim the body and pay the balance.

The night grows darker and the Duke tells Sparafucile he has decided to spend the night at the inn and retires to a room upstairs. But Maddalena, Sparafucile's sister, who has been used to bait the trap, now has fallen under the spell of the amorous Duke and she begs her brother to spare his life. But Sparafucile has made a bargain and intends to keep it. Finally Maddalena persuades him to kill the first stranger who knocks at the inn door and to substitute the body for that of the Duke.

In the meantime, Gilda, wearing a man's costume with boots and spurs, has returned to the road outside the inn and she hears this bargain being made and determines to sacrifice her life for that of her faithless lover. The storm grows in violence as a clock strikes midnight.

Gilda knocks at the inn door and asks for lodging for the night. The door is opened and as she steps inside, she is stabbed and falls to the ground.

And so, when Rigoletto returns, the assassin hands him his own daughter's body conveniently tied up in a sack. But just as Rigoletto is about to drag off the sack and dump it into the river, he hears the voice of the Duke in his room singing again, *"La donna è mobile"*.

Both mystified and horrified, he tears open the sack to discover his dying daughter. She has still enough breath to sing her final farewell to earth, *"Lassu in cielo"* ("In heaven above"). As she dies, Rigoletto realizes that the old Count Monterone's curse has really found its target. Once more he cries, *"Ah, la maledizione!"*, and he throws himself in anguish over the body of his daughter.

Il Trovatore

(The Troubador)

by GIUSEPPE VERDI (1813–1901)

Four Acts. Libretto by Commarano, based on drama by
Gutiérrez.
First produced in Rome, 1853.

Leonora, a lady of the court of Aragon	*Soprano*
Manrico, a soldier in the army of Biscay	*Tenor*
Count di Luna, a nobleman of Aragon	*Baritone*
Azucena, a gypsy woman	*Mezzo-soprano*
Ferrando, captain of the guard	*Bass*
Inez, companion to Leonora	*Soprano*
Ruiz, lieutenant to Manrico	*Tenor*

Soldiers, gypsies, nuns, attendants.

TIME: *Fifteenth Century.*
PLACE: *Aragon and Biscay in Spain.*

ACT ONE

SCENE ONE: *A vestibule in the Aliaferia Palace.*

A fierce civil war is being fought between the two princi-
palities of Biscay and Aragon. The Queen of Aragon is in
residence in the palace of Aliaferia and it is there that the
first act takes place. The first scene is in the murky courtyard of the palace where the night guard is on duty. A fire
in the center of the stage throws great weird shadows
against the grim stone walls. Count di Luna is military governor of the palace, and in this melodramatic setting we
hear his captain, Ferrando, tell the guard an old story about
the di Luna family, *"Abbietta zingara"* ("Sat there a gypsy
hag").

Years before, when the present Count was but a child, a
gypsy woman had been accused of having bewitched his
brother (who was then a baby) and the gypsy was condemned to be burned at the stake. This woman had a

daughter who was determined to avenge her mother's death. The baby mysteriously disappeared and was never heard of again. Absolutely nothing is known of its fate, but among the charred embers about the stake where the witch-woman was burned were discovered the bones of a small child, presumably the infant son of the di Luna family. The soldiers comment in horror at this story, a bell tolls midnight, and the curtain falls.

SCENE TWO: *A garden in the Aliaferia Palace.*

It is still night. We hear the heroine of the story, Leonora, one of the ladies of the court, tell her companion, Inez, of her love for a soldier. She has seen him at a tournament and all she knows about him is that he is known as *"Il Trova-tore"* ("The Troubador"), and that he comes to the palace at night to serenade her. She sings of him in a melody of wistful tenderness, *"Tacea la notte placida"* ("The night, calm and peaceful").

The ladies go into the palace just as Count di Luna, himself bent on serenading the lovely Leonora, comes into the garden. But he has barely taken his station beneath her window when the mysterious troubador appears on the same errand. The Count hides and listens to the song of the Trou-bador, *"Deserto sulla terra"* ("Alone on the earth"), which is so effective that Leonora comes out to greet her lover. She is met by the Count, who is in a fine rage. Manrico (the Troubador) defies him, and raises the visor of his helmet, revealing that he is an enemy knight in the service of Biscay. Unable to restrain their jealous passions, the two men rush at one another with drawn swords and the curtain falls swiftly as the duel is in progress.

ACT TWO

SCENE ONE: *A gypsy camp in the mountains of Biscay.*

Manrico wins the duel in which he and Count di Luna were engaged when the curtain fell on the first act, but having his rival at his mercy, he spares his life. Shortly after that, another battle in the war between Biscay and Aragon takes place and Manrico is seriously wounded. Rescued by Azucena, the gypsy woman who has reared him since earliest childhood, Manrico has been taken to a gypsy camp in the mountains of Biscay and there he has slowly regained his health.

This is the situation when the curtain rises on the second act. Azucena is crouching before a fire and Manrico is lying on a couch. It is early dawn and the gypsies begin moving about to begin their day's activities. Some of the men go to their forges and in a few minutes we hear the well-known *"Zingarella"* ("Anvil Chorus") sung by the gypsies as they pound on their anvils.

The gypsy woman, Azucena, still sits brooding over the embers of the fire and when the gypsies finish their chorus, she sings again of the flames that consumed her mother's body many years before. This is the famous aria, *"Stride la vampa"* ("Fierce flames are soaring"). This, of course, is the same incident Ferrando has told us about in the first scene, and after the other gypsies have left, Azucena tells Manrico (who regards her as his mother) the rest of the tale. She tells of how she had stolen the infant child of the di Lunas, intending to throw it into the fire, but she now confesses that in her half-crazed condition she had mistakenly thrown her *own* son into the flames. "Then tell me," cries Manrico, "am I not your son?"

She insists that he is her son and reminds him of all the love and care she has bestowed on him and how it was she who had found his wounded body on the battlefield and had brought him to the gypsy camp and nursed him back to health and strength.

Now Manrico has a story to tell. In the tenor aria. *"Mal reggendo all 'aspro assalto"* ("At my mercy lay the foe"), he relates how he had had Count di Luna lying wounded at his feet, but some strange mysterious force seemed to hold back his arm and he had spared the life of his rival. Azucena is horrified at this, and warns Manrico never again to permit this deadly enemy to escape.

But now Manrico is again called into battle—this time by Ruiz, one of his soldiers, who brings orders for Manrico to defend the palace of Castellor. The message also tells him that Leonora, believing Manrico to have been killed in battle, is about to become a nun and enter a convent. The curtain falls as Manrico rushes off to rescue Leonora and to take his place with the army once more.

SCENE TWO: *The cloister of a convent near Castellor.*

Count di Luna and a troop of his soldiers are waiting outside the convent where Leonora is about to become a nun, planning to abduct her. He places his men in readiness nearby and while he waits, sings the aria *"Il Balen"* ("Her bright smile").

The voices of the nuns can be heard singing within the convent before they come out to lead Leonora to the chapel to take her vows. And as she bids farewell to her friend Inez, di Luna, at the head of his men, rushes forward to seize her.

But again Leonora is saved by the arrival of Manrico, accompanied by soldiers from the army of Biscay, *"Per me ora fatal"* ("O, fatal hour"). The conflict is a fierce one, but Manrico manages to fight his way to Leonora and carries her away to safety as the soldiers of the rivals turn the peaceful cloister into a bloody battlefield and once more the curtain falls to the sound of clashing arms.

ACT THREE

SCENE ONE: *The camp of Count di Luna.*

After the fight that closed the preceding act, Manrico took his beloved Leonora with him to the fortress Castellor, where he is now being besieged by the forces of the Count di Luna.

The scene opens with the military march known as *"Bugles and Trumpets"* sung by di Luna's men. The Count himself, however, is in a very bad humor, and presently the gypsy Azucena, who has been lurking near the camp, is brought in to him a prisoner.

In a dramatic scene, he questions the old woman, and he begins to suspect that this is the gypsy who threw the baby into the flames when her mother was being burned at the stake. His old retainer, Ferrando, corroborates the suspicions of the Count, and although Azucena violently denies all knowledge of the crime, *"Giorni poveri"* ("I was poor, yet uncomplaining"), she is treated very roughly, and when she calls on the name of Manrico for help, the Count cries out, "So you are the mother of Manrico! Through you, I'll have revenge!"

SCENE TWO: *A chamber in the castle of Castellor.*

Under the impression that the attack is not to come until the next morning, Manrico is preparing to marry Leonora at once. She is scarcely in the mood of an expectant bride, for the violence of the events around her has horrified her. But Manrico, in a soothing melody, reassures her. It is the aria, *"Amor, sublime amore"* ("Love, divine love"), and now the tones of the organ in the chapel are heard and the marriage ceremony is about to begin.

But suddenly Ruiz, Manrico's lieutenant rushes in. "Manrico," he shouts. "They have captured the gypsy and are leading her to the stake." Hastily Manrico tells Leonora that his mother is in danger and he orders an immediate attack. He vows to rescue Azucena and he sings his very dramatic aria, *"Di quella pira"* ("Tremble, ye tyrants"). Bidding a hasty but passionate farewell to Leonora, he rushes off at the head of his men to rescue Azucena.

ACT FOUR

SCENE ONE: *Battlements of the Aliaferia Palace.*

On one side we see the chapel—on the other, the ominous high walls of the prison rise grimly. Manrico's sortie to rescue Azucena was unsuccessful, he was captured and he and Azucena are now prisoners in Count di Luna's castle. Alone, to this gloomy spot, comes Leonora—to be near her doomed lover—and she sings her plaintive air, *"D'amor sull'ali rosee"* ("On rosy wings of love"), in which she bids the breezes never to let Manrico know that she has come to offer herself to the Count di Luna in return for her lover's life.

We hear the ominous tones of the death bell, and in the chapel the priests intone the prayer for those about to die. It is the beginning of the famous *"Miserere"*. Above the prayer, we hear the voice of Leonora expressing the horror and desolation that these words strike in her heart, and off-stage, from the prison window, comes floating the farewell plaint of Manrico, the troubador, accompanying himself on his lyre, *"Ah, che la morte"* ("Ah, that death"). The grim, determined rhythms of the orchestra, the minor-keyed chanting of the priests, the wild despairing phrases of Leonora, and the calm, resigned farewells of Manrico all combine together to create one of the greatest and most popular ensembles in all opera.

And now the Count di Luna comes in and orders Manrico to be beheaded at dawn, while Azucena is to be burned at the stake. He is suddenly confronted by Leonora, who begs for the life of her lover. When she offers herself in exchange for her lover's freedom, *"Mire di acerbe"* ("Witness my tears of agony"), di Luna finally agrees. She begs to be allowed to go to Manrico's cell and notify him of his release. Di Luna consents, but before they enter the palace together, Leonora, unseen by di Luna, drinks some poison she has concealed in a ring which she is wearing—for she would rather die than be wed to the hated di Luna.

SCENE TWO: *In the prison tower.*

Azucena lies on a couch in the gloomy dungeon she shares with Manrico. Suffering has unhinged her mind and she is haunted by the memory of her mother's death. To comfort her, Manrico murmurs that he is taking her back to freedom in the mountains of Biscay. This is the beautiful duet. *"Ai nostri monti"* ("Home to our mountains").

And now Leonora enters the prison cell, telling Manrico he is free and must fly at once. She cannot, however, go with him, and Manrico's suspicions are aroused as to how she has purchased his freedom. But the poison Leonora has taken begins to take effect. She tells Manrico that she is dying, and as she sinks into his arms, Count di Luna enters. He sees what has happened and immediately orders Manrico off to the executioner's block. He then drags the half-unconscious Azucena to the window to witness the execution. A gleam of wild triumph lights the face of Azucena and she laughs madly, crying, *"Egli era tuo fratello!"* ("He was your brother!"). Knowing that her mother is at last avenged, Azucena falls lifeless to the ground.

La Traviata

(The Strayed One)

by GIUSEPPE VERDI (1813–1901)

Four Acts. Libretto by Piave, based on Dumas' *The Lady of the Camellias.*
First produced in Venice, 1853.

Violetta Valery, a courtesan	*Soprano*
Alfredo Germont, a young gentleman	*Tenor*
Giorgio Germont, his father	*Baritone*
Flora Bervoix, friend of Violetta	*Mezzo-soprano*
Annina, Violetta's maid	*Mezzo-soprano*
Dr. Grenvil, Violetta's physician	*Bass*
Baron Douphol	*Baritone*
Marquis d'Obigny	*Bass*
Gastone, Viscount of Letorières	*Tenor*

TIME: *About 1850.*
PLACE: *In and near Paris.*

ACT ONE

SCENE: *The salon of Violetta's house in Paris.*

When the curtain rises, a gay party is in progress in the luxurious apartment of Violetta Valery, a reigning beauty of Paris in the 1830's. Among the party we meet several people who will play an important part in the story, including Flora Bervoix, Violetta's closest friend, Baron Douphol, her jealous admirer, and Dr. Grenvil, her physician, and a young man from the country who has recently come to Paris, named Alfredo Germont.

The guests greet the hostess, seat themselves at tables, and are served food and wine, and shortly afterwards the young man from the country is prevailed upon to sing a rousing drinking song, *"Libiamo, libiamo"* ("Let us drink"), and soon the hostess and all the guests join him in the song. It expresses the spirit of Violetta's whole life —let us drink and be merry.

232

But at the end of the jolly song, Violetta has an attack of coughing and seems to be on the point of fainting. Her guests are solicitous but she assures them she will be all right in a few minutes and urges them to continue their gaiety by dancing in the adjoining room. Alfredo, who had never before met her, stays behind with her and in the tender melody, *"Un dì felice"* ("One happy day"), tells her how he has loved her from the first day he saw her, although he has never before spoken to her. She tries to treat his declaration lightly (as can be heard in the gay melody with which she responds to his pleading words), but she is obviously much moved and promises to see him the next day. Heretofore, her life has been devoted to a feverish pursuit of pleasure. Now, for the first time, serious love is offered to her. She takes a flower from her bouquet, gives it to him and tells him he may return to see her when the flower has faded.

The party begins to break up, and after all the farewells have been said, she is left alone and she thinks about this earnest young man from the country who offers love with such obvious sincerity. Her famous aria, *"Ah, fors' è lui"* ("Can it be he?") expresses her joy and wonder over finding one man who may have real love to offer, and she repeats the tender melody Alfredo has sung to her, *"Di quell' amor"* ("From such love").

But a moment later she decides, "No, no, my life is dedicated to pleasure" and she bursts into the brilliant *"Sempre libera"* ("Ever free") aria. Her song is interrupted by the voice of Alfredo, singing in the garden beneath her window, repeating again the passionate melody in which he first declared his love. In spite of her determination to keep her old life, she is more than a little fascinated by the offer of a true love.

ACT TWO

SCENE: *Garden of a country house.*

Three months have passed since the first act, and Alfredo is living very happily with Violetta in her pretty little house in Auteuil, a suburb of Paris. In the garden of this establishment, Alfredo voices his happiness in the aria, *"De' miei bollenti spiriti"* ("Fevered and wild my dream of

youth"). Annina, Violetta's maid tells him that Violetta
has been living beyond her means in this idyllic life, and has
been selling her jewels to pay their living expenses. Suddenly, struck with remorse for failing to carry his share of
the burden, Alfredo decides to go to Paris to raise some
money, and he tells Annina that he will be back in a few
hours.

After he has left, Violetta comes into the garden, a far
sweeter and calmer Violetta than the gay and frivolous
pleasure-lover we knew in the first act. Going through her
mail, she comes on an invitation to a party at the house of
her Parisian friend, Flora. This, she says, she certainly will
not accept.

Just then Giorgio Germont, Alfredo's father, enters. His
mission, Violetta soon learns, is to break up his son's love
affair, and at first he is very stern and most insulting. It does
not take long for him, however, to discover that Violetta is
genuinely in love with his son and possesses a character as
strong as it is tender. The immediate cause of his visit is
that Alfredo's younger sister is about to be married and
Germont is afraid that her happiness will be endangered
by this scandalous affair. In a long and very beautiful duet,
"Pura siccome un angelo" ("Pure as an angel"), he pleads
with Violetta to give him up of her own accord, for the
sake of Alfredo's family, for the sake of his future, and,
finally, for the sake of her own great love for Alfredo.

Greatly agitated, she sees the justice of his plea; and
though her heart is breaking, she at last consents and
Germont, now full of sympathy for her, takes a tender
farewell.

Left alone, Violetta dashes off an acceptance to Flora's
invitation and another note to Alfredo to tell him she is
leaving him forever, but giving no reasons. Just as she
finishes, Alfredo himself returns, much sooner than he is
expected. He is greatly troubled because of a severe letter
he has received from his father. Hiding her own far greater
troubles, Violetta tries to console him, but she breaks down
for a moment and, in a great burst of emotion, cries,
"Amami, Alfredo" ("Love me, Alfredo").

When she is gone, Alfredo sees her note. He reads it and
immediately wants to rush off after her, but is interrupted
by the return of his father. In the well-known aria, *"Di*

Provenza il mar" ("Thy home in fair Provence"), the elder Germont attempts to persuade his son to return to their quiet family life on their estate in Southern France. It is of no use, for Alfredo is foolishly convinced that Violetta has left him for the Baron Douphol. He rushes off to find her at Flora's party and his father follows him sadly.

ACT THREE

SCENE: *Terrace of Flora's villa.*

Another gay party is in progress, this time at the home of Flora Bervoix. Entertainers, costumed as gypsies, dance, sing, and tell fortunes. At one side of the terrace are gambling tables. Alfredo enters and in response to questions replies that he knows nothing whatever of Violetta and what is more, he does not care. He strolls over to the gaming tables and joins in a game of cards.

Violetta enters on the arm of Baron Douphol. She is startled when she sees Alfredo and warns Douphol not to quarrel with him. Alfredo and Douphol greet each other very coldly. The Baron sarcastically compliments Alfredo on his luck at cards and challenges him to a game. They play and Alfredo wins consistently, the Baron losing large sums of money each time. The ill-will between the two men is only too evident and a duel is avoided only by the announcement of supper in an adjoining room.

Violetta remains behind and sends for Alfredo to persuade him to leave lest the duel actually take place. Yes, says the angry Alfredo, he will leave provided Violetta comes with him. Violetta pleads that she has promised not to, and Alfredo's suspicions are, he thinks, confirmed. Does she love Douphol? And poor Violetta, who may no longer avow her true love for Alfredo, stammers out, "Yes".

In a great rage, Alfredo summons the entire company, denounces Violetta in the strongest terms before them all, and finally hurls his winnings at her feet, saying that now they can all see that he has repaid what he owes her— *"Ogni suo aver tal femmina"* ("All she possessed, this woman here"). Everyone is shocked by such behavior on Alfredo's part, and most shocked of all is the elder Germont, who enters at this moment, for he is the only one who knows how Violetta really feels and why she has left Alfredo.

The Baron Douphol flings his gloves—the conventional challenge to a duel—at the feet of Alfredo. Alfredo picks up the gloves, thus accepting the challenge.

The act closes in a very remarkable ensemble, *"Di sprezza degno"* (" 'Tis shame to manhood"), in which all take part, but in which all express different emotions. Violetta's heart is broken and she sings of her despair, while her friends try to console her; Douphol expresses his jealous rage; Alfredo, his sorrow and remorse; Germont, his compassionate pity. Germont leaves with his son, the half-fainting Violetta is led away by her friends, and the guests at the gay party which has ended so disastrously depart slowly as the curtain falls.

ACT FOUR

SCENE: *A plainly furnished bedroom.*

No longer the gay, pleasure-loving courtesan, Violetta is living in a small apartment in an unfashionable part of Paris. The jewels she once wore are all gone now, and the money they brought in is almost gone, too. And worst of all, her illness has advanced to an alarming degree.

As the beautiful orchestral *Prelude* begins, Violetta lies in bed, apparently asleep. Her faithful maid, Annina, drowses by the fireplace. Violetta awakens and Annina opens the shutters. It is early morning and the sunlight brightens the sickroom. Dr. Grenvil enters and Violetta assures him that, although she is weak, her mind is at peace. Dr. Grenvil and Annina assist her from the bed to the sofa and make her comfortable. Dr. Grenvil tells her that she will soon be well, but Violetta smiles sadly, as she knows this is not true. As the doctor leaves, he whispers to Annina that it is now only a matter of hours.

It is carnival time in Paris, and Violetta hears the sounds of singing in the streets. She sends off Annina to distribute half of her last remaining coins to the poor, and then she rereads—for the hundredth time—a letter she has received from the elder Germont—*"Teneste la promessa"* ("You have kept your promise"). The duel has taken place, writes Germont; the Baron has been wounded but will recover;

and he, himself, has told Alfredo of Violetta's true love and her sacrifice. Both father and son are coming to beg her forgiveness. But it is getting late, and they do not come, she says, and she sings the sad little aria, *"Addio del passato"* ("Farewell to the past"), in which she bids farewell to her happiness, and in which the orchestra underlines her growing illness by taking up the melody when she becomes too weak to finish it.

A moment later, announced by Annina, Alfredo rushes in, and with a great surging return of strength, she joins him in the ecstatic duet, *"Parigi, o cara"* ("Far from gay Paris"), as they plan a future of love and happiness.

But the effort is too great for her. She tries to put on a gown to go out with Alfredo, but falls back, telling him how near to death she really is. Germont and Dr. Grenvil now come in, but it is too late. Violetta gives the unhappy Alfredo a miniature of herself, *"Prendi, quest'è l'immagine"* ("Alfredo, receive this parting gift"); a present for the girl he will some day marry, and he must give it to her and tell her that it represents an angel who is praying for them in heaven. High up in the violins, we hear the beautiful melody of the first-act duet as Violetta rises once more. She is under the deathly illusion that she is well again, and she cries, "But I return to life, oh joy". Then she falls back, dead, her grief-stricken lover kneeling broken-heartedly beside her.

Un Ballo In Maschera

(A Masked Ball)

by GIUSEPPE VERDI (1813–1901)

Four Acts. Libretto by Somma.
First produced in Rome, 1859.

Riccardo, the King	*Tenor*
Renato, his secretary	*Baritone*
Amelia, Renato's wife	*Soprano*
Samuele	*Bass*
Tomaso	*Bass*
Oscar, page to the King	*Soprano*
Ulrica, a sorceress	*Contralto*
Silvano, a sailor	*Bass*

A judge, townspeople, courtiers.

TIME: *Eighteenth Century.*
PLACE: *Sweden.*

ACT ONE

SCENE: *Audience chamber in the royal palace.*

From the opening chorus, we learn that among the nobles there are two factions—one devoted to the king, Riccardo, another (headed by two conspirators named Samuele and Tomaso), planning to assassinate him. The king's entry is announced by Oscar the page, a foppishly dressed youth whose part is always sung by a coloratura soprano. Oscar presents a list of guests invited to a masquerade ball shortly to be given and when the king comes to the name "Amelia", he goes into a reverie, *"La rivedrà nell'estasi"* ("I shall behold her once again"). For he loves Amelia, even though she is the wife of his close friend and adviser, Renato.

He dismisses the court, and when they have departed, Renato himself comes in to warn the king concerning the plot on his life, *"Alla vita che t'arride"* ("To a life that is favored"). The generous high-spirited prince refuses to hear even the names of his supposed ill-wishers, for he fears that he might have to punish them.

As they speak, a judge comes in to get the king to sign an order for the deportation of one Ulrica, an astrologer. Oscar boldly speaks up and says Ulrica is quite harmless, in fact she is consulted by many quite respectable people who have faith in her ability to foretell the future. The king orders the judge to pardon Ulrica.

The incident has given Riccardo an idea and he calls back the courtiers and proposes that everyone put on some kind of disguise and visit the fortune-teller that very afternoon. Renato thinks this a very dangerous prank, while the conspirators think it may give them a chance to carry out their plot. The scene ends as they all leave to prepare for their visit to Ulrica.

ACT TWO

SCENE: *The home of Ulrica, the fortune-teller.*

The interior of the large hut where Ulrica practices her incantations is a weird place, dark and mysterious. A small crowd has gathered to watch the witch and, if possible, learn something of the future. Ulrica herself is a terrifying object, all in rags and very dirty, as she bends over a large caldron and sings her incantation aria, *"Re dell'abisso affrettati"* ("King of the abyss, O hasten").

While this is going on, a stranger strides into the room remarking that he is the first to arrive. The watching crowd frowns at this interruption, and the stranger, who is Riccardo, stands scornfully in the background as Ulrica announces that she has finally summoned the mysterious presence that can predict the future.

A brash young sailor named Silvano comes forward and asks to have his fortune told. Ulrica examines his palm and tells him his future will be excellent. The king hears all this and surreptitiously slips a brand-new officer's commission in the Royal Navy into the sailor's pocket; and so it happens that when Silvano wants to pay Ulrica for her favorable predictions, he discovers those predictions have already been fulfilled. Everyone is delighted.

And now, there is a knock at a secret door and to Riccardo's surprise, Amelia's servant is admitted. He tells Ulrica that Amelia is waiting outside and desires a private consultation with the witch. Ulrica dismisses the company and they all leave except Riccardo, who hides in a dark corner to overhear what is going on. Amelia has come to consult Ulrica because she finds herself in love with the king and she wants to forget him, for she is the wife of the king's most trusted friend and counsellor.

Ulrica's advice is frightening to the timid lady. She must go at midnight to a point outside the city where executions take place. There, underneath the gibbet, she must collect certain herbs, and these will cure her of her guilty love, *"Della citta all'occaso"* ("In the shadow of the gibbet"). The king, overhearing this, resolves that Amelia shall not go on this mission alone.

But now we hear impatient voices outside; Amelia leaves, and Ulrica admits all the courtiers, disguised, of course, as the plan had been. The king, who is wearing a sailor's costume, demands to hear his fortune. As he is dressed as a sailor, it seems appropriate for him to express his request in the form of a barcarolle, or boat-song, *"Di' tu se fidele"* ("Will the waves faithfully carry me"). Ulrica examines his palm. It is, she says, the palm of a man who is far more important than his costume suggests—but she refuses to say anything about his fate. When, however, the high-spirited king insists, she hesitatingly tells him that he is doomed to be killed by a traitor—by the next man who shakes his hand.

"That is all nonsense," says the king, but everyone else is greatly impressed and refuses to take his proffered hand. That is, all except Renato, who, arriving after the prediction has been made, takes his friend's hand readily. That clinches the matter for the king: Renato is his best friend —and besides, Ulrica has not even been able to foresee her own danger that morning when she was in danger of being deported. Good-naturedly, he tosses her a purse—and the act closes as everyone sings a chorus in praise of their generous-hearted monarch.

ACT THREE

SCENE ONE: *A snow-covered plain.*

It is a moonlit night outside the city at the place of execution, and here, under the gibbet, Amelia comes to gather the herbs that Ulrica has said will cure her of her love for the king. She is frightened by the gruesomeness of the spot, and as a clock strikes midnight, she thinks she sees a ghost approaching—but it is the king. He declares his love for her, and insists on her telling him that she loves him too, and finally she does so, but in the same breath asks him to save her from herself. The duet *"O qual soave brivido"* ("Like dew thy words fall on my heart") reaches a passionate climax when Renato appears.

Immediately, Amelia hides her head in a veil, while Renato tells the king that the conspirators have learned that he is in this lonely spot and are about to murder him. Renato urges the king to escape while there is yet time, but at first the king refuses. It is only when Amelia begs him to save himself that he agrees to do so, provided that Renato will conduct the lady back to the city without once looking at her face. This Renato swears to do and Riccardo goes off, first changing cloaks with his friend.

But as Amelia and Renato are about to leave, the conspirators find them and are disappointed to discover that the man who wears the king's cloak is only Renato. At least, says Samuele, we'll have a look at the lady. But Renato, true to his oath, threatens to attack anyone with a sword who dares lay hands on the unknown lady. There is about to be a fight when Amelia, to avoid bloodshed, removes her veil.

Renato is, of course, astounded and dismayed, while the conspirators think it a great joke that Renato should have an assignation with his own wife outside the city. Before the curtain falls, Renato tells Amelia that he will keep his oath—he will accompany her back to the city. But his voice, Amelia remarks, sounds like a warrant of death.

SCENE TWO: *A room in Renato's home.*

Renato has brought his wife home, and now he tells her bitterly that she has been unfaithful to him and that she must die. Amelia tries to assure him of her innocence, and when he grows even more furious, she begs only to be allowed to say farewell to her little son. When she is gone, he turns to a large picture of the king that is hanging on the wall. He realizes that his royal friend is even more guilty than his wife. He swears speedy vengeance against this false man; as for himself, his peace of mind is gone forever. This is the great aria, *"Eri tu"* ("Is it thou?").

Samuele and Tomaso, the two conspirators, now come in as they had agreed to, and Renato proves to them that he knows of their plots. Furthermore, he says, he will join them now. He won't give his reasons, but he offers his child as hostage for his good faith. Finally, the two men believe him and each demands the right to kill the king for himself. To settle it, they decide to draw lots.

At that moment Amelia comes in to say that Oscar has arrived with an invitation from the king. Ironically, Renato bids his wife draw the paper from the urn—and it is Renato's name which comes up. Amelia shudders over this, but there is nothing she can do. The young page, Oscar, enters gaily and presents the invitations for the masked ball which is to take place that night—*"Ah, di che fulgor che musiche"* ("Ah, what dazzling light, what music").

"Will the king be present?" asks Renato, and when the answer is "Yes", all three conspirators (for there are three now) promise to be present also, and the curtain descends as they make their final plans for recognizing each other despite the masquerade costumes.

ACT FOUR

SCENE ONE: *A room in the palace.*

It is the evening of the masked ball, and the king is alone, seated at his desk. He has decided to act honorably and end all chance of his being unfaithful to his friend; and he signs a paper which will send both Renato and Amelia on a mission to England. It is a sad decision for him, and he sings a brief aria, heart-brokenly, *"Ma se m'è forza perderti"* ("But for me life is finished"). Oscar enters now and brings him a letter from an unknown lady, as he says (though it isn't hard for us to guess that the lady is Amelia). It warns him that there is a plot to kill him at the ball and that he should not come. But the king disdains being taken for a coward; and we hear the first strains of the festal music as he prepares to attend.

SCENE TWO: *The grand ballroom.*

Throughout most of this final scene, dancers are moving about, and there is music both on the stage and from the orchestra pit, suggesting the joyous background to the dark deeds that are to be performed. The conspirators whisper together briefly; they have been unable to find the king or penetrate his disguise.

Oscar happens to meet Renato and says that he recognizes him, whereupon Renato snatches away Oscar's mask and immediately begins plying him with questions as to his master's whereabouts. First Oscar refuses to tell Renato anything; but when Renato insists that he has important business with the king and must find him immediately, Oscar describes the costume, a black domino with a red rosette.

On the other side of the stage, Riccardo and Amelia meet, and she begs him to leave the ball as there is a plot to kill him. The king refuses and he bids her a sad and fond farewell, *"T'amo, t'amo"* ("I love you, I love you"), telling her of his plan to send both her and Renato to England. Just as he does so, Renato steps up and stabs him. For a moment the dance music goes on—then all see what has happened, gather around the king, and seize Renato as a traitor. But with his dying breath the king forgives Renato, gives him the commission to go to England and pardons all who have plotted against him. And as everyone mourns him in a great musical climax, the curtain descends.

La Forza del Destino

(The Force of Destiny)

by GIUSEPPE VERDI (1813–1901)

Prologue and Three Acts. Libretto by Piave.
First produced in St. Petersburg, 1862.

Marquis of Calatrava	*Bass*
Leonora, his daughter	*Soprano*
Curra, her maid	*Mezzo-soprano*
Don Alvaro, a young nobleman	*Tenor*
Don Carlo, brother of Leonora	*Baritone*
Father Guardiano	*Bass*
Brother Melitone, a friar	*Bass*
Trabuco, a muleteer	*Tenor*
Preziosilla, a gypsy	*Mezzo-soprano*
A military surgeon	*Baritone*

Soldiers, peasants, beggars, pilgrims, monks, dancers, an innkeeper and his wife.

TIME: *Eighteenth Century.*
PLACE: *Spain and Italy.*

PROLOGUE

SCENE: *Room in the house of the Marquis of Calatrava in
Seville.*

As the curtain rises, the Marquis is bidding an affectionate goodnight to his daughter, Leonora. As soon as
he is gone, we learn from Leonora's agitated conversation
with her maid, Curra, that she has promised to elope that
very night with a mysterious young man, the heroic Don
Alvaro—"*Ah! sequirti fino*" ("Ah! I will follow"). No
one knows precisely what this man's antecedents are, and
for that reason, as Leonora knows, her aristocratic father
could not possibly approve the match.

Don Alvaro enters through the balcony window, but
just as the lovers are about to flee, the Marquis returns,
sword in hand. Don Alvaro draws a pistol to defend him-

self, then reconsiders and throws it aside. Quite by accident it goes off, and the bullet finds the heart of the noble Marquis. Cursing his daughter, the old man dies, and Don Alvaro drags Leonora off with him through the balcony window as the curtain falls on the Prologue.

ACT ONE

SCENE ONE: *An inn near the Spanish village of Hornachuelos.*

In the pursuit and flight at night, following the death of the Marquis, Don Alvaro and Leonora have been separated and each believes the other to be dead. Searching for a haven of rest, Leonora has assumed men's clothing to make her lonely journey less dangerous and, in the course of her wanderings, comes to the large inn at Hornachuelos —*"Al suon del tamburo"* ("To the sound of the tambourine"). In the crowd there she recognizes her brother, Don Carlo. She does not reveal herself to him but overhears him tell the story of her father's death at the hands of her lover, *"Son Pereda"* ("I'm Pereda"), and hears his oath of vengeance.

SCENE TWO: *The mountain church and monastery of Madonna degli Angeli.*

Leonora has at last come to the place that a certain Father Cleto had told her of, a place where she hopes to find sanctuary and all that now remains for her in life, the existence of a hermit. Still clad in men's clothing, she kneels before the cross that stands before the church and devoutly thanks heaven for leading her there. It is the prayer to the Virgin, the *"Madre, pietosa Vergine"* ("Mother, Virgin full of pity"), she sings. In the middle of this beautiful aria, the organ and choir of priests within the monastery chant a hymn which forms a musical background to Leonora's prayer.

Fortified by the courage this gives her, Leonora knocks on the door of the monastery. Brother Melitone answers her, a stout, peasant-like figure of a man, lazy and not too good-humored. He would like, if he had the courage, to turn her away and not be bothered, but he doesn't quite

dare go that far, and he summons the abbot, Father Guardi-
ano. This abbot has heard something of Leonora's story
from Father Cleto, who has sent her there. Full of compassion for the wretched woman, he agrees to bring her the
costume of the Franciscan order, and to let her take up the
life of a hermit in a nearby cave. She is never to see anyone
in the cave, but he himself will bring her a weekly allowance
of food.

Thereupon he summons the entire brotherhood from the
monastery. Solemnly he tells them that Leonora will dwell
in the cave, but that no one is ever to come near it. He
gives her a blessing, and the scene closes with a most impressive ensemble, Leonora's voice rising high over the
chorus of the priests. It is a prayer to the Virgin for protection, *"La Vergine degli angeli"* ("The saints and holy
guardians").

ACT TWO

SCENE ONE: *A battlefield near Velletri, Italy.*

Both Don Carlo and Don Alvaro, unknown to each
other, have joined a Spanish brigade which is fighting in
Italy in a war against the Germans. When the curtain rises
on this scene, Don Alvaro is alone on the stage, in the
uniform of a captain. His soliloquy tells us that he believes
Leonora to be dead and, in his aria, *"O, tu che in seno"*
("Oh, sainted soul"), he longs for death in exile rather
than life without Leonora.

Sounds of a quarrel are heard off-stage and there is the
clash of weapons and Don Alvaro rushes away to see what
is happening. He brings back with him, of all people, Don
Carlo, who has been set upon by a group of gamblers
and whom he has rescued. The two men do not know each
other, for each has taken an assumed name in this adven-
turesome war, and they swear eternal friendship.

Now a battle rages off-stage; soldiers and a surgeon,
looking over a wall, report its progress; there are shots and
running about, and the Germans are thrown back. But
Don Alvaro, who has been in the thick of it, is carried
back on a litter, mortally wounded as everyone believes.
He is left alone with his newly found friend, Don Carlo,
and Alvaro makes Carlo swear to destroy a letter he will

find on him without reading it. The two unite in the popular tenor-baritone duet, the *"Solenne in quest' ora"* ("Swear in this solemn hour").

But something Alvaro has said makes Don Carlo suspect who he may really be. And when the wounded man is carried off-stage, it is with difficulty that he refrains from breaking his vow and opening the letter. Instead, he rummages among Alvaro's belongings and finds a small portrait of his own sister, Leonora. His suspicions are confirmed: the man *is* Alvaro, who slew the Marquis of Calatrava, father of Don Carlo. Just then, the surgeon returns and reports that the wounded man will recover. Now Carlo can have his revenge, and in a burst of passion, he sings his aria, *"Ah, egli è salvo"* ("Ah, he lives").

SCENE TWO: *The camp at Velletri.*

There are bright colored tents and booths for the sale of food and drink. It is dawn. Don Alvaro enters and is met by Don Carlo who inquires if he has fully recovered from his wounds. When Don Alvaro assures him that he has, he is amazed when Don Carlo asks him if he is well enough to fight a duel. Don Alvaro accuses him of reading the letter which he had promised to destroy unopened. Don Carlo denies this, but says that the picture of Leonora which he found among Alvaro's papers revealed the truth to him. Don Carlo has sworn an oath of vengeance, but Don Alvaro reminds him that they also swore an oath of friendship which he, for one, refuses to break. Don Carlo tells him that he has learned that Leonora is not dead but has fled to relatives. Both men draw their swords, Don Carlo aggressively, Don Alvaro reluctantly, but other soldiers rush in and prevent the duel.

The camp is now fully awake and there is a lively scene with gypsies, vendors, and others moving about among the troops. One gay group dances a "Tarantella", and at the end of the scene all join in a sturdy marching song, *"Rataplan"*.

ACT THREE

SCENE ONE: *Courtyard of the monastery of Madonna degli
          Angeli.*

Brother Melitone, of goodly girth and stout bass voice,
is dishing out soup to a crowd of beggars from a great
caldron. He does it not only with ill humor, but with every
show of incompetence. He becomes more and more ex-
asperated as the beggars crowd around him and when it
is at last empty, kicks over the caldron.

Finally the beggars go off, and the abbot reproves Melitone for his bad manners. Then they briefly discuss a new
member of the brotherhood, the dark and mysterious
Father Raffaello, a kindly man, they agree, but no one
seems to know who he is or where he came from. Actually,
as we learn later, it is Don Alvaro who, like Leonora, has
come to the monastery to end his life in seclusion.

Don Carlo, who has traced Alvaro here, now enters and
demands to see this Brother Raffaello. Don Alvaro then
comes on in a monk's gown and with a shaven head. Raging, Don Carlo challenges him to fight then and there, and
offers him the choice of two swords he has brought with
him. Alvaro tries his best to avoid the fight. He suffers
being called a coward, he even kneels before the enemy he
does not wish to hurt. Don Carlo casts an insult on Alvaro's birth. This makes him accept the sword, but only
for a moment. He casts it aside again and insists on keeping to his holy vows. Finally, Don Carlo strikes Don Alvaro, and this is more than the ex-soldier can bear. Seizing
the sword from the ground, he rushes outside—still in his
priest's gown—to fight with Don Carlo, as the curtain falls.

SCENE TWO: *Outside Leonora's cave near the monastery.*

Leonora comes out of the cave where she has lived as
a hermit for five years and sings her last touching prayer,
the great *"Pace, pace, mio dio"* ("Peace, peace, oh my
Lord"), confessing that she still loves Alvaro and hoping
now only for death. She hears sounds of fighting off-stage
and quickly retires.

Don Carlo and Don Alvaro are having their grim duel.

They fight furiously across the back of the stage; we hear their swords clashing as they disappear behind a huge rock, and a moment later Don Alvaro appears alone. He has run Don Carlo through with his sword and is seeking help for him. Leonora, frightened, rings the bell that will summon the abbot in time of danger, and then she sees Don Alvaro. The two lovers, parted so long, recognize each other in this tragic, hurried moment. Quickly Alvaro explains what he has done, and Leonora rushes off, behind the rock, to her brother. But Don Carlo, unforgiving even in death, stabs her to the heart even as she leans over him. She comes back, mortally wounded and supported by the abbot, who has heard her summons.

Now Alvaro curses fate, but the abbot gently reproves him; and Leonora, dying, says that Heaven has granted her power to promise Don Alvaro pardon. Broken-hearted, he kneels beside her, and the curtain slowly falls as the abbot says, *"Salita a Dio"* ("She has risen to God").

Aïda

by GIUSEPPE VERDI (1813–1901)

Four Acts. Libretto by Ghislanzoni.
First produced in Cairo, 1871.

Aïda, an Ethiopian slave	*Soprano*
Rhadames, an Egyptian Captain	*Tenor*
Amneris, daughter of the King of Egypt	*Mezzo-soprano*
Amonasro, King of Ethiopia	*Baritone*
Ramfis, Egyptian High Priest	*Bass*
King of Egypt	*Bass*

Priests, priestesses, soldiers, slaves, dancers, Egyptians, Ethiopian prisoners.

TIME: *Ancient Egypt during the reign of the Pharaohs.*
PLACE: *Memphis and Thebes.*

ACT ONE

SCENE ONE: *A great hall in the palace of Pharaoh at Memphis.*

Egypt and Ethiopia, hereditary enemies, are again at war, and an Egyptian army is about to set forth on a new campaign. Rhadames, a young Captain, and Ramfis, the High Priest, are in conversation in the royal palace. Ramfis tells the young man that the goddess, Isis, has chosen the man who is to lead the Egyptian army and that he is now on his way to announce the choice to the King. Something in the manner of the High Priest leads Rhadames to suspect that he may be the chosen one.

Left alone, Rhadames thinks of what the future may hold for him, and his thoughts turn to the beautiful Ethiopian slave girl, Aïda, brought back as captive from one of the former campaigns. Rhadames is in love with Aïda in spite of the fact that she is a slave, and he thinks that a victorious campaign may bring him the right to marry her. He does not know, nor do any of the Egyptians, that she is the daughter of the King of Ethiopia. Rhadames sings of his love for Aïda in one of the most famous arias in opera, *"Celeste Aïda"* ("Heavenly Aïda").

He is so absorbed in his reverie that he does not notice that Amneris, daughter of the Egyptian king, has entered the hall and is watching him closely. She loves him, but realizes that he does not return her love. And then a third person joins them—Aïda, the slave.

In an impressive trio, the three characters express their thoughts and feelings: Aïda her love and anxiety about the coming campaign, Amneris her love for Rhadames and her jealousy of Aïda, and Rhadames his hopes and fears for the future.

The king and his retinue enter, and the king announces that Rhadames has been chosen to lead the Egyptian army against Ethiopia. All cry out for war, and the monarch inspires his men to battle and they all march out leaving Aïda alone. Horrified at the turn of events, she sings the beautiful aria, *"Ritorna vincitor"* ("Return victorious"), blaming herself for the words of good will she has given Rhadames, who is about to make war against her own people and yet, at the same time, she confesses to herself her great love for him. She knows that her father, the Ethiopian king, and her beloved Rhadames will soon meet in battle and she is almost overcome with her conflicting emotions. As the scene ends she implores the aid of the gods in a pathetic and touching melody, *"Numi, pietà"* ("Merciful gods, look from on high").

SCENE TWO: *Interior of the Temple of Vulcan in Memphis.*

An impressive ceremony takes place in the dimly lit temple where Rhadames is to be invested with the sacred armor to lead the Egyptians against the Ethiopians. Ramfis stands before the high altar, and we hear in the distance the voice of the High Priestess, invoking divine aid. Ramfis and his priests join in the chant and there is a solemn mystic dance before the altar.

Rhadames enters, unarmed, and approaches the altar, where a silver veil is placed on his head and a sword is put in his hand by the High Priest. The scene ends as Rhadames repeats the prayer to the gods and the whole assembly breaks into a great triumphant shout.

ACT TWO

SCENE ONE: *The palace apartments of the Princess Amneris.*

On a sunlit terrace in her luxurious apartments, Amneris reclines on a couch, waited on by slaves. Soon she dismisses them all except Aïda. Amneris tells her that the war against Ethiopia has ended with complete victory for the Egyptians. She is apparently full of sympathy for Aïda and incidentally tells her (falsely) that Rhadames has been killed. Her trick is successful and Aïda bursts into tears at the news. Amneris knows now that what she has suspected is true— her slave is in love with Rhadames. She turns on the unhappy girl, tells her that Rhadames really lives and pours scorn and insult on the slave for daring to be the rival of a princess. Aïda can barely refrain from proudly declaring that she too is the daughter of a king. Her pleas for pity meet only with contempt from Amneris. Suddenly they hear a hymn of triumph announcing the return of the victorious

Egyptian army. Aïda is left alone and once more she sings the heart-breaking prayer to the gods for pity.

SCENE TWO: *Great entrance to the city of Thebes.*

This is one of the most spectacular scenes in all opera. A great open square near the city wall is thronged with people celebrating the return of Rhadames and his victorious army. They sing a majestic chorus of praise to Isis who has brought victory to Egypt. The triumphal army enters in a great procession to the music of the famous *"Grand March"* accompanied by an imposing array of banners, arms, chariots, sacred vessels, and religious idols and passes before the two elevated thrones where sit the King of Egypt and the Princess Amneris. Finally, Rhadames, the conquering hero, comes on. He steps from his magnificent chariot; the king comes down from the throne to embrace him and Amneris crowns him with laurel. The king tells him that whatever he asks will be granted. The wretched Ethiopian captives are brought forward and Aïda recognizes with horror her own father, Amonasro, King of the Ethiopians. He embraces her tenderly but whispers that she must not disclose his rank. In a dignified plea he asks the Egyptian king to be merciful and Rhadames asks that the Ethiopian slaves be freed. The king agrees, demanding however that Amonasro remain as hostage.

He then announces that to celebrate the peace he will bestow on Rhadames the hand of his daughter Amneris. The crowd cheers as the king descends from his throne and Amneris proudly accompanies Rhadames as the royal party departs, leaving Aïda alone with her father, both of them in despair.

ACT THREE

SCENE: *The banks of the river Nile.*

Through the palm trees bordering the moonlit river comes a boat bearing the Princess Amneris and the High Priest Ramfis, for Amneris is to spend the night in prayer in the nearby Temple of Isis before her wedding to Rhadames. When the royal party has gone into the temple, Aïda creeps in cautiously, hoping for a final farewell to Rhadames and she sings her beautiful and poignant aria, *"O patria mia"* ("O my fatherland"), when she is interrupted by her father, Amonasro. He tells her that Ethiopia is preparing to attack the Egyptians again and that the war is to be resumed. All they need to know is which road the Egyptians will take against them. In a long and highly dramatic duet, her father persuades her to try to find out this military secret from Rhadames. As Rhadames comes in, Amonasro hides himself. Aïda, using all her wiles and her real love for the young Egyptian general, persuades him to fly with her, and by the path the army is to take—*"Fuggiam gli ardori"* ("Ah! Fly with me").

This he finally agrees to do and mentions the road, the Pass of Napata. Amonasro now steps forward, reveals that he is the King of Ethiopia and announces that he will order his troops to proceed to the Pass of Napata at once. Rhadames, aghast, realizes that he has unwittingly played the traitor. At this exciting moment, with the Ethiopian king and his daughter trying to persuade Rhadames to join them in flight, Amneris and Ramfis come out of the temple, with the cry of "Traitor! Traitor!" on Amneris's lips. Amonasro and Aïda escape, but Rhadames turns and with a dramatic gesture, surrenders his sword to Ramfis.

ACT FOUR

SCENE ONE: *The Judgment Hall in the Palace.*

Amneris stands in deep dejection at the entrance to the subterranean hall of justice from which comes a sinister reddish glow of light. The trial of Rhadames is about to begin and Amneris is determined to make one last desperate effort to save him. When he is led in by the guards, she begs him to save himself and to plead his innocence. But Rhadames has no desire to live without his beloved Aïda. "Never!" he replies to Amneris, and the guards lead him down the stone steps to the judgment hall.

We hear Ramfis, the High Priest, solemnly bring the accusation of treason against Rhadames and the priests call upon him to defend himself, *"Discolpati"* ("Defend thyself")—they cry three separate times, but there is only silence from the prisoner. He is guilty and his sentence is pronounced—he is to be buried alive. Amneris is overwhelmed with grief and remorse as the procession returns from the crypt and, as they pass, she hurls her curses at them.

Scene Two: *The Temple of Phtha.*

The stage is divided into two levels, the upper one, the temple itself, and the lower one the tomb where Rhadames is buried. While religious rites are enacted in the temple, we see workmen fitting the last stone into place in the floor of the temple, which is at the same time the ceiling of the tomb. Rhadames, in the dark mysterious cell, thinking he sees a vision of Aïda, sings the glorious aria, *"La fatal pietra"* ("The fatal stone"). It is Aïda herself and not a vision. Explaining that she has preceded him into the tomb and hidden herself there to die with him, they sing the duet, *"Morir! si pura e bella"* ("To die! So pure and beautiful"). The weird chant of the priestesses interrupts the stillness.

Aïda, in a sublime ecstasy of love, sings of the Angel of Death approaching and the voices of the two lovers join together in a farewell to earth, *"O terra addio"* ("Farewell, O earth"). As Aïda and Rhadames die in each other's arms in the darkness below, we hear the priests solemnly chanting an invocation and the voice of Amneris in prayer imploring peace.

Otello

by GIUSEPPE VERDI (1813–1901)

Four Acts. Libretto by Boïto, based on Shakespeare's play, *Othello*.
First produced in Milan, 1887.

Otello, a noble Moor in the service of Venice   *Tenor*
Desdemona, Otello's wife   *Soprano*
Iago, Otello's ensign   *Baritone*
Cassio, Otello's lieutenant   *Tenor*
Emilia, Iago's wife and Desdemona's   *Mezzo-soprano*
    companion
Montano, Otello's predecessor as Governor of Cyprus   *Bass*
Roderigo, a Venetian gentleman   *Tenor*
Lodovico, Ambassador of Venice   *Bass*
A herald   *Bass*

People of Cyprus, Venetian soldiers and sailors, ladies and gentlemen, servants.

Time: *Fifteenth Century.*
Place: *Cyprus.*

ACT ONE

Scene: *The harbor of a seaport in Cyprus.*

The island of Cyprus belongs to the proud city of Venice, then at the height of its power and glory. The first act takes place outside of the castle of Otello, Governor of Cyprus, overlooking the harbor and the Mediterranean. The curtain rises on one of the most famous storm scenes in all opera. Venice has been at war with the Turkish Empire and a great crowd of people, in spite of the storm, has collected on the waterfront.

A ship bringing their great general Otello home from a victorious battle with the Turks is nearing the harbor. Otello appears from the beach with a group of his soldiers

255

and sailors. He is a great popular hero and he sings proudly of the victory he has won, *"Esultate"* ("Rejoice"). The crowd cheers. He enters the castle where his bride, Desdemona, awaits him. The storm subsides and the rejoicing populace builds a bonfire on the beach in celebration of victory—*"Fuoco di gioia"* ("Joyous fire").

Iago, the villain of the story, now starts his evil work. Rankling in his mind is the thought that his comrade in arms, Cassio, has been promoted over him to the post of lieutenant to Otello. He plans to get Cassio into trouble and goes about it in a devious way.

There is a young Venetian nobleman connected with the army named Roderigo, and Iago knows that this young man is infatuated with Otello's young and beautiful wife, Desdemona. Iago tells Roderigo not to despair—Desdemona will soon tire of Otello—but first they must get rid of Cassio, who also loves Desdemona. He works on the jealousy of this impressionable young man, making him believe that Cassio is his rival for the affections of Desdemona.

When Cassio comes in, the crafty Iago puts his plot into action. In the friendliest way he congratulates Cassio on his promotion and invites him to drink. The crowd on the beach is in a festive mood and they all join Iago in a jolly drinking song, *"Inaffia l'ugola"* ("Then let the cannikin clink"). Cassio is carried along with the spirit of the occasion and drinks with Iago, although he hesitates at first, saying "I drink but poorly." Iago urges more and more drink on poor Cassio, until he loses control of himself and from being a jolly good fellow, becomes abusive and quarrelsome.

The ill feeling between Roderigo and Cassio, which has been carefully cultivated by Iago, now bursts into flame and the two men insult each other and then draw swords. Just at this moment, Montano, Otello's predecessor as Governor of Cyprus, comes on the scene and attempts to intervene. Furiously; Cassio turns his sword against Montano, while Roderigo runs off to sound the alarm bell and in a few minutes all Cyprus has been awakened by the uproar.

Montano lies wounded when Otello comes out from the castle and demands an explanation. Cassio, sobered and ashamed, has nothing to say in his own defense and is apparently the guilty man. Angrily, Otello dismisses him from his service. Iago's plot has succeeded.

Desdemona has come out from the castle following Otello and, when the crowd disperses, they are left alone and the act closes with a tender love-scene between Otello and Desdemona, a scene which contains the beautiful duet, *"Già nella notte densa"* ("The night is dark").

ACT TWO

SCENE: *A richly furnished room in Otello's castle.*

Iago has brought about the demotion of Cassio, but he is not satisfied. His bitter hatred demands that Cassio be entirely ruined. And this he accomplishes by pretending to be his friend. When the curtain rises on the second act, Iago is conversing with Cassio and telling him that his best chance of mending his broken fortunes lies in getting Desdemona to intercede for him. Cassio accepts the suggestion and goes to seek Desdemona in the garden which we see through an arched doorway at the back of the room.

Iago then sings the famous *"Credo"* aria in which he tells of his cynical philosophy of life. "I feel no remorse—Evil is my creed," he says, and he has only contempt for the so-called virtues. Then Desdemona appears in the garden and as she and Cassio are conversing, Otello enters the room and glances out into the garden just in time to see Desdemona and Cassio stroll out of sight. Iago now begins to plant the seeds of jealousy in the mind of Otello. The latter questions Iago, but all he gets are some cleverly evasive answers as if Iago were shielding a friend which, of course, merely serves to increase Otello's uneasy suspicions.

And now Desdemona reappears in the garden surrounded by women and children who bring her flowers and gifts and sing her praises, *"Dove guardi splendono"* ("Where splendor reigns"). At the end of it, Desdemona comes through the doorway into the house, followed by her serving woman, Emilia, who is Iago's wife. Naturally, Desdemona hasn't an inkling of the suspicions Iago has planted in Otello's mind and she does the very thing Iago had hoped she would. She begs Otello to reinstate Cassio.

Otello is greatly agitated at this, and Desdemona takes her handkerchief—a very special handkerchief that her husband had given her, with little strawberry designs embroidered on it—and tries to soothe him by mopping his brow, whereupon Otello angrily snatches the handkerchief from her and throws it on the floor. Emilia picks it up and a little later Iago quietly forces her to give it to him. The others leave Otello alone and he sings a bitter soliloquy, *"Ora e per sempre addio"* ("Now and forever farewell") —farewell to peace of mind, to ambition and to the love of Desdemona. He now firmly believes his wife is guilty.

Iago reappears and pours fuel on the flame of Otello's jealousy by declaring that he has seen Desdemona's handkerchief in Cassio's home. He caps the climax by telling that he has heard Cassio in his sleep uttering Desdemona's name. Otello becomes frantic with rage and the act closes with a great scene in which Iago offers to help him to vengeance. Kneeling side by side, they swear an oath never to pause until the guilty shall be punished, *"Si, pel ciel"* ("We swear by heaven and earth"), and with this great "Vengeance duet", the act comes to an end.

ACT THREE

SCENE: *Great hall of the castle.*

We see a large and magnificent room of state with vast marble floor, rich dark walls, and heavy columns and arches, through which shows the deep clear blue of the Mediterranean sky. Almost immediately the voice of a herald is heard from the terrace outside the portico; a galley has been sighted, bringing the Venetian ambassador to Cyprus. But Otello has no interest in anything now but his own insane jealousy. Iago tells him that very shortly he will have absolute proof of Desdemona's faithlessness. As Iago leaves, Desdemona enters and there follows one of the most dramatic scenes in the opera, in which Otello tries to trap Desdemona into confessing her love for Cassio, a love which, of course, doesn't exist, *"Dio ti giocondi"* ("God rejoices").

Innocently, she attempts once more to speak on behalf of Cassio, but Otello ignores this and, telling her he has a cold, begs to borrow her handkerchief. She hands it to him but he says it is not the one he wants. He must have the handkerchief with the strawberry design on it which he had given her. She says it is in her room and he orders her to go and get it and angrily dismisses her. Hurt and bewildered, Desdemona leaves the room.

Iago returns and whispers to Otello to watch and listen from behind a column. Soon Cassio approaches and the artful Iago draws him into conversation. He finds a pretext to speak of the handkerchief Cassio has in his doublet and the innocent Cassio produces the fatal handkerchief, saying he had found it in his room, all unaware that it was secretly placed there by the crafty Iago—*"Quest' è una ragna"* ("This is a spider's nest").

Otello sees the damning evidence. Now there is no doubt that his wife is guilty. There can be but one outcome. Desdemona must die.

A flourish of trumpets is heard, signaling the arrival of the Venetian ship. There follows a scene full of pomp and ceremony. The large hall fills with courtiers and soldiers and the Venetian ambassador enters. He brings news that Otello has been recalled to Venice for still greater honors and that Cassio has been appointed Governor in his place. Desdemona appears distressed at this turn of affairs and Otello interprets her distress to mean that she cannot bear the thought of being parted from Cassio. Otello is almost out of his mind and insults Desdemona and flings her to the ground, *"Silencio, demonio!"* ("Silence, demon!"). The onlookers recoil with horror and when the crowd disperses, Iago and Otello are alone. Otello cracks under the strain of his violent emotions and slumps to the floor. We hear the crowd outside shouting, "Hail to Otello, the Lion of Venice!" Iago stands looking down at the prostrate figure, a sneer on his face and he says cynically, *"Ecco il Leone!"* ("There lies your Lion of Venice!"), as the curtain falls.

ACT FOUR

SCENE: *Desdemona's bedroom.*

Desdemona is being attended by her maidservant, Emilia, and is about to retire for the night. She has a premonition of death. She tells Emilia of an old sad song of her childhood, the song of a maiden who waited in vain for the return of her lover, and she sings the pathetically beautiful *"Salce, Salce"* ("Willow, willow"). Left alone, Desdemona kneels down and sings the lovely "Ave Maria"— *"Prega per chi adorando a te"* ("Pray for her who kneels in prayer before Thee").

After she is asleep, Otello quietly comes into the darkened room, bends over and kisses his wife. She wakens. Otello tells her darkly to prepare for death. There is an agonizing scene as she protests her innocence. But Otello will not believe her and strangles her. At once there is a loud knocking at the door and Emilia rushes in, accuses Otello of being a vile assassin and calls for help. Others come in, including Iago. Otello brings out the fatal handkerchief as proof of his wife's faithlessness and Emilia understands what has happened. She denounces Iago's perfidy, whereupon the villain makes his escape through the nearest door, followed by pursuing attendants. Otello, overcome by remorse, bends over the bed sobbing, "I kissed thee ere I killed thee; no way but this, killing myself." Drawing a dagger from his girdle, he stabs himself and falls lifeless over the body of Desdemona.

Falstaff

by GIUSEPPE VERDI (1813–1901)

Three Acts. Libretto by Boïto, based on Shakespeare's *The Merry Wives of Windsor* and *King Henry IV*.
First produced in Milan, 1893.

Sir John Falstaff	*Baritone*
Mistress Meg Page	*Mezzo-soprano*
Mistress Alice Ford	*Soprano*
Anne Ford, Mistress Ford's daughter	*Soprano*
Dame Quickly	*Mezzo-soprano*
Fenton, a young gentleman	*Tenor*
Ford, a wealthy burgher	*Baritone*
Dr. Caius	*Tenor*
Bardolph } Falstaff's henchmen	*Tenor*
Pistol }	*Bass*
The host of the Garter Inn	*Tenor*

TIME: *Reign of Henry IV.*
PLACE: *Windsor in England.*

ACT ONE

SCENE ONE: *A room in the Garter Inn.*

Sir John Falstaff is outwardly fat and jolly but inwardly cynical and utterly without principle. We meet him first in the Garter Inn accompanied by his two disreputable followers, Bardolph and Pistol, and surrounded by a number of empty wine bottles. He is busy sealing a couple of letters.

Dr. Caius enters almost at once and accuses Sir John of having beaten his servants, injured his horse, and broken into his house. Dr. Caius then turns on Bardolph and Pistol and accuses them of having robbed him. They deny his charges, and eventually lead him out of the door with a ludicrously pious "Amen".

So now Falstaff gets down to business. He tells the two scoundrels that the artistry of stealing consists of nothing more than choosing the correct moment—*"Rubar con garbo e a tempo"* ("Steal with grace and at the correct time"). His bills are high and his purse is dangerously low, what with the expense of supporting his two hangers-on—*"Sei la mia distruzione"* ("It will be my destruction") —and he tells them that he has written a couple of letters to two lovely and wealthy ladies—Mistress Alice Ford, the wife of a wealthy citizen of Windsor, and Mistress Margaret Page, the wife of another. Through them he hopes to repair his ailing fortune—*"O amor! sguardo di stella"* ("O love! look at the stars"). Will the two fellows be good enough to deliver the letters for him? But much to his surprise they both refuse on the grounds that it wouldn't be honorable. Honor among such rascals is something Falstaff had never heard of, and he gives the letters to Robin, the page, to deliver. Then he turns on his two henchmen and calls them sniveling cowards and drunken sots as well as thieves. "Honor!" he cries. "Honor is of no practical use in the world and is merely a word. And a word you have no right to use," *"L'onore! Ladri!"* ("Honor! Thieves!"). Seizing a broom, he chases Bardolph and Pistol out of the inn.

SCENE TWO: *The garden of Ford's home.*

Ford's wife is one of the two ladies to whom Sir John has sent his amorous letters; and when the curtain rises, she has already received hers and is about to share its contents with her friend, Mistress Page, who has received one that—it turns out—is word for word the same as the other, except, of course, for the names. But Alice Ford and Margaret Page are not the only ones to make merry over the letters. With them are Anne Ford, Mistress Ford's pretty daughter, and Dame Quickly, a wise and merry middle-aged gossip who is a friend of theirs. In the famous quartet, *"Quell'otre! Quel tino! Re delle panice!"* ("What a gourd! What a king of panic!"), they discuss the manner in which they will make a laughing stock of the amorous Sir John.

As the four ladies go off to another part of the garden, five men come in. They are Sir John's two disloyal followers, Bardolph and Pistol, Dr. Caius, Ford, who is Mistress Ford's wealthy husband, and young Fenton, who is in love with Anne Ford. These five men voice their hatred of Sir John Falstaff in the quintet, *"E un ribaldo, un furbo, un ladro"* ("He is a knave, a swindler, a thief"). Pistol tells Ford that Falstaff has written his wife a letter asking for a rendezvous and points out that he and Bardolph, being gentlemen of honor, refused to deliver it. The women return briefly, but soon young Fenton and Anne are left alone and sing a charming little love duet, *"Labbra di foco! Labbra di fiori!"* ("Lips of passion! Lips of flowers!"), which is interrupted when Mistress Ford, Mistress Page, and Dame Quickly return.

They have discussed their plan to make a fool of Sir John. Dame Quickly will carry a letter to him making an appointment for him to meet Mistress Ford. What will happen after that is part of their plot. The men return and they too have a plot. Ford will call on Falstaff at the Garter Inn in disguise, and will be introduced to him under a false name. All are sworn to secrecy and in a merry ensemble, *"Del tuo barbaro diagnostico"* ("With your barbaric diagnosis"), everyone discusses his or her part of the plot.

ACT TWO

SCENE ONE: *The Garter Inn.*

Bardolph and Pistol are trying to convince Falstaff that they are sorry and desire to be taken back. Dame Quickly enters with a flattering message from Mistress Ford. It seems (and this is all according to the plot concocted in the previous scene) that Mistress Ford is pining away for love of Sir John Falstaff, and as Master Ford is always out between two and three in the afternoon perhaps the knight would pay a call then. And, what's more, adds Dame Quickly a moment later, Mistress Page is also pining for love of Falstaff, but unfortunately *her* husband is almost never out. Greatly pleased with himself, Sir John dismisses Dame Quickly and sings a monologue in praise of himself, *"Va, vecchio John, va!"* ("She goes, old John, she goes!")

Bardolph introduces Ford to Sir John, under the name of Brook; and Brook tells the fat man he needs his help. He wants to woo a certain Mistress Ford (his own wife, of course); and since his own efforts have been so far useless, perhaps Sir John, with his great experience in such matters, would help him. Money is no hindrance and Ford (alias Brook) lays a bag of it on the table, *"Io l'amo e lei non m'ama"* ("I love her, but she doesn't love me"). Ridiculously pleased with himself and his reputation, Falstaff promises his new friend success, for he (so he says) has already made some progress with Mistress Ford. And off he goes, taking the money with him, to dress himself properly for his conquest, *"Il diavolo se lo porti all'inferno"* ("The devil himself will take him to hell").

While he is gone, Ford sings a monologue on the subject of the faithlessness of women and how he plans to get a real revenge on Falstaff—*"È sogno? O realtà?"* ("Is it a dream? Is this reality?"). He works himself up into a great rage, but hides all of it when Falstaff returns, and the scene ends as both go out of the door together, arm in arm.

SCENE TWO: *A room in Ford's house.*

And now we shall see the climax of the women's plot against poor Falstaff. It takes place in a large room in

Ford's house, with doors, screens, staircases, and other things necessary for a scene of high farce. The ladies are discussing the coming fun, Dame Quickly reporting in detail on her visit to Sir John—*"Giunta all'Albergo della Giarrettiera"* ("The arrival of the host of the Garter Inn") —and Mistress Ford ordering in a large clothes hamper which is to be thrown out of the window and into the river when she gives the order later.

Only Anne Ford is not in good spirits, for her father, she reports, insists on her marrying the very unattractive Dr. Caius; but even she is cheered up into taking part in the fun when the others assure her of their help in her own love affair with Fenton. It is now after two o'clock, and the other ladies leave Mistress Ford alone in the room to give the expected Sir John a chance to get on with his wooing. He comes in and begins making love in the most ridiculous fashion. When Mistress Ford speaks of his extreme corpulence, he responds by claiming that once upon a time (if not now), when he was a page to the Duke of Northumberland, he was very slim indeed, *"Degno d'un Re"* ("Worthy of a King"). And, when Mistress Ford taunts him with really preferring Meg, Sir John swears that he hates the lady.

But just then, they are interrupted first by Dame Quickly and then by Mistress Page, who reports that Ford is on his way home in a terrific rage. Falstaff, who by this time has hidden behind a screen, overhears this and trembles; and a moment later Ford comes in accompanied by Bardolph, Pistol, Fenton, and Dr. Caius.

They look everywhere for Falstaff (except behind the screen, where he is), and while they are upstairs searching, he changes his hiding place to the interior of the clothes-basket. Taking advantage of this situation, Anne Ford and Fenton retire behind the screen for a bit of youthful love-making, singing a charming duet, *"Vien qua. Che chiasso!"* ("Come here. What an uproar!"). And so it happens that when the party of searchers descends from upstairs, they think it is Falstaff and Mistress Ford behind the screen making sounds of billing and cooing. They marshall their forces together with what looks like needless care and ferocity—only to discover the young lovers, who earn a denunciation from Ford for their behavior, *"Se t'agguanto! Se ti piglio!"* ("If I catch you again!").

Meantime, the women have piled various items of soiled laundry on top of Falstaff, who lies almost suffocating in the basket; and when the men go off again in search of their prey, Alice Ford calls in the servants and orders the basket taken up and heaved out of the window. Outside that window, as we learn from the dialogue, is the river Thames. And so, when the men come back from their search, Mistress Ford calls them to the window and points out the poor, bedraggled knight crawling up the muddy bank.

ACT THREE

SCENE ONE: *Outside the Garter Inn.*

Poor old John Falstaff sits sadly meditating on the rascally world, the vile world, which has sent so noble a fellow as himself to be doused ignominiously in the river— *"Mondo ladro. Mondo rubaldo."* ("Villainous world. Pilfering world!"). Dame Quickly visits him and quickly persuades the fatuous old fool that Mistress Ford had no part in his misfortunes, that she is much distressed by them, and in fact, she has a letter asking him to keep an appointment at midnight under Herne's Oak in Windsor Park. Falstaff is completely taken in.

Now Dame Quickly and the fat knight go inside the Inn to discuss the appointment in more detail, while the others come in to discuss their new plot. It will be a sort of masquerade aimed at Falstaff's further discomfiture. Mistress Page, in green, will be a wood nymph; Anne Ford, in white, will be Queen of the Fairies; Dame Quickly will be a goblin; and Mistress Ford will lead in a group of children dressed up as supernatural imps to make life miserable for Falstaff. Meantime, Ford takes Dr. Caius aside and assures him that he shall marry Anne Ford, for Anne will be dressed in white with a green scarf and, at the right moment, Caius shall lead her up to Ford who will bless them as bride and groom. Dame Quickly, coming out of the inn, overhears this little counter-plot, and resolves at once to save pretty Anne Ford from the terrible fate of having to marry the unattractive Dr. Caius when she is so dreadfully in love with handsome young Fenton.

Scene Two: *Windsor Park at Herne's Oak.*

Fenton is the first of the conspirators to arrive and he sings a kind of serenade, *"Da labbro il canto estasïato vola"* ("From your lip the song of ecstasy flies"), in praise of love, with Anne, in the distance, joining her voice with his at the end. Mistress Ford comes in and gets Fenton to become part of her plot to foil Ford in his plans of marrying Anne Ford to Dr. Caius—and Fenton puts on a monk's hood as a disguise.

Falstaff now comes to keep his appointment with Mistress Ford. He wears a great cloak with deer's antlers fastened to his head and, finding himself alone, is properly frightened of the place and the hour. Here Mistress Ford meets him and again he starts to make ridiculous love to her. But they hear Mistress Page calling for help. Mistress Ford runs off to find her friend, while the frightened knight simply throws himself on the ground in terror. Demons, he thinks, are coming—and they do, too; for Anne Ford, in disguise, of course, leads in the group of children; and presently everybody joins them. Fairies, imps, hob-goblins, all sorts of fantastic creatures pinch, poke, and pummel the poor fat knight until they think they have had enough of this fun, and then finally take off their disguises and show him the lesson of humility he should have learned by now.

But meantime, Dr. Caius has gone off to find Anne according to his agreement with Ford; and he brings in a white-robed figure to ask for the marital blessing. Mistress Ford brings in another couple, also in robes, and asks her husband to make this a sort of double wedding. And after he has agreeably done so, disguises are removed and the second couple turns out to be, of course, Anne Ford and young Fenton, while the first is Dr. Caius and—of all people—the red-nosed Bardolph, who palmed himself off, in a white robe, as Anne! Ford is willing to take his defeat in good grace; and now Falstaff, whose good nature is the most irrepressible part of him, leads everyone in a jolly fugue, *"Tutto nel mondo è burla"* ("All the world's a stage"), the conclusion of which is, "He laughs best who laughs last."

Tannhäuser

by RICHARD WAGNER (1813–1883)

Three Acts. Text by Wagner.
First produced in Dresden, 1845.

Hermann, Landgraf of Thuringia	*Bass*
Elisabeth, his niece	*Soprano*
Tannhäuser	*Tenor*
Wolfram }minstrel knights	*Baritone*
Biterolf	*Bass*
Venus, goddess of Love	*Soprano*
A shepherd boy	*Soprano*

The Three Graces, sirens, naiads, nymphs, bacchantes, nobles, knights, ladies, pilgrims.

TIME: *Early Thirteenth Century.*
PLACE: *In and near the castle of Wartburg, Thuringia, Germany.*

ACT ONE

SCENE ONE: *A mountain grotto.*

We are in a mysterious cave or grotto deep in the heart of the mountain known as "Venusberg". Here Venus, pagan goddess of love, holds her court, surrounded by nymphs, bacchantes, satyrs, and fauns. The grotto is illuminated faintly by multi-colored lights; a soft rosy mist seems to envelop it. Venus reclines on a couch, with Tannhäuser at her feet. Sirens and nymphs dance, growing more and more riotous in their frenzy. The wild Bacchanale is interrupted for a moment by the distant sound of an amorous Chorus of Sirens, contrasting strongly, in its voluptuous quiet, with the frenzied activity of the Bacchanale.

The Bacchanale is resumed, reaches a violent climax, and then subsides. The bacchantes and dancers sink down to rest, and a mist slowly fills the cave until only Venus,

Tannhäuser, and the Three Graces are visible in the foreground. The Graces dance languorously as in the background appear two visions illustrating mythological stories, one of Europa and the White Bull, the other of Leda and the Swan.

The Graces disappear and Venus and Tannhäuser are alone. Tannhäuser starts up restlessly and Venus, caressing him tenderly, asks what is troubling him. He replies that he dreams of his life on earth, of the sound of bells and the song of the nightingale. Venus hands him his harp and bids him sing of the joys of love and he does so passionately in his *"Dir töne Lob"* ("Hymn to Venus").

The voices of the Sirens are heard again softly from the distance. Tannhäuser repeats his praise of Venus, but insists that he is weary and must have his freedom. A year of sensual indulgence has brought satiety and he longs for human life, with sorrows as well as pleasures. Venus pleads with him to remain, then threatens him, but Tannhäuser replies that his faith lies in the Virgin Mary and at his mention of the name of the Virgin the profane spell of Venus is broken. In one of the most strikingly dramatic scenes in all opera, the magic grotto with its perfumed atmosphere disappears and Tannhäuser, without moving a step, finds himself standing in a mountain valley near the Castle of Wartburg.

Scene Two: *A mountain valley.*

It is a bright spring morning and the whole valley is flooded with sunlight. On a hilltop in the background, sharply outlined against the clear blue sky, is the Wartburg, with a winding pathway leading down from it. Near the spot where Tannhäuser is standing is a wayside shrine to the Virgin Mary. The tinkle of sheep bells is heard and on a grassy knoll a young shepherd boy plays his pipe and sings a simple song in praise of springtime.

A band of pilgrims passes by on their way to Rome, chanting their *"Pilgrims Chorus"*. Tannhäuser, who has not moved up to this moment, suddenly falls on his knees in front of the shrine and prays that his sins may be forgiven, as the song of the pilgrims slowly dies away in the distance.

Now a new and different sound is heard—the sound of

hunting horns drawing nearer. Soon a group of knights enter, returning from a hunt. Tannhäuser springs to his feet and they recognize him with astonishment and joyfully welcome him back to his home. They are curious to know where he has been for the past year, but he answers them evasively and says that he is doomed to wander alone and cannot stay. But his old friend, Wolfram, begs him to remain and tells him that the Princess Elisabeth has been pining for him and his songs and has not even entered the Hall of Minstrels since Tannhäuser's mysterious disappearance, *"Als du im kühnem Sange"* ("When for the prize we were contending").

At the mention of Elisabeth's name, Tannhäuser embraces Wolfram and greets the Landgraf and the other knights. Still more knights enter and join in the joyful reunion and in a few minutes the whole company sets out for the Wartburg.

ACT TWO

SCENE: *Hall of the Minstrels in the Wartburg.*

Landgraf Hermann has decreed a contest of song in honor of the return of Tannhäuser, the greatest singer of them all. The prize for this contest is to be the hand of the Landgraf's niece, Elisabeth, who, as we know, already loves Tannhäuser, and who is loved by Tannhäuser's friend, Wolfram. The contest is to take place in the great hall of the Castle of Wartburg, with its high Romanesque arches, its handsome throne for the Landgraf and Elisabeth, its great tiers of seats for the knights and their ladies.

Elisabeth, splendidly costumed, enters the hall alone and sings the ecstatic aria, *"Dich, teure Halle, grüss ich wieder"* ("Once more, beloved Hall, I greet thee"), and then Wolfram brings in Tannhäuser and stays quietly in the background as the happy pair sing their duet of reunion, *"Gepriesen sei die Stunde"* ("O blessed hour"). The penitent Tannhäuser begs Elisabeth never to mention the year of separation or to inquire where he has been. It is enough that he has returned and that they love each other. Overhearing this, Wolfram realizes that his own love for Elisabeth is hopeless.

Soon it is time for the contest to begin, and the Landgraf

and his niece greet every knight and lady in the court as they file in to the grandiose choral music and trumpet fanfares that has become familiar as the *"Tannhäuser March."* On the right sits the listening court, with the royal pair on the throne above them, and on the left are the six competing knights of song, attended by pages, with Tannhäuser and Wolfram among them.

The Landgraf gives them a speech of welcome, and Elisabeth draws from an urn the name of the man who is to sing first. The lot falls to Wolfram, who takes his harp and sings a song in praise of spiritual love, his "Eulogy of love"—*"Blick' ich umher"* ("Gazing on this fair assembly")—which is really the devoted but undeclared love he bears Elisabeth.

Tannhäuser has grown restless during Wolfram's song and at its conclusion, he seizes his harp and rises to his feet to express his scorn for such a pallid love as that of which Wolfram sings. Carried away by emotion, like one in a trance, he breaks into a boastful paean to sensual love, *"Dir Göttin der Liebe"* ("Thou, goddess of love"). There is consternation among the court as Tannhäuser's song grows ever wilder. One knight, Biterolf, more hot-headed than the others, interrupts Tannhäuser and rebukes him angrily. When Tannhäuser continues his song, Biterolf draws his sword.

The Landgraf bids Biterolf put up his sword, order is restored, and an attempt is made to go on with the contest. Wolfram starts to sing again, but is interrupted by Tannhäuser, who repeats his *"Hymn to Venus"*, saying that he alone of all those present knows the real joys of love, for he has learned them from Venus herself.

By this they know that Tannhäuser has visited the Venusberg. The ladies all flee from the hall in horror, all except Elisabeth, who seems too stricken to move. As the knights draw their swords and threaten to kill the erring Tannhäuser, she rushes down from her throne and intercedes for him, begging them to forgive him—*"Ich fleh' für ihn"* ("I plead for him").

Finally, the Landgraf rises and pronounces the sentence of banishment on Tannhäuser for his blasphemy, and demands that he join a band of pilgrims about to set out for Rome to seek absolution from the Pope. Tannhäuser by this time is full of remorse for his conduct. He throws himself down at Elisabeth's feet and then rises to join the band of pilgrims whom we hear chanting outside in the valley. With the words "To Rome!" he accepts the Landgraf's decree and, as the curtain falls, the knights repeat his cry.

ACT THREE

SCENE: *Before the shrine at which Tannhäuser prayed in Scene Two of Act One.*

It is autumn in the valley of the Wartburg when the curtain rises, and like the season, the day is dying. There, before the roadside shrine, Elisabeth prays silently for the salvation of Tannhäuser—"Elisabeth's Prayer", *"Allmächt'ge Jungfrau"* ("Almighty Virgin"), a devotional duty she performs every day, as we learn from Wolfram in his opening soliloquy. Soon we hear the pilgrims chanting on their return from Rome—they have won their salvation by grace. Elisabeth rises from her prayers and peers anxiously into the faces of the returning pilgrims. As the last one passes by, she realizes that Tannhäuser has not returned. Sadly, she kneels once more and in a deeply moving prayer begs the Virgin Mary to take her up to Heaven so that she may there plead for Tannhäuser's salvation. The prayer over, Wolfram asks to conduct her home, but she gently declines this offer and goes slowly up the woodland path to the castle.

Left alone on the slowly darkening stage, Wolfram sings the famous "Song of the Evening Star", *"O du mein holder Abendstern"* ("O thou sublime, sweet evening star"). At its close Tannhäuser enters in a wretched condition, so disheveled and distracted that we can hardly recognize him. He tells his old friend, Wolfram, what has happened—his pleadings to the Pope for forgiveness elicited only this answer: "If thou hast shared the joys of Hell where Venus dwells, thou art forevermore accursed. As my barren staff shall never flower again, so shalt thou never gain salvation." His hope gone, Tannhäuser's one remaining desire is to return to Venus, and a vision of the goddess and of the Venusberg rises in the background. Wolfram tries to hold back his friend, but Tannhäuser has ears only for the seductive song of the goddess of Love, and he is about to rush to the Venusberg again when Wolfram mentions the name—"Elisabeth!" As if by magic, the vision disappears, and Tannhäuser is overcome with remorse.

Down the winding path comes a slow procession bearing the body of Elisabeth, who has met death even as she had prayed for it. Now a new band of pilgrims appear. A miracle has been wrought, for they bring with them the staff of the Pope which has blossomed forth with fresh green leaves. This is a symbol of Tannhäuser's forgiveness and salvation, and it has been won for him by the devotion even unto death of Elisabeth. Tannhäuser falls by the bier as the pilgrims sing of his salvation. Sacred love has triumphed.

Lohengrin

by RICHARD WAGNER (1813–1883)

Three Acts. Text by Wagner.
First produced in Weimar, 1850.

Elsa, princess of Brabant	*Soprano*
Lohengrin, a knight of the Holy Grail	*Tenor*
Count Telramund of Brabant	*Baritone*
Ortrud, his wife	*Mezzo-soprano*
King Henry of Germany	*Bass*
A herald	*Bass*

Nobles of Brabant, Thuringia and Saxony, pages, ladies and gentlemen of the court, attendants.

TIME: *Tenth Century.*
PLACE: *Antwerp.*

ACT ONE

SCENE: *An open meadow outside the city of Antwerp.*

Brabant is a small principality, a part of the larger realm ruled over by King Henry. The king has come to Brabant, and when the curtain rises (after a very beautiful orchestral prelude) we find him holding court under a giant oak tree outside the medieval city of Antwerp beside the river Scheldt.

The late ruler of Brabant has left two children: a daughter, Elsa, and a younger brother, Gottfried, the latter being the actual heir to the throne. The guardian of the orphans, and the Regent of Brabant, is Count Telramund. The evil influence in the story is Ortrud, Telramund's wife, who is plotting to get rid of the two orphans and place her husband, Telramund, on the throne.

The young prince Gottfried has disappeared, and no one knows what has become of him. Telramund has accused Elsa of having done away with her brother. Elsa is called in to defend herself. She comes in, accompanied by her ladies in waiting. According to the custom of that far-off time, she must submit to what we call "trial by combat". Telramund, the accuser, will fight a duel with some knight who will volunteer to fight in defense of Elsa. But Elsa says she has no defender, except one who has appeared to her in a dream. In a very beautiful aria, known as *"Elsa's Traum"* ("Elsa's Dream"), she tells that "In my dream a knight in shining armor approaches me with words of consolation. He shall be my champion."

The trumpets sound a fanfare, the herald summons the champion, but there is only an uneasy silence. Twice the call is made, and then for the third time the herald makes his proclamation. This time there is murmuring among the crowd of onlookers, increasing to great excitement. A swan is seen swimming down the river, drawing a small boat by a golden chain, and in the boat stands a "knight in shining armor".

The knight steps ashore, bids farewell to the swan, *"Nun sei bedankt, mein lieber Schwan"* ("Now farewell, beloved swan")—a touching and beautiful passage—and then turns to the king and announces that he has come to fight for Elsa. He then asks Elsa to become his wife after he has won the fight. But there must be one condition—she must *never* ask his name, nor whence he came—*"Nie sollst du mich befragen"* ("These questions ask me never"). Elsa, almost in a trance, readily agrees.

Then follows a dignified and moving prayer, *"Mein Herr und Gott, nun ruf' ich dich"* ("My lord and God, I cry to thee"), in which the king implores God to see that justice is done, a prayer finally joined in by all present. An open space is marked off for the combat, trumpets are sounded, and the king strikes his shield three times with his sword as a signal for the duel to begin.

It is a very brief one. Almost at once Lohengrin strikes Telramund to earth with a mighty blow but spares his life. The crowd shouts its acclaim to the victor, Lohengrin embraces Elsa joyfully, and the act ends with great rejoicing by all except Ortrud and Telramund.

ACT TWO

SCENE: *Courtyard of the fortress of Antwerp.*

Three buildings surround the courtyard: in the background is the dwelling of the knights, on the left the Kemenate (the women's quarters), and on the right the impressive front of the cathedral. It is night. Telramund and Ortrud are lurking in the shadows and we hear a long argument between them as they blame each other for the disgrace that has led to their imminent exile. Telramund, in bitter anger, blames their downfall on Ortrud's plotting, but she is equally scornful of him and says that if he had drawn but one drop of blood from Lohengrin, then the "knight in shining armor" would have lost his magical power.

But she insists that all is not yet lost. It is obvious that Lohengrin's supernatural power is somehow bound up with the secret of his name and, if this can be found out, then he will be as other men. One person can draw the secret from him—Elsa; and Ortrud and Telramund swear an oath of vengeance for their disgrace.

And now Elsa appears on the balcony to sing of her supreme happiness, *"Euch Lüften, die mein Klagen"* ("Ye wandering breeze"). Dismissing Telramund, Ortrud begins to work her wiles on the innocent maiden. She comes as a friend, she says, and wishes Elsa only happiness. She expresses her repentance for any unintentional evil she and Telramund may have wrought, but even as she is speaking of her good will, she is sowing in Elsa's mind certain doubts about her bridegroom's origin. But Elsa is too full of her own joy to be suspicious, and she bids Ortrud to wait, while she returns to her chamber. During this brief wait, Ortrud calls upon Odin and Freia, her pagan gods, with a wild appeal.

Elsa has descended from the balcony and now appears at the door of the Kemenate with two ladies in waiting and invites Ortrud to come with her to prepare for the wedding ceremony.

Dawn is breaking and as the skies grow lighter, trumpet calls are heard from various parts of the fortress, and the day's activities begin. Slowly the courtyard fills up with soldiers, knights and members of the court. A herald proclaims the banishment of Telramund and the marriage of Lohengrin and Elsa.

In stately procession, Elsa and her attendants emerge from the Kemenate and start to cross the courtyard but before they reach the cathedral steps they are stopped by Ortrud, who haughtily says she will no longer cringe before Elsa like a servant but will take her rightful place. Then she challenges Elsa to tell the name of the man she is to marry. Elsa replies proudly that her husband-to-be is a stainless knight who conquered Telramund in fair fight and spared his life. But Ortrud insists that the unknown warrior is an evil sorcerer.

At this moment, King Henry, Lohengrin, and other knights come into the courtyard. Ortrud is ordered away and once more the bridal procession moves forward, and once more is interrupted, this time by Telramund. The other knights cry out against him, but he angrily demands to be heard and repeats Ortrud's accusation that Lohengrin is a sorcerer and has won by evil magic. Lohengrin replies that his honor is not questionable and that he is responsible to no one but Elsa. The king and the other knights crowd around Lohengrin in approval and Telramund and Ortrud are ordered to be gone.

The bridal procession is reformed after this stormy scene and moves once more toward the cathedral steps. Telramund and Ortrud stand aside, but they know that they have sowed the seeds of suspicion in Elsa's mind. And Lohengrin, greatly troubled, knows it too, for he has seen in Elsa's eyes a look of fear and doubt. Just as the bridal pair reach the portals of the cathedral, Ortrud lifts a threatening hand, and the orchestra thunders out the stern music suggesting the fatal questions Elsa has promised not to ask.

ACT THREE

SCENE ONE: *The bridal chamber.*

The stirring orchestral Prelude to the third act brilliantly suggests the excitement of the great medieval military wedding that has just taken place between Elsa and Lohengrin; and when the curtain rises we hear the familiar strains of the "Wedding March" (*"Treulich geführt"*), perhaps the best-known melody in all opera. Into the bridal chamber come the bride and groom, the king, and many attendants, and after a few brief ceremonies the happy pair is left alone.

There follows a long and beautifully melodious duet in which the two express their happiness and confidence in each other, *"Das süsse Lied verhallt"* ("The sweet song dies away"). And yet, the seed of doubt remains in Elsa's mind concerning the name and origin of her knight and champion. Tenderly he tries to reassure her, but all in vain. Elsa imagines she sees the swan approaching to take her husband away from her and desperately, as though some demonic power were driving her on, she asks the fatal question: "What is thy name? Whence dost thou come? What is thy origin?"

But even before the grief-stricken knight can answer, Elsa sees Telramund enter the room with drawn sword. "Defend thyself!" she cries to Lohengrin and hands him his sword. With one magical blow, Telramund is slain, but sorrowfully, heart-broken, Lohengrin says, *"Weh! Nun ist all' unser Glück dahin"* ("Alas, now all our joy is fled").

SCENE TWO: *Same as Act One.*

Once more the king stands under the judgment oak, and all the nobles of Brabant are gathered together. The body of Telramund is borne in and Lohengrin is adjudged right in having slain his enemy. But now, says the hero, he must tell them that Elsa has asked the fatal question and he must answer.

Then, in the famous passage known as "Lohengrin's Narrative"—*"In fernem Land"* ("In distant land"), he tells them that he comes from Monsalvat, the home of the

Knights of the Holy Grail—that he himself is one of those knights, that Parsifal, leader of the knights, is his father, and that his name is Lohengrin. Now the swan once more draws the boat to the shore and is sorrowfully greeted by Lohengrin. Then turning to Elsa, he bids her a heartbroken farewell and gives her his horn, his ring, and his sword for her brother Gottfried, should he return.

Lohengrin then sinks to his knees in silent prayer and in the orchestra we hear the theme of the Holy Grail as the white dove of the Grail descends from heaven and hovers over the boat. Perceiving it, Lohengrin springs up and unfastens the chain which binds the swan to the boat, whereupon the swan immediately sinks, and in its place there stands on the river bank a handsome youth in gleaming silver garments. "Behold your ruler!" cries Lohengrin.

At the sight of the young Prince Gottfried, Ortrud sinks down with a shriek for it is she who, by evil magic, changed the Prince into a swan, falsely accusing Elsa of having murdered him. Now all her evil plotting has come to naught. Lohengrin steps into the boat and the dove (in place of the swan) seizes the chain and draws the boat down the stream. Elsa gives a last despairing cry, "My husband, my husband!" as the figure of Lohengrin recedes into the distance.

Tristan und Isolde

by RICHARD WAGNER (1813–1883)

Three Acts. Text by Wagner.
First produced in Munich, 1865.

Tristan	*Tenor*
Isolde	*Soprano*
Brangäne	*Mezzo-soprano*
Kurvenal	*Baritone*
King Marke	*Bass*
Melot	*Tenor*
A shepherd	*Tenor*
Voice of a young sailor	*Tenor*

Sailors, soldiers, knights, attendants.

TIME: *Middle Ages.*
PLACE: *On shipboard, in Cornwall and Brittany.*

ACT ONE

SCENE: *Deck of a ship at sea.*

When the curtain rises, it is not an ordinary ship's deck which we see, but a kind of royal pavilion which the sailors have set up for the Irish princess, Isolde, and her serving-maid, Brangäne. Rugs cover the deck, there are rich hangings and tapestries and a luxurious couch. A large curtain strung across the back of the scene hides the after-part of the ship.

As the act begins, Isolde is reclining on the couch, while Brangäne stands at the rail, gazing off to sea. All we know at the moment is that Isolde is being taken across the sea from Ireland to Cornwall in England to marry the king of the latter country in an effort to bring about peace between the two countries which have been at war. As the act progresses, however, we learn that the situation is not as simple as it appears to be, for much has happened to the chief characters before the curtain rises.

The first music we hear is the voice of a sailor who occupies the lookout's post high up on the mast. He sings a sailor's "chantey" about the Irish girl he left behind, *"Westwärts schweift der Blick"* ("Westward sweeps the eye"). This is a kind of folk-song, but to Isolde it seems like a studied insult. In a black mood, she declares that she is suffocating and tells Brangäne to draw the curtains.

Brangäne does so, and now we see for the first time the after-part of the ship. Sailors are grouped about the main mast, while on the lofty after-deck is a group of knights with their leader, Tristan, at the helm. Isolde tells Brangäne that she wishes Tristan to come to her. It is not a request, but an order.

Brangäne delivers the message, but Tristan replies that he cannot leave the helm until he has brought the ship safely into port. Kurvenal, Tristan's devoted henchman, answers Brangäne rudely and sings a song in praise of his master and the sailors join in the rousing chorus. Brangäne closes the curtains hastily.

In a long scene between Isolde and Brangäne we now learn the beginning of the story—*"Weh! dies zu dulden"* ("Ah! an answer so insulting"). Isolde, the Irish princess, had been engaged to marry a noble knight named Sir Morold. During the course of the long warfare between Ireland and Cornwall, Morold had been killed by the Cornish knight, Tristan, who cut off the slain knight's head and sent it back to Ireland. But Tristan himself had been severely wounded in the combat and his wound did not heal. We also learn that Isolde and her mother were famous as sorceresses and their potions were reputed to have magical power. She tells how the wounded Tristan went to Ireland and placed himself in her care. He called himself Tantris, but Isolde soon discovered his real identity, for a broken fragment of steel taken from the dead Morold fitted exactly into a nick in the sword of the wounded knight, Tantris. But though Isolde felt impelled to revenge the death of her fiancé, now that his murderer was in her power, she could not bring herself to do the deed, for she realized that she had fallen in love with the wounded knight and felt that he also loved her.

And so she nursed him back to health and he left, vowing eternal gratitude, but never mentioning love. Shortly after that he returned to Ireland, not as a lover, but as a messenger from his uncle, King Marke of Cornwall, entrusted to bring back to Cornwall the Irish princess who was to marry the king. And now the voyage is nearly over, and Tristan has not spoken to Isolde, or acknowledged in any way that they had ever met before. Isolde broods bitterly over this strange behavior, which she regards as the basest treachery. By refusing to obey her command, Tristan has now added insult to injury, and Isolde's sense of outrage and betrayal is more than she can endure. She declares that she will never reach Cornwall alive to be married to "the old and weary king". But her own death will not be enough to wipe out the betrayal—Tristan also must share the atonement with her.

She reminds Brangäne of some magic potions her mother had given her as she set out on the unhappy voyage. Brangäne brings the casket and Isolde selects the death potion and orders Brangäne to prepare it in a goblet of wine. Kurvenal now appears and tells the ladies they are approaching port and orders them to prepare for a speedy landing.

Again Isolde sends a message to Tristan that she would speak with him before leaving the ship. Kurvenal delivers the message and this time Tristan complies. He enters the pavilion with great dignity. Isolde demands vengeance for the death of Morold, and Tristan offers her his sword so that she may strike the fatal blow herself. But she refuses and, instead, invites him to drink a toast with her. Tristan understands all too well the real meaning of her invitation, but he accepts, knowing that it will mean death. But, unknown to Isolde, Brangäne has put a love potion in the goblet of wine instead of the death potion. The young lovers drink and their despair is changed into ecstasy just as the ship enters the harbor. They are oblivious to what is going on around them as we hear the shouts of the sailors making ready to go ashore.

ACT TWO

SCENE: *Garden of King Marke's castle.*

It is a beautiful, luminous summer night. A single large torch lights up the terrace and entrance to the castle while on the right-hand side of the stage we catch a glimpse of dark woods. The king has gone on a hunt and we hear the sound of hunting horns going farther and farther away until they are lost in the distance. Isolde is impatiently awaiting Tristan. But Brangäne warns her mistress that this is a false hunt, that Melot, a henchman of the king's, has set a trap to catch the lovers, for Melot himself is more than half in love with Isolde.

But Isolde refuses to believe this. She extinguishes the torch—the signal for Tristan to come—and mounting the steps, waves her long white scarf for him. Brangäne goes up into the castle tower to keep watch for the two lovers. The music grows more fervid and Tristan rushes in. The lovers throw themselves into each other's arms.

With passionate intensity, they sing of the ecstasy of their love, *"Isolde!" "Tristan!" "Geliebter!"* ("Isolde!" "Tristan!" "Beloved!"). At length the music sinks down to a gentle murmur and the two lovers seat themselves on a garden bench in silent bliss. We hear the soft sound of a fountain, and very tenderly, very quietly, the two lovers sing of the peace and beauty of the night, which holds truth and love for them as opposed to the harsh lying cruelty of day, *"O sink hernieder, Nacht der Liebe"*, ("Descend upon us, night of love").

Twice during this duet, we hear the voice of Brangäne as it floats down from the watch tower, *"Habet Acht!"* ("Beware"). The warning goes unheeded by the two lovers. Through all their ecstasy runs the dark threat of death, and in the midst of their joy they long to die together.

Suddenly, the love music is rudely interrupted. From the watch tower Brangäne shrieks in terror. Kurvenal rushes in shouting a warning to Tristan. "Save thyself," he cries, but it is too late. King Marke, Melot, and the other huntsmen come in hastily. Tristan springs to his feet and holds his mantle before Isolde, hiding her from curious and malicious eyes. For a few moments, no one moves or speaks, until Tristan murmurs to himself, "Hateful day—for the last time!"

Melot breaks the silence by a proud boast that his suspicions have proved correct and his trap has been successful. But King Marke stands in stunned sorrow at this betrayal. When he speaks, it is not revenge but grief that he expresses. Tristan, his nephew, most trusted of his knights, the very soul of honor! If honor does not dwell with Tristan, where can it be found? When he cries out to know why this blow has befallen him, Tristan answers sadly that there is no answer.

Tristan tells Isolde that he must go "to a dark country" and asks if she will follow him there, *"Wohin nun Tristan scheidet"* ("Where Tristan now is going"). She quickly assents. This is more than Melot can bear and he attacks Tristan with his sword. Tristan, dropping his guard, is wounded. Melot would kill Tristan then and there but is restrained by King Marke. Isolde throws herself on the body of the wounded knight as the curtain falls.

ACT THREE

SCENE: *Courtyard of Tristan's castle in Brittany.*

Tristan's castle is on a promontory thrusting out into the sea. In the center of the courtyard is a large linden tree and, lying on a couch in the shade of the tree lies the wounded Tristan, wrapped in a blanket and watched over by the anxious Kurvenal. From nearby comes the mournful sound of a shepherd's pipe, playing a melancholy song. Over the ramparts we can see the blue waters of the ocean stretching off to the empty horizon. The scene is one of utter loneliness and desolation.

The shepherd stops his piping long enough to slip in quietly to ask if Sir Tristan has wakened yet, but Kurvenal replies that he fears that if he wakes, it will only be to die. He bids the shepherd to return to his post to keep watch over the sea and reminds him that if he sees a ship, he is to change his tune and play a joyful melody.

After the shepherd has left, Tristan wakens. At first, he does not know where he is, and Kurvenal reminds him of the scene in the garden of King Marke's castle and tells the wounded knight that he has brought him home to recover. More than that, Kurvenal says that he has sent a message to Isolde, asking her to come with her magic potions and nurse Tristan back to health, as she did before. Half delirious, Tristan sings again of the hateful day and the blessed shadows of the night. He recalls the few brief moments of happiness he and Isolde enjoyed together and the cruel fate that brings such suffering to them. The excitement of old emotions is too much for him and he sinks back exhausted.

Suddenly, the shepherd's tune, which has been heard at intervals, changes from its mournful cadence to a merry little ditty. It is the signal that a ship is entering the harbor. Kurvenal rushes to the ramparts and looks down. It is Isolde who is coming. Tristan can no longer control his excitement. Crying "The ship, the ship!" he springs to his feet and wildly tears the bandages from his wound. Isolde hurries in and takes him in her arms, but it is too late. They have barely time to greet each other, when Tristan sinks dying at her feet.

And now another ship is entering the harbor and this time it is King Marke who is coming. Kurvenal calls on the other henchmen of the castle to help him defend it. He makes a hasty effort to barricade the entrance to the courtyard, but as he does so, Melot rushes in. Kurvenal kills him with one mighty blow and then runs out, sword in hand, to fight the other attackers. We hear the sounds of combat and in a moment Kurvenal staggers back into the courtyard, mortally wounded, and falls dead beside the couch of his master, Tristan.

His death is in vain, for King Marke has come not to separate the lovers, but to unite them and give them his blessing, for Brangäne has told him of how she substituted the love potion for the death potion.

Through all this, Isolde remains oblivious to everything, holding the body of her beloved Tristan in her arms. Almost in a trance, she sings the transcendently beautiful *"Liebestod"* ("Love-death"), a great paean of reconciliation between love and death. The music, in ascending phrases, seems to rise to Heaven itself and at its end, Isolde sinks lifeless by the side of her beloved, as King Marke sadly blesses the two ill-fated lovers, united at last in death.

Die Meistersinger

(The Mastersingers)

by RICHARD WAGNER (1813–1883)

Three Acts. Text by Wagner.
First produced in Munich, 1868.

Walther von Stolzing, a young knight		*Tenor*
Eva, daughter of Veit Pogner		*Soprano*
Magdalene, her companion		*Mezzo-soprano*
Hans Sachs, shoemaker		*Bass-baritone*
Veit Pogner, goldsmith	Master-	*Bass*
Sixtus Beckmesser, town clerk	singers	*Baritone*
Fritz Kothner, baker		*Bass*
David, apprentice to Hans Sachs		*Tenor*
Night watchman		*Bass*

Mastersingers, journeymen and apprentices of the guilds, townspeople, and children.

TIME: *Middle of the Sixteenth Century.*
PLACE: *Nuremberg.*

ACT ONE

SCENE: *Interior of St. Katherine's Church.*

It is St. John's Eve and a religious service is just coming to an end. Accompanied by organ music, the congregation is singing the closing chorale of the service, *"Da zu Dir der Heiland kam"* ("When to thee our Saviour went"). Standing by a pillar in the rear of the church is the young knight, Walther von Stolzing. He takes no part in the service but is trying to attract the attention of the young girl, Eva Pogner, who, with her maid and companion, Magdalene, is occupying one of the rear pews. It is obvious that she is well aware of the handsome young man who is gazing at her so intently.

The chorale over, the congregation begins to leave the church and Walther approaches the two young women and begs a word from Eva. They have only recently met and he asks her anxiously if she is already betrothed. She tells him frankly that her father, who is an ardent member of the Mastersingers' Guild, has promised her as the prize in a contest of song which the Guild is to hold on the following day. David, a young apprentice, now joins the group and tells them that he must prepare the church for a meeting of the Mastersingers, who have promised to hear a number of apprentices who wish to join the Guild. David and Magdalene are much in love with each other and feel very sympathetic toward the two other lovers. Walther decides to compete for membership in the Guild, thus making him eligible for the contest for Eva's hand, and David promises to help him all he can. Walther and Eva agree to meet that evening and the two young women leave the church.

Other young apprentices now begin to arrange benches for the meeting of the mastersingers. After the benches are lined up, they set up in front of them a small platform with a chair on it and a table, on which they put a large slate. Around this platform is hung a dark curtain and behind this curtain is to sit the "Marker" who will mark down on the slate all the mistakes made by the candidate for membership. Opposite the Marker's chair is another large and rather ornate chair where the candidate is to sit during his audition.

While the Marker's booth is being arranged, Walther sits in the candidate's chair and listens while the friendly David gives him an elementary lesson in the complex old-fashioned rules of music and poetry which must be strictly adhered to by anyone rash enough to aspire to membership in the Mastersingers' Guild. Far from being a "mastersinger", Walther has never had any formal training in either music or poetry and he is somewhat dismayed by the technical requirements which must be met before he can be called a "master".

The apprentices have not made a very good job of their work and David has to interrupt his instructions to Walther in order to take down the Marker's booth and set it up all over again. This is finished just in time, as the mastersingers enter and greet each other in friendly fashion and seat themselves on the benches. Fritz Kothner calls the roll and all twelve members of the guild report "present". They are all craftsmen of various trades and prize most highly their membership in the guild of music and poetry.

One of the mastersingers, Veit Pogner, a goldsmith, makes a long and rather pompous speech, *"Das schöne Fest"* ("The beautiful feast"), in which he announces that his most precious possession, his daughter Eva, will be the prize at the contest of song to be held on the morrow. Hans Sachs speaks up and says that the young lady herself should have something to say about it and anyway, why should they, the mastersingers, make their own decisions according to their own rules? Why not let the public decide who the winner is? This suggestion causes great consternation among the other mastersingers and after considerable argument, a compromise is agreed upon. The opinion of the public will be considered, but only members of the guild will be eligible to compete, and Eva is to have the privilege of rejecting the winner if she chooses to do so.

Walther is now introduced as a candidate for membership. When they ask him where he studied the arts of music and poetry, he proudly replies that he drew his inspiration from an old book by a famous minstrel, Walther von der Vogelweide, and from the beaties of nature—*"Am stillen Herd in Winterzeit"* ("By the silent hearth in wintertime"). The mastersingers are not much impressed with this. One of them, the crotchety and sour-visaged town clerk, Beckmesser, steps into the Marker's booth, but before he draws the curtain, he holds up the slate and grimly calls attention to the fact that the candidate is allowed only seven mistakes. "Now begin!" he says spitefully, as he yanks the curtains in place.

Walther, seated in the candidate's chair, picks up the words as the theme of his song, *"Fanget an!"* ("Now begin, sings the spring in the forest"). As he proceeds, we hear Beckmesser marking down dozens of mistakes on his slate. Walther, it seems, has broken practically every rule of both music and poetry. Suddenly, Beckmesser jerks the curtain aside angrily and holds up the slate which is completely covered with marks, and demands an end to the farce. The mastersingers express their disapproval in unmistakable terms and Walther is voted down unanimously. Only Hans Sachs has the sensitivity and genius to recognize that despite Walther's violation of the formal rules, his song shows extraordinary talent. And so the meeting breaks up with Walther very angry and defiant at the treatment he has received, and wise old Hans Sachs discouraged at the narrow-mindedness of his colleagues.

ACT TWO

SCENE: *A street in Nuremberg.*

It is evening of the same day. On the right is the large house of Veit Pogner, the goldsmith, shaded by a big linden tree. Across the street is the humble home and workshop of Hans Sachs, the cobbler, with an elder tree in full bloom beside it. A group of young apprentices is busy putting up the shutters at the windows of the various shops along the street, among them David. Magdalene slips out of Pogner's house to inquire from David the outcome of the audition and David tells her that Walther has been unanimously rejected by the Mastersingers.

The street becomes quiet as the apprentices leave for their homes. Pogner and Eva stroll in and seat themselves on a stone bench under the branches of the linden tree. After a few minutes, Pogner enters his house and Magdalene tells Eva the sad news about Walther's failure. Through the open door of his shop, Sachs can be seen working on a pair of shoes. As he does so, he meditates on the beauty of the summer evening, the air sweetly perfumed by the blossoms of the elder tree, *"Wie duftet doch der Flieder"* ("The elder's scent is waxing").

Eva speaks to him of the mastersingers' rejection of Walther and it is not difficult for Sachs to perceive her real feelings toward the handsome young knight. Sachs is a widower and has long loved his young neighbor, whom he has known since childhood, but he recognizes the fact that he is too old for her and resolves to do what he can to help the two young people. He retires into the back of his shop and Magdalene comes to call Eva home. She tells her that Beckmesser is planning to serenade her that very evening and the two young women agree that Magdalene is to don Eva's clothes and appear at the window to receive the serenade, while Eva is to meet her lover under the linden tree.

Before Eva can enter her home, Walther appears and the two young lovers, recognizing the hopelessness of their position, plan to elope that very night. But Sachs overhears their plans. He determines to prevent such a rash solution of the problem and flings open the door of his shop so that his light shines brightly across the street. When Beckmesser appears to sing his serenade, Sachs takes matters into his own hands still more by moving his workbench out into the street. As Beckmesser tunes his lute and attempts to sing, *"Den Tag seh' ich erscheinen"* ("I see the dawning daylight"), Sachs hammers away at his work singing lustily.

When Beckmesser angrily protests, Sachs says that he will act as Marker and will only hammer when Beckmesser makes a mistake. This only makes matters worse, as Sachs evidently finds as many flaws in Beckmesser's music as the latter had found in Walther's earlier in the day. Neighbors are aroused by the noise and heads in nightcaps begin appearing at the windows of the houses along the street. Among them is David, who recognizes Magdalene as she leans from the upstairs window of Pogner's house posing as Eva. David rushes out and picks up a stick with which he belabors poor Beckmesser; other neighbors join in, and in a few moments the street is full of a brawling mob. Eva and Walther attempt to escape in the confusion, but are intercepted by Sachs, who takes Walther into his house, while the irate Pogner takes charge of his daughter.

At the climax of the hubbub, the nightwatchman's horn is heard and the crowd disappears as suddenly as it gathered. Doors and windows are closed as the nightwatchman strolls through the quiet street, intoning his old call announcing that it is eleven o'clock and all is well. A full moon has arisen above the housetops as the nightwatchman disappears down the street.

ACT THREE

Scene One: *Interior of Sachs' workshop.*

Sunlight floods the room. Sachs sits in an armchair reading a large book which he holds on his lap. He is so absorbed that he does not notice the arrival of David who comes in timidly to ask forgiveness for his part in the brawl the night before. Sachs closes his book and orders David to dress for the St. John's Day festival, which is about to begin. Musing over the folly of mankind, Sachs sings his famous monologue, *'Wahn, Wahn, überall Wahn'* ("Mad, mad, all the world's mad").

Walther has spent the night in Sachs' house and now enters and tells Sachs of a beautiful dream he has had. Sachs suggests he put the dream into poetry and music and he writes down the song as Walther sings it, making comments and suggestions as he goes along. It is the famous *"Preislied"* ("Prize Song"), which we hear in its entirety later on.

Sachs and Walther go into the inner room to dress for the festival and Beckmesser enters, still stiff and sore from the drubbing he had received the evening before. He spies the manuscript on the table and, thinking it an original composition by Sachs, the best of the mastersingers, hides it in his doublet. When Sachs enters, Beckmesser accuses him of bringing about his discomfiture, so that Sachs himself can enter the contest and win the fair Eva. But Sachs, realizing that Beckmesser can never live up to Walther's beautiful poem, makes him a present of it and Beckmesser, overjoyed, limps out with the song that he thinks will bring him victory.

Now Eva enters, dressed all in white, and complains that her new shoes do not fit, but Sachs knows full well the reason for her visit, for when Walther appears, splendidly dressed for the festival, the two young lovers gaze at each other rapturously. Suddenly, impulsively, Eva throws her arms around Sachs' neck exclaiming that she has always loved him. But Sachs gently frees himself from her embrace and tells her that he knows too well the story of *Tristan and Isolde,* in which a young woman marries a middle-aged man, and he has no wish to play the role of King Marke. David and Magdalene enter the room and Sachs declares that David is no longer an apprentice, but this day becomes a journeyman shoemaker, giving him the traditional box-on-the-ear, as David kneels before him. The two pairs of young lovers, Eva and Walther and Magdalene and David, join with Sachs in a happy quintet, *"Selig wie die Sonne"* ("Blessed as the sunlight").

SCENE TWO: *A meadow outside the town walls.*

At one side of the stage is a large platform, gaily decorated with flags and bunting. A crowd of townspeople has
assembled and there is dancing and merrymaking, which
is interrupted by the arrival of the various guilds, each
marching to its own music and carrying its own banner.
The tailors, the bakers, and the other tradesmen are wel-
comed by the crowd. Last of all come the mastersingers,
who take their places on the platform, giving a place of
honor in the front row to Eva. For a moment, there is a
solemn hush, and then the crowd and the mastersingers
join in a beautiful chorale, *"Wach auf"* ("Awake, the day
is dawning").

Now comes the great event of the day—the contest for
the hand of the fair Eva. Sachs, as master of ceremonies,
introduces Beckmesser as the first contestant. A grassy
mound has been prepared for the singers and Beckmesser
takes his place on it nervously, fingering his lute and trying
to refresh his memory by consulting the manuscript which
he has concealed in his doublet. He is a ludicrous but rather
pathetic figure and his efforts to sing are greeted by laughter
from the crowd, subdued at first but growing louder as the
unfortunate man gets more and more confused. Finally,
Beckmesser hurls the manuscript at Hans Sachs, shouting
that he is the author of the ridiculous poem, and rushes
wildly from the scene, followed by shouts of derision.

Then Sachs declares that the real poet is young Walther
von Stolzing and calls on him to sing the song. Walther
stands on the grassy mound and sings the "Prize Song"—
"Morgenlicht leuchtend im rosigen Schein" ("Morning
dawns in rosy light"). As he finishes, the crowd and the
mastersingers shout their approval and he is declared winner of the contest. Eva places the laurel wreath on his
brow and Pogner brings forward the gold chain which proclaims him a mastersinger. But Walther angrily refuses to
allow the chain to be placed around his neck, as he is still
rankling at the treatment he received from the mastersingers the day before.

But Hans Sachs wisely and kindly advises the young man
to restrain his fiery temper and not to despise the rules of
the masters, which have preserved the sacred standards of

the arts. And Walther, deeply touched by Sachs' words, consents to receive the gold chain from Pogner. Then all turn in homage to Sachs and the curtain falls to a joyous chorus, *"Heil Sachs!"* ("Hail to Sachs!").

Das Rheingold

by RICHARD WAGNER (1813–1883)

One Act, Four Scenes. Text by Wagner.
First produced in Munich, 1869.

Wotan, ruler of the Gods		*Bass-baritone*
Fricka, wife of Wotan, goddess of marriage and the home		*Mezzo-soprano*
Freia, goddess of youth		*Soprano*
Froh, god of youth		*Tenor*
Donner, god of thunder		*Baritone*
Loge, god of fire		*Tenor*
Erda, goddess of wisdom		*Contralto*
Alberich, a dwarf of the Nibelung race		*Baritone*
Mime, brother of Alberich		*Tenor*
Rhinemaidens	Woglinde	*Soprano*
	Wellgunde	*Mezzo-soprano*
	Flosshilde	*Contralto*
Giants	Fasolt	*Bass*
	Fafner	*Bass*

Nibelung dwarfs and slaves.

TIME: *Legendary.*
PLACE: *Northern Europe.*

(First of the four music dramas comprising "The Ring of the Nibelungs.")

SCENE ONE: *At the bottom of the Rhine.*

A faint bluish-green light penetrates into the dark depths of the river from the surface far above. Rough rocks indicate the bottom of the river. Dimly seen through the murky waters, three figures are swimming about. They are the Rhinemaidens and they are frolicking in the water as they guard a precious treasure of pure gold which has been confided to their care.

Clambering over the rocks at the bottom of the river is Alberich, an ugly dwarf of the Nibelung race, with matted hair and unkempt beard. He tries awkwardly to embrace the Rhinemaidens, who one by one float enticingly near him but always elude him and laugh at his clumsy efforts.

A soft, rosy glow begins to light up the waters of the river. It is the mysterious Rhinegold. Fascinated, Alberich questions the Rhinemaidens about it, and they foolishly reveal to him the mystery of the treasure they are guarding. The Rhinegold, forged into a ring by anyone bold enough to become its possessor, will confer upon him an unlimited power over the whole universe, for he will be even mightier than the gods themselves, but this power will be his only if he renounces love forever.

Alberich climbs slowly and painfully to the top of the rock and cries, *"Der Welt Erbe gewänn ich"* ("I renounce love forever"), and wrenches the gold from its rocky base. With a burst of mocking and triumphant laughter, he clambers down the rock and disappears with his treasure. Now that the magic gold is gone, the river is plunged in darkness and we hear the despairing cries of the Rhinemaidens.

SCENE TWO: *An open space on a mountain height.*

As the orchestra continues with a symphonic interlude, the dark murky waters of the Rhine seem to disappear and are replaced by heavy clouds of fog, and when these clear away we find ourselves on a rocky height. Far away, on the summit of a high mountain, stands a castle with numberless pinnacles glittering in the rays of the rising sun. Wotan and Fricka, reposing on a hillock, awaken and contemplate the castle which has just been completed by the giants, Fasolt and Fafner, according to Wotan's orders. But the bargain which Wotan made with them now returns to plague him.

Foolishly, in his desire to live magnificently, as befits the ruler of the gods, Wotan promised to give to the giants Fricka's sister, Freia, goddess of youth, love, and beauty. Fricka reproaches him for his folly and urges him to protect Freia and to persuade the giants to take some other reward for their labors. Freia, herself, now rushes in and begs Wotan to protect her. The two giants, huge shaggy creatures armed with enormous clubs almost as big as young trees, come lumbering across the mountainside in search of their reward.

They seize Freia and attempt to carry her off, but her brothers, the gods Froh and Donner, bar their way. Wotan, raising his spear, forbids them to fight and just at that moment, a newcomer appears on the scene and offers a solution to the dilemma. It is Loge, the shrewd and crafty god of fire. It was Loge who urged Wotan into his ruinous agreement with the giants and as the time approached for the fulfilment of the bargain, Wotan sent Loge all over the world in search of some compensation to offer the builders in exchange for the radiant goddess. But Loge reports that he has found nothing which anyone would be likely to prefer to woman and youth. Only one single creature, the dwarf Alberich, has renounced those precious things for the gold which bestowed power, and he has cursed love.

The avarice of the giants is excited at this story and after a long consultation, they offer to exchange Freia if Wotan will get for them the magic gold. But in the meantime, they will hold Freia as hostage, and, seizing her roughly, they take her away. Now the stage grows dark and the faces of the gods seem to grow old, for it was Freia who had supplied them with eternal youth. Wotan resolves to descend into the gloomy kingdom of the Nibelungs and to gain the magic Ring, not to restore it to its rightful owners, the Rhinemaidens, but to use it for his own purpose— for the ransom of the goddess Freia. Accompanied by Loge, he descends into a cleft in the rock.

SCENE THREE: *The subterranean caverns of Nibelheim.*

Through the orchestral interlude, the stage seems to be hidden by an opaque curtain of steam as Wotan and Loge penetrate into the depths of the earth. Soon we hear the sounds of hammers and anvils. We are approaching the workshop of the Nibelungs, who are craftsmen slaves of the merciless Alberich.

As the vapors clear away, a rocky subterranean cavern is seen. This is the realm of Alberich who, thanks to the magic of the Ring which he has forged from the Rhinegold, rules over the other Nibelungs and makes them dig in the depths of the earth to extract more and more wealth. He has forced one of them, his brother Mime, a skillful smith, to forge for him an enchanted helmet, the "Tarnhelm", which makes its wearer invisible. Mime wants to keep it for himself, but Alberich makes himself invisible, beats Mime unmercifully, and leaves him cowering in terror.

And now Wotan and Loge enter the cavern by a cleft in the rock, and Alberich returns with the Tarnhelm at his best, wielding a whip and driving before him a flock of pitiful dwarfs carrying sacks of treasure, *"Hieher! Dorthin! Hehe! Hoho!"* ("Hither! Thither! Hallo!"). When Alberich sees Wotan and Loge, he turns his fury upon them, warning of the vengeful plans he has formed against their race, now that he has supreme power. The outraged Wotan raises his spear against the audacious dwarf, but the tricky Loge restrains him. He flatters Alberich and congratulates him on his good fortune but intimates that he is not wholly convinced that Alberich has as great power as he thinks he has. "Does the magic helmet really make you invisible, or transform you into any shape you wish?" he asks.

Anxious to exhibit his powers, Alberich dons the Tarnhelm and disappears in a cloud of smoke and immediately a great and loathesome snake appears on the floor of the cavern. The gods express their great admiration and ask if he can transform himself into a toad. He does so and Wotan at once puts his foot on him while Loge tears the Tarnhelm from his head. Binding him tightly, the captors lead him upward through the entrance of the cavern.

SCENE FOUR: *The rocky height of Scene Two, but the background is now veiled in mist.*

Wotan and Loge, dragging their prisoner, emerge from the dark caverns to the light of day. Alberich is mad with rage, but they mock him and order him to deliver up the treasure which he has amassed. Protesting, but powerless, Alberich uses his magic power to summon the Nibelung dwarfs from the depths of the earth, and soon they come in carrying the great bags of gold. Alberich begs to have the Tarnhelm returned to him, but Wotan refuses and demands that Alberich give him the magic Ring. Alberich is furious as he has counted on the Ring to bring back the power he lost. "Take my life," he cries, "but not the Ring." Roughly,

Wotan tears the Ring from his finger and Alberich shrieks out a terrible curse. "May this Ring bring anguish and death to all who possess it, envy to those who do not, until it returns to the hand of the Nibelung, its rightful owner. Thus do I curse the Ring." He rushes off in a fury of rage and hate,—*"Bin ich nun frei"* ("Am I now free?")—as Wotan slips the Ring on his own finger.

Now, the giants appear with Freia to exchange her for the promised treasure. At the approach of the goddess, the other divinities feel their youth and vigor returning and welcome her joyfully. The giants demand that the treasure be heaped up in front of her until she is no longer visible. After every nugget of the hoard has been piled up, Freia's gleaming hair can still be seen. Loge is forced to yield up the Tarnhelm, but now Fasolt discovers a small opening through which he can see the bright eyes of the goddess. He demands the Ring which Wotan is wearing, but Wotan refuses. In violent anger, the giants threaten to take Freia away. Suddenly, the air darkens and the divinity, Erda, the ancient spirit of the earth, who knows all things past, present, and future, appears in the depths of a grotto among the rocks, faintly illuminated by a pale and ghostly light.

She already foresees the end of the gods. *"Flieh' des Ringes Fluch"* ("Yield the Ring"), she warns. "You are in danger, the end of your power is in sight. Hear me, Wotan, yield the Ring." Then she disappears and daylight returns to the mountain. Wotan throws the Ring on the piled-up treasure, and the giants gleefully prepare to carry it away. But Alberich's curse takes effect almost at once. The giants quarrel over the division of the treasure and Fafner kills Fasolt with his club. Then, he turns, gathers up all the treasure and strides away with it.

The gods prepare to enter Valhalla, their new home. Donner, god of thunder, swings his hammer, there is a blinding flash of lightning and a deep roll of thunder, and the fog lifts from the mountain and the towers of Valhalla appear on the distant mountain top gleaming in the afternoon sunlight. A great rainbow covers the valley and this serves as the entrance of the castle. As the gods move over it, there arises from the depths of the valley, where the Rhine flows, the sound of the Rhinemaidens, calling for their lost gold. "Bid them be silent," says Wotan to Loge, and their voices die away as the gods enter Valhalla, all but the crafty Loge, for he despises his fellow deities, and plans to raise his own fortunes on the ruin of theirs.

Die Walküre

(The Valkyrie)

by RICHARD WAGNER (1813–1883)

Three Acts. Text by Wagner.
First produced in Munich, 1870.

Siegmund	*Tenor*
Sieglinde	*Soprano*
Hunding, husband of Sieglinde	*Bass*
Wotan	*Bass-baritone*
Brünnhilde, daughter of Wotan	*Soprano*
Fricka, wife of Wotan	*Mezzo-soprano*

Eight Valkyries, sisters of Brünnhilde.

TIME: *Legendary.*
PLACE: *Northern Europe.*

(Second of the four music dramas comprising "The Ring of the Nibelungs.")

ACT ONE

SCENE: *The interior of Hunding's dwelling.*

The orchestral prelude depicts the raging of a storm and when the curtain rises we see the interior of a primitive dwelling built around the trunk of a huge ash tree. In the foreground is a hearth, before which is a heap of skins forming a kind of couch. At the foot of the tree are a rustic table and stools. Suddenly, the door at the back of the room is opened, and a young man, Siegmund, staggers in out of the storm and falls exhausted in front of the hearth.

A young woman, Sieglinde, enters from an inner room and is surprised at the sight of the stranger. She brings him a drink and as he revives he tells her that his sword is broken and that he has fled weaponless, from his enemies. She tells him that she is the wife of Hunding, owner of the house. A mysterious feeling of sympathy arises between them, but he sadly says that he must leave the house, as he brings misfortune wherever he goes. But she answers that he cannot bring sorrow to this house as it has long been a dweller there.

Then Hunding, master of the house, appears. He is a black-visaged glowering man and gazes suspiciously at this blond young stranger, but true to the ancient laws of hospitality, he invites him to share their evening meal. As they sit at the table, Hunding asks Siegmund what brought him here and Siegmund tells of his early life—how as a child he lived in the forest with his father, mother, and twin sister. But one day, on returning with his father from a hunt, he found their dwelling reduced to ashes and his mother slain. As for his sister, no trace has ever been found of her. For a time he and his father lived in the forest, and then the father, too, disappeared and the young man was left alone in the world.

From the first words of this story, to which Sieglinde has been listening with deep emotion, Hunding recognizes in the fugitive an enemy of his tribe. Still abiding by the laws of hospitality, the unwilling host allows his unwelcome guest to remain overnight, but warns him that in the morning he must fight for his life.

Hunding and his wife, Sieglinde, retire to the inner room for the night, leaving Siegmund in despair as he is weaponless. He remembers that his father once promised him a sword in his hour of need. "Wälse, Wälse," he cries, "Where is your sword?" At this moment, the fire suddenly blazes up brightly on the hearth, throwing its light on the ash tree and revealing the hilt of a sword, the blade of which is completely sunk in the tree. But Siegmund does not see the sword and, in a moment, the fire dies down.

In a few minutes Sieglinde returns and tells how she has given her husband a sleeping potion and urges Siegmund to escape while there is still time. But when he refuses to go, she calls his attention to the sword hilt in the tree trunk, and tells how at her marriage to Hunding, a marriage forced upon her by a tribe who had abducted her as a young child, an aged man had entered the room, had driven his sword into the tree, and then departed. Since then many men had tried to draw the sword from the tree but none had succeeded.

Siegmund realizes that this is the sword promised him long ago "in his hour of need". At this moment the great doors at the back of the room fly open revealing a woodland bathed in bright moonlight. Clasping Sieglinde in his arms, Siegmund sings his beautiful Spring Song, *"Winterstürme wichen dem Wonnemond"* ("Winter storms have waned in the month of May"). *"Du bist der Lenz"* ("Thou art the spring"), responds Sieglinde ecstatically. "The sword in the tree is for you and Siegmund is the name I have treasured so long." Their memories are awakened together. They are the children separated so long ago and it was their father who had placed the sword in the tree. Siegmund wrenches the sword loose: " 'Needful' I christen this sword!" he cries, and embracing Sieglinde fervently they rush out into the night.

ACT TWO

SCENE: *A wild rocky height.*

We hear the joyous battle-cry—*"Ho-jo-to-ho"*—of Brünnhilde, one of the Valkyries, the warrior goddesses, standing on a high rock with shield and spear and great eagle wings on her helmet. Wotan, chief of the gods, tells her that she must defend Siegmund in his coming fight with Hunding, with whose wife, Sieglinde, he has fled. But Fricka, goddess of marriage, appears and reproaches Wotan for condoning a wrong and she convinces him that he must punish the young couple who have broken the law of marriage—*"Deiner ew'gen Gattin"* ("Your eternal consort's holiest honor"). Wotan sorrowfully reverses his instructions to Brünnhilde, and tells her she must not interfere in the fight to save Siegmund.

Alarmed at Wotan's obvious distress, Brünnhilde begs him to confide in her, and he tells her the whole humiliating story of his greed—the theft of the Rhinegold treasure from Alberich and the curse upon it, and his hope that his mortal son, Siegmund, might be the means of salvation, *"Was keinem in Worten ich künde"* ("What lies in my breast untold"). Brünnhilde is much moved and begs him to let her save Siegmund's life, but he sternly refuses and leaves her. Looking down from the rocky height, she sees Siegmund and Sieglinde climbing slowly and she disappears into her cave.

Siegmund and Sieglinde are exhausted by their long flight over the mountain and Sieglinde is hysterical with fear and dread. With a piercing cry, she faints in Siegmund's arms. He holds her unconscious body tenderly as he sits down on a broad rock. The stage grows dark and soon, in an unearthly light, Brünnhilde stands before him and tells him that only heroes destined to die in battle may gaze upon her, and that his death is near and that she has come to carry him to Valhalla to live with the gods—*"Siegmund— sieh' auf mich"* ("Siegmund, see'st thou me"). But when he learns that Sieglinde cannot accompany him, he refuses to go, and he shows such nobility and courage that her heart is touched and she decides to disobey Wotan's instructions.

Darkness has fallen on the mountain and we hear the sound of Hunding's horn coming nearer. Soon he appears, seeking vengeance. The duel between Siegmund and Hunding is illuminated by fitful flashes of lightning. Brünnhilde is seen shielding Siegmund, but Wotan also appears standing on a rock overlooking the combat. He stretches forth his spear and the sword of Siegmund is shattered. And so Hunding slays his enemy, but with a contemptuous wave of his hand, Wotan, the god, slays Hunding also. Brünnhilde rushes to the aid of the distracted Sieglinde and, taking her in her arms, carries her away.

ACT THREE

SCENE: *The Valkyrie's Rock.*

There is an orchestral introduction, one of the most famous and thrilling passages in all Wagnerian music, *"The Ride of the Valkyries"*. When the curtain rises it is on a scene of wild grandeur, a great overhanging rock at the summit of a mountain. Here, the nine warrior goddesses, the Valkyries, daughters of Wotan and Erda, are wont to assemble as they carry home to Valhalla the bodies of heroes slain in battle. Dark storm clouds move across the sky as the Valkyries come in one by one until eight of them are there. Then they see the ninth approaching. It is Brünnhilde, but she brings not a hero but a woman, Sieglinde.

Brünnhilde tells her sisters about the fight, saying that Wotan is pursuing her in a great rage determined to punish her for vainly attempting to save Siegmund against his express commands. There is great agitation among the Valkyries and their fear of Wotan's wrath is greater than their love for Brünnhilde or sympathy for Sieglinde. Sieglinde, in despair, reproaches Brünnhilde for not allowing her to die with Siegmund, but her despair is changed to hope and joy when Brünnhilde tells her she is to become the mother of a great hero and she must endure everything for his sake—*"So fliehe denn eilig"* ("Then fly with all swiftness"). The sympathetic Valkyries tell her of a cave where she may hide until the child is born. Brünnhilde gives her the broken pieces of Siegmund's sword and tells her she must keep it for her son who will forge from it a new and stronger weapon. Bearing the broken sword, Sieglinde makes her escape—*"O hehrstes Wunder"* ("O radiant wonder").

Wotan comes striding in and the Valkyries vainly endeavor to conceal Brünnhilde in their midst. The king of the gods commands her to stand forth, and now the great final scene of the opera begins. The eight Valkyries flee in terror and Brünnhilde, kneeling at Wotan's feet, asks her father if her offense was indeed so great. The storm has subsided, the sky clears, and a calm twilight descends. Wotan's rage has departed now, but no pleading, no tender love he bears his child can now turn him from his course. First in great gloom, then with a warm tenderness, he bids her a final farewell. This is to be her punishment—he will take her divinity from her and she will become a mortal woman. He will put her in a magic sleep on the rock that stands at the summit of the mountain and the first man who awakens her shall claim her for his own. One concession only does he allow—at Brünnhilde's request, he agrees to encircle her with a ring of magic fire so that only a fearless hero may find her. The eloquent music of Wotan's "Farewell" is one of the most beautiful of Wagner's inspirations —*"Leb' wohl, du kühnes, herrliches Kind"* ("Farewell, O valiant child, we can never meet again"). He clasps her in his arms, ends her godhood with a kiss and leads her to the rock under a solitary pine tree. She sinks into slumber and he places her gently on the rock, with her helmet on her head, her shield on her breast, and her spear in her hand.

Then he climbs to the highest peak of the mountain, strikes the rock three times and summons Loge, the god of fire. Tongues of flame appear on all sides of the mountain as the orchestra plays the wonderfully enchanting *"Magic Fire Music"*. Dimly seen through the flickering flames and smoke we discern the unconscious body of Brünnhilde reclining on the rock as Wotan strides majestically away.

Siegfried

by RICHARD WAGNER (1813–1883)

Three Acts. Text by Wagner.
First produced in Bayreuth, 1876.

Siegfried	*Tenor*
Brünnhilde	*Soprano*
Wanderer (The god Wotan in disguise)	*Bass-baritone*
Mime	*Tenor*
Alberich	*Baritone*
Fafner (the dragon)	*Bass*
Forest bird	*Soprano*
Erda (the earth goddess)	*Contralto*

TIME: *Legendary.*
PLACE: *Northern Europe.*

(Third of the four music dramas comprising "The Ring of the Nibelungs.")

ACT ONE

SCENE: *A cave in the forest.*

By means of his magical power, Fafner has transformed himself into a dragon and lives in a cave in the forest, guarding the treasure taken from Wotan, as told in "Das Rheingold." The first scene of "Siegfried" is another cave nearby in the same forest. It is the home of the dwarf Mime, who has left Nibelheim. On one side of the stage we see the forge, bellows, and anvil, and on the other side is a couch covered with the skins of animals. At the back of the stage there are large natural openings through which is visible the bright verdure of the sunlit woods.

At the rise of the curtain Mime is hammering away at a sword blade and complaining bitterly at his hard lot, *"Zwangvolle Plage! Müh' ohne Zweck!"* ("Forced undertaking! Toil without fruit!"). Every sword he makes is immediately smashed to bits by the boisterous youth Siegfried. He possesses the broken pieces of a sword called *"Nothung"* ("Needful") and he knows that if he could only reforge the broken pieces he would have a weapon with which the dragon Fafner could be slain and then Mime could seize the treasure which he covets. But the broken sword resists all his efforts to remake it.

Suddenly, Siegfried, a tall handsome youth, come bounding into the cave leading a bear by a rope. He roars with laughter at Mime's terror, but soon tires of this sport and drives the bear out of the cave. Picking up the sword Mime has been working on, Siegfried smashes it with one sturdy blow and rages at the dwarf for being so stupid. Mime, trying to put him in a good humor, brings him food, but Siegfried petulantly knocks the dish from his hand and expresses his hatred and contempt for the dwarf. Mime whines that he has devoted his life to feeding and clothing the boy and has met with nothing but ingratitude. Siegfried knows that he has nothing in common with this repulsive creature and finally seizes Mime by the throat and vows he will choke the life out of him unless he tells him who his real father is.

Mime then tells him how years before he came upon a young woman in the forest and sheltered her in his cave until she gave birth to a child and then died. But before she died she told Mime the child was to be called "Siegfried" and had given the dwarf the broken pieces of a sword which was to be his weapon when grown to manhood. Of Siegfried's father, Mime could tell him nothing except that he had been killed in a combat in which the sword had been broken. Siegfried commands Mime to repair the broken sword at once and he rushes off into the forest leaving Mime in despair.

Soon a stranger enters the cave heavily muffled in a dark cloak, and having on his head a wide-brimmed hat which covers part of his face. This stranger is none other than the god Wotan, but he tells Mime that he is a "Wanderer" and asks if he may rest awhile in the cave. The Wanderer challenges Mime to a battle of wits. Each is to ask the other three questions, and if his opponent fails to answer, his head shall be forfeit. Mime, who has a high opinion of his own wits, agrees. His three questions are: "Who dwells in the depths of the earth? Who dwells on the earth's surface? And who dwells on the cloudy heights?" "The Nibelungs live in the depths," replies the Wanderer, "the giants live on the earth's surface, and the gods live on the mountain heights." "And now it is my turn," says the Wanderer. "Tell me the name of those whom Wotan loves and yet treats so harshly." "The Wälsungs, Siegmund and Sieglinde," replies Mime. "And what is the name of the sword with which Siegfried will kill the dragon?" "Needful." And the third question is, "Who will forge the broken pieces of the sword?" Mime is terror-stricken as he does not know the answer. "Only he who knows no fear shall forge the sword," replies the Wanderer. And, laughing scornfully, he leaves the cave.

And now Siegfried returns and demands the new sword. Mime tries to instill fear in his heart by telling him of the fearful dragon who lives nearby. "Give me the pieces," cries Siegfried. "I will forge the sword and slay the dragon." He goes to work and as he works at the forge he sings lustily, *"Nothung, Nothung, neidliches Schwert."* ("Needful, Needful, conquering sword.") When the sword is complete, Siegfried raises it high over his head and then brings it down with a terrific blow which cleaves the anvil in two.

ACT TWO

SCENE: *Another part of the forest.*

It is night in the forest near the cave in which Fafner hides his treasure, a treasure from which he derives no benefit as he spends his whole life guarding it. Through the gloom, we catch a glimpse of the skulking figure of

Alberich, the dwarf, who prowls about hoping in some way to regain the magic Ring. A mysterious light flashes through the forest—it heralds the approach of the god Wotan, still in the guise of the Wanderer. Wotan tells Alberich that at this very moment Mime is bringing to the cave a young man who will slay the dragon and he suggests that Alberich may yet have an opportunity to gain the treasure before Mime gets there. Alberich calls into the cave that he will be content to let the dragon keep the treasure if he will only give up the Ring, but the dragon drowsily refuses. Wotan laughs mockingly at Alberich and both he and Alberich leave the spot.

Day is dawning as Siegfried, sword at his side, comes in, accompanied by Mime. Mime is afraid to get too close to the dragon's cave and warns Siegfried that the monster's breath is poison. Mime leaves and awaits the outcome of the conflict at a safe distance. The bright morning sunlight penetrates through the green leaves and Siegfried, instead of being in fear of the dragon, lies down under the spreading branches and reflects on the beauty of the forest. And now, we hear in the orchestra, the lovely strains of the *"Waldweben"* ("Forest Murmurs").

The song of a forest bird drifts down. Siegfried cuts a reed with his sword and makes a pipe on which he tries to imitate the bird, but realizes it is useless. Then he blows his hunting horn and the noise awakens the dragon who appears at the entrance of the cave breathing fire and smoke as well as defiance. Siegfried draws his sword and the battle is a short one. The sword is plunged into the dragon's heart and he dies, first warning Siegfried that the one who plotted this deed is planning also to end Siegfried's life. Siegfried sees a spot of the dragon's blood on his hand and instinctively puts it to his lips. The blood is magic and enables Siegfried to understand the language of birds. At once the song of the bird high up in the trees becomes clear to him. It tells him of the Tarnhelm and the magic Ring. Siegfried enters the cave and takes out these magical objects, leaving the rest of the treasure in the cave. Alberich and Mime now return and immediately start quarreling about the division of the treasure but when Siegfried emerges from the cave, they scurry away into the underbrush. In a moment Mime returns bringing Siegfried a soothing drink. But Siegfried realizes that underneath his obsequious manner Mime intends to murder him. With loathing and contempt he kills the dwarf and flings his body into the cave.

Siegfried is overcome with weariness and with loneliness. He has never known human companionship. "Is there no one on earth who will be my companion?" he sighs wearily, and at once the voice of the forest bird answers him. "A glorious bride awaits you," she sings and offers to guide him to her. Joyfully Siegfried springs to his feet and follows the flight of the bird toward Brünnhilde's rock.

ACT THREE

SCENE ONE: *A wild region at the base of Brünnhilde's rock.*

In the deep and narrow gorge the Wanderer appears and, raising his spear, summons Erda, the earth goddess. She appears dimly within the rock, awakened from her slumber. Wotan inquires from her what the future will bring but she will not tell. He knows all too well that the power of the gods is waning and that soon they all will perish. Erda sinks back into her eternal slumber, and from down the mountainside, we hear the sound of Siegfried's horn. As he sets foot on the steep pathway leading to the top of the mountain, Wotan stops him. "Who forged the sword you carry?" he asks. "I did," replies Siegfried. But the young hero has no time for idle, and to him, meaningless conversation. "Out of my way," he demands arrogantly. But Wotan interposes his spear to bar the way, and warns Siegfried that his sword has once before been shattered by this very spear. "Now I have found my father's enemy," cries Siegfried, and with a mighty blow he cuts the spear in two. There is a flash and a roar as of thunder. Sorrowfully, Wotan picks up the broken pieces of his former symbol of power. He knows that his power is gone and the end of the gods is near. "Go your way," he says. "I cannot stop you."

SCENE TWO: *The summit of Brünnhilde's rock.*

Once more we hear the *"Magic Fire Music"* (last scene of *Die Walküre*). Siegfried passes unharmed through the flames and reaches the top of the mountain where he stands surveying the scene. It is a day of brilliant sunlight, and distant mountain peaks stretch off to the far horizon. Under the solitary pine tree on the mountain-top, Brünnhilde still sleeps her magic sleep. Siegfried approaches her with awe. He has never seen a woman before. Gently, he removes her helmet and shield. He kneels beside her and presses his lips to hers. Brünnhilde awakens slowly, sits up on her rocky bed and raises her hands to the sun, singing the beautiful melody, *"Heil dir Sonne"* ("Hail to thee, O Sun"). She turns to Siegfried and greets him as the son of the mother she had defended against Wotan, hailing him as "Siegfried, blessed hero!" But she realizes she is no longer a goddess, but a mortal woman, and she begs Siegfried to leave her in peace. But she cannot resist his impetuous ardor and, in a magnificent duet, *"Leuchtende Liebe, lachender Tod!"* ("Love that illumines, laughing at death"), they sing of the love that has come to them.

Götterdämmerung

(The Twilight of the Gods)

by RICHARD WAGNER (1813–1883)

Prologue and Three Acts. Text by Wagner.
First produced in Bayreuth, 1876.

Siegfried	*Tenor*
Brünnhilde	*Soprano*
Gunther, King of the Gibichungs	*Baritone*
Hagen, his half-brother	*Bass-baritone*
Gutrune, sister of Gunther	*Soprano*
Waltraute, a Valkyrie	*Mezzo-soprano*
Alberich	*Baritone*
Three Norns	*Soprano* *Mezzo-soprano* *Contralto*
Three Rhine-maidens	*Soprano* *Mezzo-soprano* *Contralto*

Gunther's vassals and Gutrune's women attendants.

TIME: *Legendary.*
PLACE: *Northern Europe.*

(Fourth of the four music dramas comprising "*The Ring of the Nibelungs.*")

PROLOGUE

SCENE: *Brünnhilde's Rock.*

It is night and through the darkness we can dimly make out three ghostly figures in front of the cave where Siegfried and Brünnhilde sleep. They are the Norns or Fates who weave the golden cord of Fate by which are determined the destinies of men and gods. As they weave they sing of the sorrows of mankind due to the treachery of the gods and they predict the downfall of Valhalla and the end of the gods. Suddenly the rope of destiny breaks. With a cry, the three veiled figures sink into the earth, their task ended.

And now dawn comes to the mountain top. When the sun has fully risen, Siegfried and Brünnhilde emerge from the cave. He is clad in full armor and is about to go forth into the world to prove himself a hero among men. In parting he gives her, as proof of his love, the magic Ring made from the Rhine-gold, and she, in turn, gives him her horse Grane on which, in the days of her godhood she used to ride the skies, *"Zu neuen Thaten"* ("Did I not send thee"). There is a last farewell and as Siegfried leads Grane down the mountainside, Brünnhilde stands on the highest point of rock gazing after him. We hear once more the sound of Siegfried's hunting-horn as the curtain falls.

There is an orchestral interlude known as *"Siegried's Rhine Journey"*.

ACT ONE

SCENE: *The Hall of the Gibichungs.*

The Gibichungs are a fierce and warlike tribe, ruled over by Gunther. His chief adviser is his half-brother Hagen, who is the son of Alberich. Gunther, his sister Gutrune, and Hagen are seated at a council table in the great Hall of the Gibichungs on the banks of the Rhine. Hagen reproaches Gunther and Gutrune for the fact that they are not married and tells Gunther that he knows of a bride for him who dwells on a mountain top surrounded by fire. Only one man, the fearless hero Siegfried, may penetrate the magic flames. Siegfried, Hagen says, is even now on his way and at any moment may arrive at the castle of the Gibichungs. Hagen then discloses his evil plan. Siegfried is to be given a magic potion which will cause him to fall in love with Gutrune. He can then be persuaded to win Brünnhilde for Gunther in order to marry Gutrune. What Hagen does not tell is that he is plotting to regain for himself the all-powerful Ring which Wotan took from his father Alberich, and that Siegfried has already penetrated the magic fire and won Brünnhilde for his bride. Nor does he explain that the magic potion which is to be given to Siegfried will erase from his mind all memory of Brünnhilde.

Suddenly, there is the sound of a horn call from the river. It is Siegfried who steps ashore from the small boat in which he and Grane have made their journey. He demands at once to see the King of the Gibichungs, to whom he offers either combat or friendship. Gunther at once chooses friendship and Gutrune comes forward with the magic potion and words of welcome. Siegfried puts the drinking horn to his lips and immediately all memory of Brünnhilde leaves him and he gazes with admiration and dawning love on the fair Gutrune—*"Die so mit dem Blitz"* ("Thou fair one"). Then Gunther tells him that he too has chosen a bride but that unfortunately she lies in magic sleep on a mountain top surrounded by fire. Her name is Brünnhilde. No flicker of memory stirs Siegfried's clouded mind. "I will help you," he says. "I will bring you Brünnhilde and Gutrune shall be my reward."

And now Hagen takes a hand in the plot. He explains to Siegfried the magic power of the Tarnhelm which Siegfried wears at his side but of whose potency he has had no knowledge. And so Hagen explains how Siegfried can don the Tarnhelm and assume the appearance of Gunther, bring Brünnhilde down from her mountain to the real Gunther, after which Siegfried will assume his real appearance and the Valkyrie will never know how she has been deceived.

Siegfried and Gunther seal the bargain by mingling drops of their blood in a drinking horn filled with wine and then they enter Siegfried's boat and set forth for Brünnhilde's rock. Gutrune gazes after the departing Siegfried and Hagen broods darkly over the successful beginning of his intrigue: "Siegfried brings Brünnhilde and with her he brings the Ring." The curtain falls and there is another orchestral interlude in which we hear many of the familiar strains including the sound of Siegfried's hunting horn.

SCENE TWO: *Brünnhilde's Rock.*

It is early evening. Brünnhilde, standing in front of her cave, is startled at a sudden roll of thunder and Waltraute, one of the bravest of the Valkyries rushes in in great distress. She tells of how Wotan and the gods are awaiting their destruction, powerless to avoid it, and she begs Brünnhilde to give the Ring back to the Rhine-maidens in an effort to avoid the curse which Alberich has put on it— *"Erzählung der Waltraute"* ("Waltraute's Narrative"). But Brünnhilde refuses to part with the pledge of Siegfried's love for her, even though Valhalla crumble into ruins. Waltraute leaves in despair.

And now Brünnhilde notices that the flames which surround the rock have increased in intensity. Someone is coming up the mountain! "Siegfried!" she cries, but is overcome with horror as she sees a stranger stand before her, his face hidden behind a helmet of chain mail. "I am a Gibichung," the stranger announces. "I have come to take you as my wife." "The Ring will protect me!" cries Brünnhilde. Siegfried overpowers her and tears the Ring from her finger and orders Brünnhilde into the cave. Heartbrokenly, she obeys. The stranger lingers on the threshold and for a moment raises his helmet. It is, of course, Siegfried, not Gunther. Drawing his sword he vows to guard the woman for Gunther. Then, lowering his helmet once more, he enters the cave, the unwitting betrayer of his own bride.

ACT TWO

SCENE: *In front of Gunther's dwelling.*

It is night, and Hagen, with spear and shield in hand, awaits the return of Siegfried and Gunther. In the darkness before him crouches Alberich. He reminds his son of the Ring's curse and makes him swear that he will regain the Ring—*"Hagen, mein Sohn!"* ("Hagen, my son"). Alberich vanishes in the shadows, and dawn begins slowly to streak the sky with light. Siegfried enters suddenly as Hagen wakens. The Tarnhelm, says Siegfried, has brought him here instantly, while Gunther and his unwilling bride, Brünnhilde, are following in the boat.

Hagen summons his vassals by horn calls, and soon the open space in front of the castle is filled with men. There is great rejoicing as Hagen announces that Gunther has won for his bride one of the Valkyries. The boat containing Gunther and Brünnhilde now touches the shore and Gunther proudly leads in his bride. Brünnhilde does not look up and her whole appearance and manner tell of her suffering and humiliation. And now another bridal pair appears—Siegfried and Gutrune. Brünnhilde sees the ring on Siegfried's finger. She cries out in horror and accuses Gunther of having taken the ring from her by force. She, of course, recognizes Siegfried, although he has no recollection of her. And now Brünnhilde realizes that Siegfried has betrayed her—that it was he who came disguised as Gunther to her rock through the flames. "Bear witness, all!" she cries furiously, "Siegfried is my husband, not Gunther." Siegfried calls for a spear upon which to make a solemn oath and Hagen offers his weapon. Seizing the spear point, Siegfried swears that Brünnhilde's story is untrue, *"Helle Wehr"* ("Spear of war"). Brünnhilde pushes her way forward, and she also seizes the spear point and cries, "Hallowed weapon! May you bring Siegfried to his death, for he has broken his vows." Siegfried is unmoved by this and enters the castle with Gutrune, while Brünnhilde, Gunther, and Hagen remain to plot their revenge. Brünnhilde tells how with her magic art she made Siegfried invulnerable except for his back, which needs no protection as he never turns it to a foe. It is planned that Siegfried is to be killed during the course of a hunt on the following day. Gunther is at first loathe to consent to this, but finally agrees when Hagen reminds him that *he* will then become the owner of the magic Ring.

ACT THREE

SCENE: *A forest glade on the banks of the Rhine.*

Siegfried has wandered away from the rest of the hunting party and comes to the banks of the river where the Rhinemaidens are swimming about. They beg him to return the Ring to them and warn him of the curse which hangs over it. If he does not restore it to them at once he will meet his death before the day is over—*"Trio of the Rhinemaidens"*. But Siegfried has never known fear and refuses, *"Im Wasser wie am Lande"* ("Alike on land and water"). They swim away and we hear the hunting horns of the Gibichungs approaching and soon the glade is filled with men carrying carcasses of the animals and game they have killed. Siegfried tells how the Rhine-maidens foretold his death and this strikes terror to the heart of Gunther. But Hagen hands him a horn of wine containing a magic potion which will clear his memory and asks him to tell them the story of his life. Siegfried tells of his life with Mime, of the forging of the sword, of the battle with the dragon and of the death of Mime. And then, he tells of the voice of the forest bird leading him up the mountain through the flames to Brünnhilde whom he takes as his bride. Gunther springs to his feet in horror. Two black ravens fly over the scene and then disappear over the river. As Siegfried turns to watch them Hagen plunges his spear into his back and he falls to the ground as Hagen rushes off. Siegfried with his last breath sings a poignant farewell to Brünnhilde. *"Brünnhilde! heilige Braut"* ("Brünnhilde! heavenly bride"), and falls back across his shield. The vassals pick up the shield and move off, slowly carrying the body of the fearless hero while, from the orchestra, we hear the magnificent *"Funeral March"* which forms an interlude between Scenes One and Two.

SCENE TWO: *Hall of the Gibichungs, as in Act One.*

Gutrune awaits the return of the hunting party full of gloomy forebodings and fears. These are soon justified when the body of Siegfried, still lying on his shield, is brought in. Gutrune wildly accuses Gunther of his murder, but Gunther denies it and accuses Hagen of plotting and accomplishing the deed. Hagen admits it, but says that Siegfried had sworn falsely and that it was but justice that the spear by which he swore should be the weapon that brought about his death. For this, Hagen demands the Ring on Siegfried's finger. "The Ring is mine!" shouts Gunther. Hagen rushes upon him suddenly and kills him with his sword, then approaches the body of Siegfried, but suddenly the arm of the dead man is raised as if in warning, and Hagen recoils in terror.

Brünnhilde now enters the scene and commands the Gibichung henchmen to pile up a funeral pyre on the river bank. She has learned from the Rhine-maidens of Hagen's treachery and Siegfried's innocence. She takes the Ring from Siegfried's lifeless finger and places it on her own; then, turning to the river, she says that soon the Rhine-maidens may regain their Ring, cleansed forever from its curse. Grane is brought forth as the body of Siegfried is placed on the pyre. In this beautiful "Immolation

Scene," a blazing torch sets the fire, and Brünnhilde rides into the flames. Her sacrifice will bring atonement for gods and men.

The great hall collapses with a thunderous roar; the Rhine overflows, and the Rhine-maidens recapture their Ring from the dead hand of Brünnhilde. As they return to the river, Hagen, like a madman, leaps into the water and the Rhine-maidens drag him under and, in a moment, one of them reappears and holds up the ring with a gesture of triumph. And now, over the ruins of the Gibichung castle, we can see a red glow in the sky where Valhalla is consumed in flames. It is the end of the ancient gods and the promise of redemption by love.

Parsifal

by RICHARD WAGNER (1813–1883)

Three Acts. Text by Wagner, based on the poem by von Eschenbach.
First produced in Bayreuth, 1882.

Parsifal	*Tenor*
Kundry	*Soprano*
Gurnemanz, Knight of the Holy Grail	*Bass*
Amfortas, King of the Knights of the Holy Grail	*Baritone*
Klingsor, a sorcerer	*Bass*
Titurel, father of Amfortas	*Bass*

Knights of the Holy Grail, esquires, boys and youths, flower Maidens of Klingsor's garden.

TIME: *Middle Ages.*
PLACE: *In and near the Castle of Monsalvat in Spain.*

ACT ONE

SCENE ONE: *A forest glade.*

To the knights of the Grail has been entrusted the Holy Grail itself, the cup from which Christ drank at the Last Supper, and also the spear which pierced his side as he hung upon the cross. Titurel, founder of the order, has grown old and has entrusted the leadership to his son, Amfortas. Through the sin of Amfortas, the knights have lost the sacred spear and their leader suffers from a terrible wound which will not heal. Near the castle of the knights is a lake, and here Amfortas is brought in the hope that bathing in its waters may assuage his pain.

The first scene is in a woodland glade by the shore of this lake. It is early morning and preparations are being made for the ritual of the bath but, before Amfortas comes to the lake, a weird figure rushes in—a woman clad in rough garments, with dishevelled hair and a strange look in her wild eyes. It is Kundry, a fantastic creature who lives to serve the knights. She has roamed the earth searching for a magical balm which may heal Amfortas' wound and she hands Gurnemanz, one of the older knights, a small phial and then sinks exhausted to the ground.

Amfortas is borne in on a litter carried by knights. Gurnemanz hands him the phial brought by Kundry, but Amfortas sorrowfully speaks of a prophecy which has been made that he will be restored to health only by an "Innocent Fool". Amfortas is borne down to the lake shore and two young esquires ask Gurnemanz about Amfortas and Kundry. In response to their questions he tells in the long narrative, *"O wunder-wunder-voller heiliger Speer"* ("O wondrous, most holy spear"), how years ago admission to the Grail Knights was denied to Klingsor, who in revenge had used his magical powers to transform a deserted spot near the castle of the knights into a luxurious garden peopled with beautiful and seductive women who enticed a number of the knights into the magical garden and kept them there. Finally, the leader himself, Amfortas, carrying the sacred spear, ventured into the garden in an effort to destroy Klingsor and his evil magic, but he fell a victim to the most beautiful of the temptresses and Klingsor stole the spear and wounded Amfortas with it—the wound which will not heal.

Suddenly, there is an interruption. A swan from the lake has been wounded in its flight and drops to the earth as several knights drag in a youth with bow and arrow. Gurnemanz reproaches him with this wanton cruelty and asks, "Who are you? Where do you come from?" To all his questions the youth replies, "I do not know." Now Kundry springs up from the ground and tells something of the boy's strange history. His father was killed in battle before his birth and he was brought up in the forest, far from mankind. But now, she says, the mother is dead and the youth is alone in a world he does not understand. And now Kundry feels the influence of some magical power which is overcoming her and she knows that the evil magician Klingsor is casting a spell over her. She cannot resist it, and unnoticed by Gurnemanz and the youth, she sinks down beneath a thicket and is seen no more. It is time now for Amfortas to return to the castle for the solemn service of the Grail, and Gurnemanz resolves to take the strange youth with him to the service, thinking that he perhaps may be the "Innocent Fool" of the prophecy.

SCENE TWO: *The temple of the Grail* (The transformation scene).

Gurnemanz leads the young man up the hill to the castle and into the temple of the Grail where he leaves him standing and staring with uncomprehending eyes at the scene before him. The knights enter in solemn procession and take their places at the semi-circular communion table before the altar. The voice of Titurel is heard, as from a tomb, bidding Amfortas to unveil the Grail. But Amfortas cries out in anguished protest, for this ritual, which brings peace and healing to others, brings only fresh agony to him, as his wound opens afresh. But he finally yields, the Grail is uncovered, and a mysterious darkness descends upon the temple. Through the darkness a shaft of light strikes down from the vaulted dome and the crystal Grail glows with rich color. Amfortas lifts the Grail and consecrates the bread and wine for the communion of the knights. This done, the light within the Grail fades and daylight returns to the temple as the Grail is again enclosed in its shrine.

The elements of communion are distributed and after the knights have partaken of them, Amfortas sinks back exhausted and is carried from the temple followed by the knights in stately procession, leaving only Gurnemanz and the strange youth who has stood motionless during the whole communion service. When Gurnemanz asks him if he understands the meaning of what he has seen, the young man is speechless and replies only by placing his hand on his heart with a sorrowful gesture. "You are a fool!" cries Gurnemanz in disgust. "Begone with you!" And he drives him from the temple. But when Gurnemanz kneels before the altar, a voice from above repeats the prophecy of the "Innocent Fool", made wise through pity, who will redeem the knights from their distress.

ACT TWO

SCENE ONE: *Klingsor's castle.*

Klingsor, the evil magician, from his dark castle tower summons Kundry to do his bidding. Still in trance-like sleep, she slowly rises from the depths. She awakens with a terrible cry and cowers before the unearthly power of Klingsor. He mockingly taunts her with her devotion to the knights of the Grail whenever he releases her from his spell. And now she is in his power again, and she must seduce the guileless young man who even now is approaching the castle. Kundry protests, but her protests are of no avail, and she sinks back into the darkness to be transformed once more by magic into a temptress who will be the tool of the wicked magician's evil designs against the knights.

SCENE TWO: *The Magic Gardens.*

Into the enchanted garden comes the strange man who Gurnemanz has ejected from the temple of the Grail. He is surrounded by a group of Kingsor's flower maidens, garlanded with flowers and dressed in floating diaphanous garments, who sing to him and gaze upon him lovingly.

But they depart laughingly when one even more beautiful than they appears. It is Kundry, and she calls to him "Parsifal!" Suddenly he remembers that this is a name that his mother called him long ago. She speaks in the ensuing monologue, *"Ich sah' das Kind an seiner Mutter Brust"* ("I saw the child upon its mother's breast"), to him again of his mother and of her death after her son had left her. "Alas," cries Parsifal, "I have caused my mother's death."

She comforts him and tells him she brings him his mother's blessing and her parting gift—a kiss. She bends over him and presses a long kiss upon his lips. Suddenly, Parsifal is enlightened. "Amfortas! The spear wound!" he cries. In vain Kundry tries to bring him back beneath her spell, appealing to his sympathy, for she tells him that when

Christ was on his way to Golgotha she had laughed at Him and since that time has been condemned to wander the face of the earth. Now, she has found her deliverer, Parsifal—*"Seit Ewigkeiten—harre ich deiner"* ("For endless ages I have awaited thee"). But he rebukes her and says he must return to Amfortas. Kundry realizes she has failed and curses him—may he never find the road back to the Grail castle.

She calls upon Klingsor to aid her, and the magician appears on the ramparts of the castle overlooking the garden. He flings the sacred spear at Parsifal, but a miracle occurs. The spear pauses in its flight and hangs in mid-air. Parsifal seizes it and makes the Sign of the Cross with it. Instantly, the castle falls in ruins, the garden withers, Kundry sinks down with a despairing cry, and Parsifal, carrying with him the sacred spear, goes on his way in search of Amfortas.

ACT THREE

Scene One: *A meadow near the Grail Castle.*

Years have passed since Parsifal rescued the sacred spear and destroyed the evil power of the magician Klingsor. It is a day in early spring and Gurnemanz, now very old, is crossing the meadow in front of the simple hut where he lives as a hermit when he hears groans coming from a nearby thicket. Peering into the thicket, he sees Kundry, no longer the beautiful temptress, but the mysterious, rough-clad woman whom Gurnemanz knows only in that guise. She is lying unconscious on the ground. He revives her and observes that a great change has come over her. Gone is the old haunted look. Her face has grown almost ethereal. She murmurs softly, *"Dienen—dienen"* ("I must serve"), and says no more.

And now across the meadow comes a knight in black armor, spear in hand. Gurnemanz bids him lay aside his spear as this is the realm of the Holy Grail. The unknown knight plunges the spear into the earth and kneels to pray. As he does so, he raises the visor of his helmet and the aged Gurnemanz recognises the youth he expelled from the temple years before. "You have brought back the sacred lance," he cries, and tells of how evil days have befallen the Grail Knights, how Titurel has died, and how Amfortas no longer unveils the Grail. Parsifal regrets the years of his pilgrimage, and sinks down on a grassy mound overcome with emotion. Gurnemanz brings water from a holy spring and Kundry kneels at Parsifal's feet, annointing them with oil while Gurnemanz extends his arms in blessing.

Refreshed by these ministrations, Parsifal announces that he will go at once to the castle and assume the responsibilities of King of the Grail Knights. As his first act of office, the new leader of the knights baptizes the weeping Kundry. Gurnemanz reminds him that it is Good Friday and that all nature rejoices in the Holy Day. From the distance is heard the tolling of bells as the three set out for the castle.

SCENE TWO: *Temple of the Grail.*

Once more, we are in the temple, but the scene has changed. The communion table no longer stands in front of the altar, as the service of communion has been discontinued. Amfortas is carried into the temple for the funeral rites for his dead father, Titurel. The knights implore him to unveil once more the Holy Grail, but he refuses and prays that the spirit of his father intercede for him in heaven so that he may be granted release from pain in death. He leaps from his couch, tears aside his robe, and exposes the unhealed wound. He begs the knights to slay him, but they draw back in horror.

Just at this moment, Parsifal strides forward and places the point of the sacred spear on the wound, declaring that the weapon which caused the wound is the only thing that will heal it, *"Nur eine Waffe taugt"* ("One weapon only serves"). Amfortas is overcome with joy at the sudden ending of his torture and the realization that his sin is forgiven. Parsifal lays the sacred spear on the altar and then takes the Holy Grail from its shrine. Once more the temple is mysteriously darkened and the Grail shines with unearthly light. Kundry sinks slowly to the ground and dies, her long bondage at an end. A white dove slowly descends from above the altar and hovers over Parsifal as he holds aloft the sacred chalice. The prophecy has been fulfilled. The "Innocent Fool" has learned wisdom through pity and suffering, and the brotherhood of the knights of the Grail has been redeemed.

Index of Titles

(Titles of operas in both English and the original language are listed here in a single alphabetical order.)